D1625769

THE
GILDED AGE

Alexis Gregory

THE GILDED AGE

The Super-Rich of the Edwardian Era

Foreword by John Kenneth Galbraith

CASSELL

A CASSELL BOOK

First published in the UK 1993
by Cassell
Villiers House, 41/47 Strand
London WC2N 5JE

Copyright © 1993 Alexis Gregory

All rights reserved. No part of this book may be
reproduced or transmitted in any form or
by any means, electronic or mechanical,
including photocopying, recording or
any information storage and retrieval
system, without prior permission in writing
from the copyright holder and Publisher.

British Library Cataloguing-in-Publication Data
A catalogue record for this book is available from the British Library

ISBN 0-304-34319-6

Printed and bound in Artegrafica, Verona, Italy

CONTENTS

—— 7 ——
JOHN KENNETH GALBRAITH,
"CONSPICUOUS CONSUMPTION ILLUSTRATED"

—— 9 ——
OVERTURE

—— 21 ——
REAL ESTATE

—— 35 ——
TRANSPORTATION

—— 57 ——
DISCOVERERS, CONSOLIDATORS,
AND MONOPOLISTS

—— 81 ——
BANKERS

—— 103 ——
MILLIONAIRES' HOUSES

—— 133 ——
COLLECTORS

—— 163 ——
TRAVEL

—— 185 ——
SOCIETY

—— 218 ——
EPILOGUE

—— 219 ——
BIBLIOGRAPHY

—— 220 ——
INDEX

—— 223 ——
PHOTOGRAPHIC CREDITS

—— 224 ——
ACKNOWLEDGMENTS

Conspicuous Consumption Illustrated
by John Kenneth Galbraith

It is now just under a hundred years since Thorstein Veblen, then at the University of Chicago, published *The Theory of the Leisure Class*. Indignation and anger were the norm in the current and later writing of the Gilded Age, the time of the great real estate tycoons and the nineteenth-century transportation and industry captains. Incredibly rich, they all were Theodore Roosevelt's Malefactors of Great Wealth as well as those who presided so majestically and disastrously over Upton Sinclair's jungle. To the writers who leveled outrage and wrath against them, Veblen was the notable exception. He looked at the excesses of the vastly rich with something approaching detached amusement. Anthropology—not economics, not social justice—was his ruling guide. It proved both more interesting and far more devastating. Now, in this new fin-de-siècle, the angry men and Ida Tarbell have retreated to the shadows. Conspicuous consumption and conspicuous waste, Veblen's deathless terms, remain alive and well to this very day.

They are much alive in this handsome volume, and with an advantage that Veblen did not enjoy. He analyzed and described; he could not illustrate. Here we see conspicuous consumption in all its visual effect. It is Veblen brought fully to the eye.

But there is much more. Alexis Gregory is a diligent and literate scholar. In the first part of the book he goes back to tell how the money was made—money that, in an economy and polity far poorer than those now, was accumulated in truly astounding volume. And it was subject to taxation that even Ronald Reagan and his economic acolytes might have thought too meager. Indeed, until the arrival of the income tax, with President William Howard Taft, it was all but nonexistent.

Succinctly and interestingly, Gregory covers real estate, railroads, oil, mining, investment banking, and other sources of great wealth, and then he goes on to his main purpose. That is to show how the money was used, how it got spent. Here, especially, the illustrations add the new dimension.

The images and the text reflect the author's acute knowledge of art and its highly diverse history. The writing is both informative and readable. But there is also the mood. Gregory sees quite a bit of this achievement as being on the thin edge of insanity. It was not enough to be rich; the wealth had to be celebrated. This was accomplished by building a bigger mansion or a longer yacht or having a more luxurious and expensive railroad car (or train) than any would-be competitor.

The Gilded Age was, very specifically, a world of competitive ostentation, in which quality and style were regularly sacrificed to mere size or some other highly visible manifestation of proclaimed expense. To this the author turns his informed and accomplished eye and his detached view, and he writes with more than a slight note of amusement.

To be sure, the expensive exercises of the very rich are frequently admired. Theirs is a legacy that we sometimes now appreciate and enjoy. As in Newport, it can be a community resource for the visitors it commands. But there is more here that provokes a gentle but well-deserved ridicule. This the great entrepreneurs could not have stood. From wherever they are now watching, they must note that the reader of this volume is often smiling, is sometimes on the brink of derisive laughter. This must be more than mildly discomforting. Having successfully passsed through the eye of that notable needle, they must surely now look down with some discontent at the reaction to what they left behind.

So I repeat: Here in text and pictures is Veblen's conspicuous consumption. It is a book of which he would have greatly approved.

OVERTURE

The subject of this book, in its simplest terms, is the making and spending of money, an ongoing activity that concerns almost everybody. The main difference between "everybody" and the titanic figures about to be evoked is one of scale, inasmuch as practically no private person before or since the nouveaux riches of the Gilded Age has been able to amass such colossal fortunes. During the heady 1980s, of course, billionaires seemed to emerge in surfeit numbers, until they had either to pay back their loans or to jump off their yachts. But a multimillionaire of the 1890s was, in fact, far wealthier than a billionaire of the 1980s, who also had to deal with income tax, inheritance tax, and a mine field of government regulations that, while unimagined a century earlier, could now be mustered to slap him in jail the moment he fell out of favor. Moreover, a tycoon of a hundred years ago belonged to a much

rarer species, considering the chasm that yawned between rich and poor, a chasm sparsely occupied by a still fledgling middle class. In the Gilded Age, unlike today, a multimillionaire was a very big deal indeed.

The time span covered by this narrative is about 75 years, from the second half of the nineteenth century to the Crash of 1929, although some of the protagonists, such as John Jacob Astor and Cornelius Vanderbilt, started their careers before and others, such as Andrew Mellon, lived on to deal even with the Great Depression. The power of these millionaires—labeled parvenus, arrivistes, and robber barons before they and their descendents became known as moguls, magnificoes, and pillars of society—culminated during a relatively short period from the 1870s until the outbreak of World War I, which all

OPPOSITE: The supreme symbol of the Gilded Age was the Crystal Palace designed by Joseph Paxton for London's Great Exhibition of 1851. The immense, iron-and-glass, hothouse-like structure, the tremendous variety of industrial as well as luxury products on display, and the other breathtaking wonders brought from every corner of the globe—all combined to endow the Great Exhibition with an atmosphere of buoyant optimism and promise.

BELOW: A fictitious assembly of the monarchs of industry and finance in the United States at the turn of the century includes both heros and villains. In reality, a gathering of this sort around one table would have been impossible, given that several of those represented here were not on speaking terms.

Page 6. The study of the great banker, J.P. Morgan, situated in his library on 36th. Street and Madison Avenue in New York City, is the very epitome of both the power and the opulence of the Gilded Age. It was from this dignified, proto-Renaissance room that the great banker- whose portrait hangs over the fireplace- guided a vast empire of interlocking trusts, monopolies and businesses. Masterpieces of Renaissance painting hanging on the walls, and the elegant bronzes on the patrician desk reminded visitors that Morgan was to his time what the Medici had been to theirs; a merchant prince of the highest order.

Poverty and oppression in the old world and a vision of the new world as a place of unlimited possibilities brought throngs of immigrants across the ocean in search of a better life. They crossed in steerage accommodations, enduring terrible discomfort, eating slop, and sleeping on vermin-infested mattresses before being unloaded on Ellis Island in New York Harbor for sorting and visa checks. Thereafter, they proceeded to the Battery for a health check (OPPOSITE). Anybody with a contagious disease was sent back on the next ship, while the others started their lives with little but a few dollars in their pockets and a handful of personal possessions in straw hampers (RIGHT). In the years to come, when the hard-working and successful returned to Europe on summer visits, they traveled in first class with their sumptuous possessions packed in Louis Vuitton steamer trunks.

but shattered the old order. This Gilded Age was known in Britain as the Edwardian period and in France as the Belle Époque, and subsequent to it the world has never seen a time of such extravagance and splendor.

The principal currents flowing right through the Gilded Age can be found in the struggle between democracy and authoritarianism, in the de-cline of the ancien régime and the triumph of the bourgeoisie, in the Industrial Revolution, in the emergence of the United States as a great economic and political power, in the discovery and development of raw materials to feed rapidly growing factories, in the agricultural crisis together with the consequent rise of the city, and in the massive migrations of an impoverished, often oppressed proletariat in search of freedom and opportunity. Particularly important was the liberation of European Jews from their ghettos and the extraordinarily rapid climb of these entrepreneurs to the very summit of international finance, as well as to leading roles in the arts and sciences of both Europe and the United States.

Never had there been a moment so golden with opportunity, and those who seized the day became outrageously rich and powerful. The first half of the book explains—with no attempt at comprehensiveness—how a few of the most representative figures became so wealthy. Thereafter follows an equally important section on how these tycoons and their families spent their fortunes—building palatial houses, buying masterpieces to fill them, traveling in high style, dressing fashionably, acquiring fabulous jewels, and, most of all, social-climbing.

Given the overriding significance of money in this story, it is essential that yesterday's wealth be understood in today's terms. That Commodore Cornelius Vanderbilt left a $100-million estate at his death in 1877 is not in and of itself very revealing. According to the traditional rule of thumb, nineteenth-century dollars should be multiplied by approximately 25 in order to translate into current devalued dollars. This would make the Vanderbilt fortune equivalent to $2.5 billion, putting its founder in the same league with several hundred billionaires named by the editors of Fortune Magazine in a recent issue. A century ago, however, Mrs. Vanderbilt's chambermaids earned $12 per month, which, if subjected to a multiple of 25, would come to $300, or the equivalent of only three days of today's wages. Meanwhile, the Commodore's suits from H. Poole in Savile Row cost £3.50, or $17.50, in contrast to the £1,750 now charged for comparable wear. The cost of the average 250-foot yacht was $200,000, while today's floating hotel of the same dimensions would take $20-25 million to build. In the same luxury vein, the entire art collection assembled by Henry Clay Frick was appraised at $30 million at the time of the steel magnate's death, whereas Pontormo's portrait of Duke Cosimo I de' Medici, which had been on loan to the Frick Collection for years, was removed in 1989 and sold at Christie's for $35 million.

In consequence, it would not be unreasonable merely to multiply any dollar figure mentioned from now on by at least 100, or a pound sterling amount by 500 for the dollar equivalent, thus making the reader's life incredibly simple. However,

The Gilded Age could scarcely have been more striking in its contradictions, as a contemporary satirist made clear in 1895 with his contrasting views of the rich (OPPOSITE) and the poor (RIGHT). Under the clothes, there seems to be little difference between those who made it and "them that didn't," except the stakes. The images are entitled *A Showdown in the 400*, referring, of course, to Mrs. Astor's choice among New York's richest and most prominent citizens and *The Draw on the Bowery*, which was the poorest section of Manhattan.

there is an obvious catch in all this, namely that the quotidian necessities of life—bread, meat, vegetables, heating, soap—cost far more than 1 percent of today's prices. On the other hand, the cost of daily bread was as irrelevant to the Gilded Age millionaire's lifestyle as it is to contemporary billionaires, who spend an infinitesimal fraction of their income at the grocery store. All things considered, therefore, Vanderbilt's $100 million would readily make $10 billion today, and one could very well argue for its being a little more than double that amount. At the time of his death, the next richest United States millionaires were John Jacob Astor and the less well-known Alexander T. Stewart, each with $40 million, but in Europe the Rothschilds jointly commanded far more capital than the three top Americans combined.

THE MIND SET OF THE RICH

Making a great fortune seems to require a particular mind set more than anything else. The ethos of John Jacob Astor is no different from that of such recent realtors as the Reichmann Brothers, the late William Zeckendorf, or Sir Charles Clore. Equally, Daniel Drew, the cattle rustler who watered his livestock, is as much a kindred soul of the junk-bond king Michael Milken as Jay Gould, the notorious speculator, is of the crooked arbitrageur Ivan Boesky. The self-made millionaire thinks of money both first and foremost, just as he never ceases, night or day, to seek out the next profitable opportunity. Wars, droughts, and revolutions provide splendid occasions for speculators, who thrive on buying low for the sake of selling high at a later date. An opportunity—especially the sort provided by general disaster—draws the entrepreneur's attention just as water pulls down the divining rod in a blighted landscape. The great

financier reads complicated balance sheets and hears melodies or sees images of paradise to which the less talented remain deaf and blind. Such a mind set is probably as much a gift from on high as a musical intelligence or a scientific bent. This natural capacity, however, must be accompanied by near-manic energy, steely ruthlessness, expansive vision, and an extraordinary aptitude for detail.

Most tycoons are also silent, secretive, or at least very difficult to communicate with. As Daniel Drew, Vanderbilt's nemesis, put it: "It's the still hog that eats the most." The penny-pinching millionaire is not always stingy by nature; he simply wants total control over the world he has created. The self-made Croesus tends to be less interested in money than in power. He can spend happy hours saving a few thousand dollars only to give away millions to charity a few minutes later. In a capitalistic society, where the greatest rewards go to the bold and astute risk-taker, the money-driven entrepreneur is considered a paragon of stability and accomplishment. Actually, robber barons are often as eccentric or mad as great artists or scientists. The latter, however, are forgiven their odd behavior, while the obsessive financier is passed off as a crank or skinflint.

Those who dream of all things wonderful that millions can buy are more than likely destined never to earn them—or to end up in the slammer if they try. To the tycoon, money is abstract; its pursuit is his total purpose, an extension of his power. For even the richest tycoon there can be no greater excitement than destroying his competitors, abusing his government, exploiting his staff, ruining the small investor by bearing markets and scooping up shares at deep discounts, outwitting his colleagues, accumulating, trading, pyramiding, bribing, syndicating, and skating to the very edge of thin ice in order to maximize his gain. Never mind booms and busts, his purpose is to clean up. When the Crash of 1929 threatened to bring down the entire world, ninety-year-old George Baker—chairman of New York's National City Bank and the true successor to J.P. Morgan as the emperor of finance—insisted that he be allowed to rise from his deathbed and return to his office on Wall Street. Baker had triumphed in nine financial crises and was not going to let this one get away. He had himself driven downtown, made millions, and lived quite happily for another two years. The energizing thrill of it all may even have helped him stand off the dread reaper a bit longer.

Such bizarre conduct was virtually universal among the first generation of the Gilded Age rich. Their descendants, however, had only to bask in the glowing legacy of inherited wealth. The male progeny might expect to have attributed to them all the virtues of intelligence, wisdom, and leadership that come automatically with a swollen bank account—provided the beneficiaries remained in their fathers' offices or engaged in philanthropy. The tycoon's daughters could marry into society or aristocracy, touching cobwebbed palaces with the magic of their trust funds and returning home auraed in the faded glory of a titled husband's feudal past. Family relations of the super-rich varied immensely according to religious affiliation. Christian plutocrats, as a rule, had little faith in the abilities of their heirs and thus chose not to involve them in their businesses, preferring to protect these interests through elaborate trusts. The exception to the rule came when sons at a very early age revealed aptitudes, or appetites, similar to their fathers', as in the relationship between Junius Morgan and his son, John Pierpont. Too, Puritans tended to believe it essential that sons make it on their own, often coddling them as children only to dunk them in a cold bath as young adults. Jews, on the other hand, embraced the concept of *mischpoche*, or tribal family, and treated it as crucial, with the result that such great dynasties as the Rothschilds and the Guggenheims moved on together as an irrepressible force. Jewish fathers took their young sons into every aspect of their business affairs, and in time the boys quite naturally extended the family's interests, gradually becoming equal partners in elaborate, multinational ventures.

The first-generation tycoons followed no particular pattern in choosing their wives, many of whom suffered from the monomaniacal fixations of the men they married. The second generation, by contrast, selected mates for dynastic reasons, principally to forge business links or attain higher social standing. For the most part, the big spending also got underway with the second generation. Wives recruited the architects, bought the furniture, battled their way into society, chose the jewels, and organized the servants, dinners, balls, and travel. Their husbands generally collected the paintings and invariably built the yachts and racing stables. All such activity *should* have been delightful, but the nouveaux riches—husbands and wives alike—competed ferociously with their peers (and even relatives) for advancement on the social scene, which often left them as much pained as pleasured. The poor little rich girl whose happiness had to be sacrificed in the interest of family ambition was a sad reality, as were the rich boys with egos crushed by domineering fathers. Furthermore, life in a Fifth Avenue mansion ruled by tutors and nannies turned out, on the whole, to be a debilitating and artificial way to raise children. Shirt sleeves to shirt sleeves in three generations was not fiction, as WASP heirs found solace in drink while their Jew-

In the Gilded Age, the real money was made on Wall Street in an ongoing battle between the Bulls, representing financial optimists, and the Bears, who rejoiced in panics or crashes. In this much-loved painting, by William H. Beard (New York Historical Society), the bears rejoice in the aftermath of one of the many crises that rocked the Gilded Age. Music, dancing, drinking, and eating were in celebration of what for many others had proved financial ruin. Needless to day, the money lost by the innocent generally went into the pockets of astute financiers.

ish counterparts supported a large segment of Freud's disciples. John D. Rockefeller told the truth when he confided to a Sunday School class: "It is wrong to assume that men of immense wealth are always happy."

THE EXTRAVAGANCES OF THE RICH

While tycoons lived in great, if sometimes tortured, opulence, a small middle class struggled for their living, and the large proletariat merely subsisted in conditions of searing poverty and degradation. Richard Wagner's *The Ring of the Nibelungen* was the Passion Play of the period, a four-opera music drama in which gnomes work underground to pull up treasure that does little but cause trouble, sitting under the cold belly of a dragon, destroying true love, and igniting the spectacular conflagration of Valhalla.

Inevitably, the abuses of the super-rich had to produce a Karl Marx and an itchy proletariat. Socialism seemed an answer, but every system has its built-in disorder. Communism's was elephantiasis, while capitalism's is still manic depression, treated since the 1930s with lithium-like doses of government intervention. Prior to the ministrations of John Maynard Keynes during the troubled 1930s, capitalism generated soul-wrenching depressions, the worst panic coming in 1873 as a result of overexpanded agriculture and speculation in railroad stocks. However, the most historic rout occurred on Black Tuesday 1929. Stock-market crises were a regular occurrence, often orchestrated by greedy robber barons for the diabolically simple purpose of swelling their own bank accounts at the expense of an uninformed and thus defenseless public. Still, despite the abuses, inequality, exploitation, and sick-making ups and

downs, the Gilded Age was a time of immense creativity and optimism, nowhere better expressed than in the great universal expositions that began in London in 1851. These were essentially showcases for the new wonders of the Industrial Revolution, exhibiting everything from heavy cannons to Lalique jewels. People came in droves, from all over the world, thanks to advances in transportation, and their need for temporary accommodation brought about the first grand European hotels. Although Paxton's Crystal Palace, erected for the 1851 fair, has not survived, Paris's Eiffel Tower, Pont Alexandre III, and Grand as well as Petit Palais still bear witness to the grandiosity of those astonishing events. The World's Columbian Exposition of 1893 in Chicago, reigned over by Mrs. Potter Palmer, marked the international recognition of the United States as a major industrial power, and to many the neoclassical architecture that Richard Morris Hunt designed for the occasion seemed to bring back the glory of ancient Rome.

The scale of the Chicago exhibition very aptly reflected the new nation's wealth and aspiration. It is no accident that the majority of tycoons in this book are American. The opportunities in the New World for bright entrepreneurs surpassed anything in Europe by light years. The United States had no customs barriers and no rigid caste system to favor the established over the capable. Equally important, the country possessed millions of acres of rich farmland ready for exploitation, as well as a mass of burning, pent-up energy suddenly set free by the resolution of the Civil War. The Republic needed reconstructing, and plenty of talent came forward to take on the job. The federal government generously supported entrepreneurs, at the same time that congressmen could be corrupted, all of which

ABOVE: The interior of the Electrical Building at the Columbian Exposition of 1893 in Chicago. This was the first world's fair ever held in the Americas, and it marked the arrival of the United States as an international power with which to be reckoned. The 600-acre site of the "Chicago Fair" contained 150 buildings, many of them clad in white marble. Exhibitors arrived from 72 different countries, and 27 million dazzled visitors felt as if they were walking in the glory of ancient Rome (BELOW).

meant that few controls and virtually no regulatory commissions stood between a potential bandit and his manifest destiny. Given these conditions, labeling a tycoon "robber baron" may be quite unfair, since, in theory at least, robbery is not illegal if tacitly sanctioned.

During the nineteenth century, laissez-faire found its most literal exponents in the United States, where any alert person willing to work hard could become rich. The great American fortunes, as the following pages show, were first made in land, transportation, and raw materials, as well as in banking, whose operatives became fantastically affluent knitting together trusts and monopolies for entrepreneurs who built railroads, mined and smelted ore, refined oil, or produced steel. A young man could step off an immigrant ship with a few dollars in his pocket, find a job peddling on the streets of Manhattan's Lower East Side, travel West in search of gold, work on a railroad or in a telegraph office, and make a financially rewarding career with remarkable ease—provided he met the challenge with clear-headed focus and unflagging industry. The country was underpopulated, underdeveloped, and essentially the fiefdom of white men, who had stolen it from the native aboriginal population. The massive flow of migrants from Europe is the obvious indicator of where true opportunity lay, and the floodgates of Ellis Island did not close until after the 1929 Crash. Only when the immigrants had made it did they return

"home," and once back in Europe they often recruited family members and friends to join them in the good life across the sea. On the eastbound journey, steerage remained forever empty, while first class overflowed with American millionaires on their way to play major roles in British society and become as legendary in Europe for their extravagance as the grand dukes of Imperial Russia.

THE BRITISH EMPIRE

Inasmuch as Great Britain governed one-quarter of the planet's humanity at the end of the nineteenth century, it would seem evident that the Empire would also develop a new and substantial plutocra-

Two engravings by Gustave Doré illustrate the dismal new urban landscape in Great Britain. The agricultural crisis and the rise of new industries in and around such cities as Liverpool and Manchester fostered slums, child labor, sooty air, inhuman overcrowding, and crime.

cy. London was the world's financial capital; furthermore, sterling was king, despite the billions being made in America. An exporter in Bombay selling cotton to a Russian merchant would, more than likely, be paid in drafts on one of London's great banks. In addition, the affairs of the Indian subcontinent, the vast Australian outback, and the incredibly rich mines of South Africa were run from boardrooms in the City and the imposing ministries in Whitehall.

As a result, there was very limited scope for the real-estate speculations or railroad land grants that formed the basis of most American fortunes. Also, Britain's strict clan system, which reserved higher education for the well-born, did much to stifle the ambitions of those who were not.

By the end of the nineteenth century, however, a fundamental change had begun to occur in the distribution of British wealth, a change that affected all strata of society. As the Empire expanded and

England's nouveaux riches, both in their composition and in the means or sources of their wealth, differed considerably from their tycoon cousins across the pond. Yet, the accession of British entrepreneurs to monumental amounts of money proved no less dramatic, although the scale of these new fortunes remained, with few exceptions, considerably smaller than that of the American accumulations. No arriviste in nineteenth-century Britain succeeded in amassing the prodigious estate of John D. Rockefeller, John Jacob Astor, or Commodore Vanderbilt—and for a host of reasons. First of all, most of the land in Great Britain belonged to families who made up the feudal aristocracy and constituted the nation's true grandees.

transoceanic transport evolved, the commodities—primarily grains—that had long supported the nation's agricultural lands encountered severe competition and thus fell precipitously in price. From 1855 to 1859, agriculture generated 20 percent of the national income, a rate that dropped to 6 percent during the next four years, in response to the cheaper wheat placed on the market by such exporting countries as Argentina, Australia, and, above all, the United States. Simultaneously, new industries burgeoned, the locomotive quadrupled in power, and the blast furnace acquired seven times more capacity. Tenant farmers, no longer able to pay their rent, moved to industrial centers and cities, there becoming the new proletariat, the ill-housed and ill-nourished denizens of an overcrowded, confused, inhuman, but rapidly growing urban world.

The population of Great Britain surged from 9 million in 1801 to 36 million in 1911, as Liverpool, Manchester, Leeds, and a good part of London became teeming slums. The great transfer of wealth from the country to the metropolis, and from the landed gentry to the rootless entrepreneur, was the main economic, cultural, and historic current of the mid-nineteenth century in Britain. While the gentleman farmer retrenched, the energetic opportunist grasped the reins of power in the most dynamic economic development the world had ever seen.

LEFT: Much of Britain's new industrial wealth flowed from textiles, woven by machines operated by dreadfully underpaid and overworked women and children.
ABOVE AND FAR LEFT: One of the most successful of Victorian Britain's entrepreneurs was Sir Thomas Lipton, a Scotsman who returned from a youthful period in the United States with enough capital to open a food shop in Glasgow. Gradually, he developed a monopoly in tea, producing and marketing one of the commodities most treasured by the nation's growing urban proletariat.

The population explosion generated many huge fortunes in Great Britain. The scornful Napoleon had characterized England as a nation of shopkeepers. If this be the case, the true sovereign of the English was Sir Thomas Lipton, who started in a small job at a Glasgow stationer's and, thanks to his brilliant entrepreneurship, became the leading yachtsman of the Gilded Age and a sporting friend

Viscount Leverhulme, kept them clean—no easy task in the grimy factories and cities of industrial Britain. Lever called his Merseyside factory Port Sunlight, and he made it the first model worker's city in the new industrial world. Lever believed good working conditions to be an essential part of a solid, efficient company, and by removing his workers from the impoverishments of the urban

BELOW AND RIGHT: William Hesketh Lever, later Viscount Leverhulme, made a fortune by manufacturing soap at a price reasonable enough to save factory workers from the ill effects of the grimy environment in which they had to live and labor.

of King Edward VII. He entertained the Merry Monarch with stories of his early days in America, where he went at age fifteen in search of greater opportunity than Britain could offer at the time. Young Lipton labored on rice plantations in South Carolina and at a food store in New York City, before returning to Glasgow six years later to invest his entire savings, £100, in a small food shop. He worked like a demon from 8:30 in the morning until 11 at night expanding his business, opening other stores, and therewith creating the first grocery chain in history. Lipton went straight to the most promising market then available to him—the new urban proletariat—on the sound theory that a poor man's 20 shillings were as good as a rich man's pound. Soon his purchasing clout was so mighty that he could cut out the middleman and thus reduce his prices dramatically. Lipton purchased directly from the main markets of England and Ireland, paying cash to buy at the lowest price. He also acquired a slaughterhouse in Chicago and developed his own tea plantations in India, importing England's national beverage duty-free. With this staple of every British household, Lipton succeeded in creating a near monopoly, its large wooden cases quickly sorted and packaged in all sizes.

While Sir Thomas Lipton fed millions of Englishmen, Sir William Hesketh Lever, later the first

environment, he hoped they would achieve their full potential. This tycoon never viewed the millions he spent on his employees' housing, education, or recreation as philanthropy but, rather, as a way of helping the underprivileged to become healthy and independent. (George Cadbury, the chocolate king who processed one-third of Britain's cocoa, similarly aided the workers at his Garden City, in Bournville near Birmingham.) Lever, a pioneer of industrial paternalism, fought for the eight-hour day, created the Employees' Benefit Fund as well as the Employees' Holiday Club, and grew enormously rich, mainly from Lifebuoy soap (introduced in 1894), Lux soap flakes (1899), and endless other consumer products sold throughout the world. Like Sir Thomas, Lord Leverhulme short-circuited the middleman for his raw materials, purchasing hundreds of thousands of acres of farmland in the Congo and Solomon Islands.

Other large fortunes were made by those willing to satisfy the needs of the urban masses. Bass ale and Guinness stout, for instance, assuaged workers' thirst, providing a pleasurable if potentially harmful way to drown the miseries of daily life. Harmsworth, Kemsley, and Beaverbrook responded to the more widespread, albeit minimal, literacy with newspapers while diminishing the standards of the medium. W.H. Smith provided for the national circulation of not only newspapers but also tobacco and candy, while Thomas Cook offered escape from the anthracite fogs of London, Liverpool, and Manchester by organizing expeditions to the seashore and countryside. Owing to the average Englishman's fear of traveling by rail, Cook could purchase large blocks of seats at a steep discount, thereby saving the new industry and launching the era of mass travel.

For the British, however, the real money was to be made beyond the confines of the British Isles. Between 1870 and 1900, the already far-flung Empire increased by half, opening immense opportunities for those willing to explore the outer reaches of civilization. In John Buchan's *Prester John* (1910), the story of a fictitious white King of Abyssinia, David Crawford, informed his uncle that, being ignorant of business, he could only get a job as a common clerk. "If you want to better your future you must go abroad, where white men are at a premium," which is precisely what a number of young people did during the second half of the nineteenth century. They would make the largest of the new British fortunes, thanks to the gold and diamond mines of southern Africa as well as to trade in India and the Far East.

Continental Europe, unlike the United States and the British Empire, comprised many sovereign states and small principalities with no common, unifying purpose and much quarrelsome distrust of one another, a situation that severely hampered the attempts of their entrepreneurs to create large fortunes based on national economies. Germany, of course, only became a true power after Bismark's unification, which finally permitted the construction of great fortunes, above all in steel, banking, and armaments. Imperial Russia was a vast expanse with incalculable riches that remained locked inside the nation's landmass until the Russian bear finally roused himself from long hibernation. But once the beast within woke up, Russia joined the Industrial Revolution with astonishing fervor, surpassing even Great Britain in its rate of growth. The ancien régimes of both Continental Europe and Russia were too involved with their estates and life at court to be attracted by the dirty

work of factories. They gladly left the fruits of industry to entrepreneurs of common origin, who, in most of Europe if not in Imperial Russia or Austria, were eventually brought into the establishment either by marriage or by patents of nobility. However, the only Continental success story on an American scale was that of the Rothschilds, precisely because they transcended fixed boundaries by sending family members to Frankfurt, Paris, London, Vienna, and Naples—becoming, in effect, the first multinational enterprise.

The Gilded Age was the best of times and the worst of times, as Charles Dickens wrote of the similarly luxurious, eerie calm before the storm of the French Revolution. Wonderful for the rich and terrible for the poor, the Gilded Age reached its apogee at the turn of the century, when the old order crisscrossed modern times and the happy few could well believe that peace and prosperity were gifts that God had bestowed forever. Above all things, it was an age of fearless, indomitable giants, and I can only pray that those I have not had the space to describe in the following pages will not return to ruin me!

BELOW: Like Lever, George Cadbury earned tremendous wealth by providing the industrial masses with a desirable and inexpensive product. And he too practiced an enlightened, benevolent paternalism towards his many employees.
LEFT: Thomas Cook pioneered the business of group travel, not only for the rich but for the working class as well, at a time when industrialization made everyone wish to "get away from it all."

REAL ESTATE

Of all the ways to amass money in the Gilded Age, owning real estate was arguably the easiest. Indeed, real estate has long been a basis for large fortunes and a traditional repository of great wealth. In purely economic terms, the magic of good property—at least, until the protracted recession of the early 1990s—is the inelasticity of supply when confronted with strong demand. An entrepreneur can always build new factories to turn out more widgets, but there is no way to lengthen New Bond Street, the Rue de la Paix, or Fifth Avenue. In general, market forces over much of the last century have propelled good property up a practically steady curve, thanks to population increase and economic expansion. Nothing involves less work than buying well-located plots and waiting for them to rise in value, and, above all, there is no need to deal with unions, disgruntled workers, exploding equipment, remodernization of factories, day-to-day management, or any other of the myriad problems faced by a rich industrialist virtually every hour of his professional life. Another secret of property wealth is that, once accumulated, only minimum intelligence is required to keep it under control; therefore, property-based assets often pass through several generations—even idle or foolish ones—without being dissipated.

Today, of course, there are many restrictions to protect tenants from greedy landlords, zoning laws to prevent entire cities from turning into sprawling and disorderly slums, and large real estate taxes that have come to form the basis of many cities' reserves. Increases in property value, evidently, have no multiplier effect on economies except for the money spent by happy owners on goods and services to enhance their lifestyles, and few were to spend as lavishly as the descendants of that king of modern real estate, John Jacob Astor (1763-1848).

FROM FURS TO LAND: JOHN JACOB ASTOR

It was the mass migration of the rural population to the great cities that created the basis of much colossal wealth in the nineteenth century, and no one took better advantage of this phenomenon than John Jacob Astor in an ever-expanding New York City. The land Astor bought made it possible for his heirs to be the social leaders of the United States, to become British lords and rule London society, and to dispense seemingly endless millions of dollars—even today—through the Astor Foundation. It is not surprising, then, that late in his career Astor said: "Could I begin my life again, knowing what I know now, and had I the money to invest, I would buy every foot of land on the Island

Nothing so perfectly bears out the American legend of rags to riches as the image of John Jacob Astor trading furs with the Indians (BELOW) in contrast to the legacy enjoyed by his descendants (OPPOSITE). Having made his first fortune in the wilderness, Astor then invested in New York City real estate, whose value would increase by virtual quantum leaps. As a result, his prominent family became the property kings of modern times. Seen on Fifth Avenue's hotel row are the giant and luxurious Savoy Plaza, now destroyed, and the Sherry Netherland, both of them once controlled by the Astor estate. The Sherry Netherland still stands opposite the Plaza, a celebrated luxury pile built precisely to challenge the Astors' large and extremely elegant St. Regis just four blocks down the avenue (see page 30).

BELOW: Patriarch John Jacob Astor as a successful fur trader. The square jaw and rough features betray both his overriding ambition and his common origins.

RIGHT: This engraving, made from a drawing by Frederic Remington, shows Indians trading in a Hudson Bay store. It suggests why young Astor was eager to branch out into other businesses. Back-packing through the dangerous, snow-bound northern wilderness to swap trinkets for furs could only be described as an exhausting and eventually monotonous, if financially rewarding, enterprise.

of Manhattan." His biographer Harvey O'Connor wrote that John Jacob Astor "could die, his descendants could sleep for a hundred years, and still the house of Astor, founded on the rock of Manhattan, would prevail against all enemies."

John Jacob Astor—from a family named Ashtor, Ashdour, or Aostor—was born in Walldorf, Germany, a small village near Heidelberg, on July 17, 1763. His father was a butcher, his mother died when he was four years old, and John Jacob never, to his dying day, mastered the English language. This did not seem to matter a great deal for by the time he died in 1848, Astor was counted the richest man in the United States and among the six wealthiest men in the world, with a fortune of $20-30 million.

Early on, Astor realized that no great future was to be had from carving up roasts in his father's shop; so, as a young man he left for the New World via London (where he worked in his brother's flute factory). John Jacob eventually saved fifteen guineas, of which five procured steerage passage across the Atlantic, five went for seven flutes, which he intended to resell at a profit in America, and five remained to help him settle into a new life. At the age of 21, John Jacob got a job in New York City peddling the bread, cookies, and cake of a German baker, George Dietrich. He sold the flutes at a profit, got a better position with Robert Borne, a Quaker furrier, and quickly learned a new trade.

It was on skins and pelts, not property, that Astor made his first fortune. At the end of the eighteenth century, Indians in upstate New York and Canada controlled the supply of furs, commodities

eagerly sought by rich gentlemen and ladies in the United States, Great Britain, and most of continental Europe (not Russia, however, which had its own supply of minks and sables). The Indians traded their pelts for gunpowder, guns, blankets, tobacco, or alcohol, which Astor first back-packed on his treks through the snowy wilderness, where he got on well with the Native Americans. It was worth the effort, since the average markup on furs was 1,000 percent, a profit that improved in 1796 when the British withdrew from their military outposts, and Canadian furs no longer had to be sent to England before being reimported into the United States or exported to Europe. The volume traded was enormous, and, through hard work, Astor quickly emerged as a dominant force in the market. Buyers came from Europe and all over the United States to his fall or spring auctions, where he might sell over 500,000 muskrat skins in a single day, not to mention the skins of beaver, lynx, fisher, otter, mink, and the occasional fox or wildcat.

For several years, Astor stored the smelly pelts in the basement of his house in New York. Growing ever richer, he bought the goods he traded with the Native Americans in mass quantities at far cheaper prices in London, cut his transport costs, and made better deals with his aboriginal friends than did his few competitors. His deals were absolutely ruthless. For example, a gun costing about one pound seven shillings was swapped for twenty beaver skins worth around 25 pounds, and two yards of cloth costing twelve shillings bought six to eight beaver skins worth eight or ten pounds. Worst of all was his trading on Maine's Mackinaw Island in whiskey, firewater that he made for five cents a gallon and sold for fifty. One of his lieutenants provided the formula: "Take two gallons of common whiskey or unrectified spirits, add to thirty gallons of water and to this add red pepper enough to make it fiery and tobacco enough to make it intoxicating, and you have a decation that will cause the Indian to give everything he possesses into the hands of the white man."

By 1800, at the age of 37, John Jacob Astor was worth $250,000, a truly substantial sum in its day. He quickly launched himself into the China trade, exporting his furs, the ginseng that grew in Indian territory, and sandalwood from Hawaii, while importing teas, silks, spices, and chinaware that he resold in North America and Europe. He soon owned two fleets of ships, one that sailed from the East Coast of America to Europe, the other from the West Coast to China via Hawaii—and the profits of their bounty bought more and cheaper trinkets in London, which purchased more furs, which piled up more cash. James Gordon Bennett, owner of *The New York Herald*, declared there was no deal that Astor, "a self-invented money-making machine," would not execute to increase his fortune. Meanwhile, his traders stirred up their Indian friends to scalp—literally—all competitors, and soon Astor had a virtual monopoly, controlling 90 percent of the market. In a few decades he had brought the population of Canada's furred species close to extinction. The time had come to invest his profits.

THE MOVE INTO PROPERTY

Astor had been dabbling in real estate since 1800, but it was only in 1834 that he made it a full-time occupation. That year John Jacob lost his wife Sarah, to whom he had been married only since 1785, and at the age of 71 he no longer felt up to a continued life of wheeling and dealing with Indians. Moreover, the fur market was shrinking and the China trade increasingly competitive. Since the opening of the Erie Canal in 1825 New York City had become boom town, to which Astor responded with an action plan of remarkable simplicity. The city's hub at the turn of the century had been on the tip of Manhattan Island, what is now the financial district and was then the center of trade and shipping. To the north were large farms, and for the city to grow, it had to move toward the undeveloped land or out to sea. Therefore, Astor bought farms for a farthing and waited for the city to come to him.

While still active in the fur trade during the early nineteenth century, Astor had made a great deal of money on land in lower Manhattan. The land belonged to Trinity Church, and Astor bought it on a long lease from Aaron Burr, who had started to default on his mortgages when he was Vice-President of the United States (a situation that would deteriorate further after Burr killed Alexander

THE CITY OF NEW YORK.
ROGERS, PEET & CO.,
BROADWAY, BROOME & MERCER STS., NEW YORK.

Hamilton in a pistol duel in 1804). Astor sublet individual plots for short terms at a large profit, and all the improvements made by the tenants reverted to him at the end of their leases. Values increased, rents went up, the poor tenants were evicted, and the richer ones gouged; thus, shortly before Astor died, those long leases bought for less than $100,000 (plus an annual rent of $269 per year paid to the church) were yielding $1.25 million per year. "Leave da land alone," said the lucky landlord, "let somebody else develop it." So much for the income needed to keep up the Astor life-style.

For long-term investment, Astor in 1803 bought the Eden Farm, an agricultural property that lay outside the city limits. Its 70 acres ran along what is now Broadway from 42nd Street to 46th, clear down to the Hudson River, and it cost $25,000. Shortly afterward he acquired the contingent properties (which would eventually house the city's theater district) for $9,000 more, and in 1809 he swallowed up the Cosine Farm, which covered the entire area between Broadway and the Hudson

BELOW: Astor made his first major property deals with United States Vice-President Aaron Burr, shown killing Alexander Hamilton in an infamous duel.
LEFT: The tip of Manhattan was the site of John Jacob Astor's early real estate investments. However, at that time—the early 19th century—the map would have shown the inhabited tip covered with orange housing and the rest in green farmland. Astor started buying about a third the way up the island and then waited for the urban spill to follow. He also bought in New York City's other boroughs, then linked by ferries rather than the great bridges that would cause property values to soar.

BELOW: John Jacob Astor, now a sedate, graying, immensely wealthy landlord, owned most of the land on midtown Broadway (RIGHT).

BELOW: Meanwhile, Astor had leased much of his less well-located property to often unreliable tenants whose houses became dark, overcrowded, and filthy slums. More by accident than by intent, Astor's heirs emerged as the city's largest slumlords, and to improve the lot of their tenants, trapped in subhuman conditions, the city had to enact legislation.

River from present-day 53rd Street to 57th, for $23,000. And, to pay the interest, Astor leased the land to farmers and then sold off a few small lots to recoup his investment. "Buy da acre, sell da lot," he liked to say, and he never wasted a penny. Comparing these prices to his final $20-million estate gives a clearer idea of what his total wealth must have encompassed. Astor also bought shallow water lots on the downtown shore for a few dollars each from bribed city officials, filled them in, and sold the properties for fortunes as the city prospered. He owned most of the Lower East Side, 500 acres of Greenwich Village, vast sections of the Bowery, Lafayette Place, and Astor Place, as well as Astoria, Queens, a large suburb on the other side of the East River.

In the ever-growing metropolis, Astor allowed much of his land to be overbuilt with housing for the urban poor, leaving his descendants to become the world's first major slum landlords, against whom the municipal government would seek legislation to improve the lot of its constituents. Often, several families found themselves crowded into a few dank rooms that were firetraps, dangerous to life and limb, and almost devoid of light and air. Owing to inadequate pressure, water could not rise beyond the first floor, which made sanitation primitive, with the result that dysentery, scarlet fever, and other infectious diseases ran rampant.

In contrast, the Astors built and owned some of the most luxurious of New York's grand hotels, starting with John Jacob's City Hotel, which occupied his land at Broadway and Vesey Street. This, however, was a modest hostelry compared with the Astor House, erected during the 1830s. Six stories high, Astor House boasted modern plumbing and steam heating, which brought comfort to three hundred rooms and seventeen bathrooms. For a generation it constituted the social and political mecca of New York City. The first truly grand hotel of the nineteenth century may have been Tremont House in Boston, but for lavishness it had a strong competitor in Astor's palace, which offered not only a bowl and pitcher in every room, quite an advance for the time, but also a novel electrical device in the lobby for signaling rooms. Luxury hotels, however, did not distract Astor from collecting his rents, extorting his tenants on renewals, and accumulating even more land for a song during the many panics that periodically shook the nineteenth-century financial world, a world dominated by robber barons.

LEFT: The corner town house on Fifth Avenue at 65th Street, photographed in 1898, was but one of the many splendid residences owned by John Jacob Astor's descendants. The patriarch himself chose to live— and die—in a far more modest brownstone in Greenwich Village.

FAR LEFT: A salon in the home of William B. Astor, Jr.

OVERLEAF: The Astor family portrayed in all their late-19th-century glory. William Backhouse's younger son, William, built a splendid residence on Fifth Avenue at 34th Street, the present site of the Empire State Building, where he poses with his family in their baronial salon. Left to right are William, his daughter Helen, his daughter Charlotte Augusta, his only son John Jacob IV, who went down on the *Titanic*, his wife, the social arbiter Caroline Schermerhorn Astor (who considered herself *the* Mrs. Astor, even though the position belonged by precedence to her sister-in-law), and his daughter Caroline. This splendid painting, still in the family's possession, is the perfect expression of upper-class comfort and demeanor in the Gilded Age.

THE SECOND GENERATION

John Jacob Astor had three daughters and two sons who lived to adulthood (three other children died young), the senior of whom—John Jacob, Jr.—was epileptic and mentally deficient, to his father's immense grief. The elder Astor insisted that his other children treat his namesake as if the boy were normal, but eventually he had to house him in his own mansion with a physician, tutor, and staff to make life as pleasant as possible. The patriarch therefore invested all hope in his younger son, William Backhouse (1792-1875), named after the English fur trader who had been a mentor to the young John Jacob. William was educated at the socially desirable boarding school of Reverend Smith in Stamford, Connecticut, then at the universities of Heidelberg and Göttingen, after which he emerged a polished gentleman unlike his father,

who balanced peas on his knife and once wiped his greasy fingers on his neighbor's crinoline during a dinner party. "Villiam vill nefer *make* money" his father said, "but he vill keep vat he has." To make sure of that, John Jacob left his heirs, principally William, his immense property in a lifetime trust designed to keep the estate from being given away or dissipated. The trust was to be watched over by five of John Jacob's friends, as well as supervised by the New York State Supreme Court. Still, William enjoyed the independence of being allowed to accumulate his own $5-million fortune, which, when added to the $15 million left in trust, would make him the richest man in the United States.

John Jacob passed his declining years in ill health, his poor digestion assuaged only by taking milk from a wet nurse, after which he was rolled in a blanket. During one such session, a rent collector informed the old man that he could not get any money out of a destitute widow. "But she must pay it, she can pay it, and she vill pay it. You don't go the right vay to vork vid her," said New York's most important landlord. The desperate lieutenant went to William, who took the rent out of his pocket and told the man to give it to his father. "Dere, I told you she vould pay it if you vent the right vay to vork vid her," said Astor before falling into a rejuvenating sleep.

John Jacob was also a skinflint when it came to philanthropy or patronage. After promising the artist John James Audubon $1,000 toward the publication of his *Birds of America*, he attempted to renege. On Audubon's sixth visit he called out sadly to William: "Do ve have *any* money in da

Various members of the Astor family had both the money and the time to enjoy a near-royal way of life, thanks to enormous revenues flowing to them from the houses and hotels they owned in New York City. BELOW: Vincent Astor's magnificent oceangoing steam yacht, the *Nahma*. RIGHT: William Waldorf, Viscount Astor, the titled head of the expatriate British line of the family, is seen at the Cunard Line's dock in New York City.

bank at all?" William shouted back: "Yes, father, we have $220,000 in the Bank of New York, $70,000 in the City Bank, $90,000 in the Merchants Bank...." Astor finally coughed up. When he died, on March 29, 1848, few grieved, and his children busied themselves quarreling over the will, which, however, was ironclad and irrefutable.

THE ASTORS' RISE IN SOCIETY

John Jacob was right about William, as well as his descendants, who, until after World War I, developed their land, collected increasingly large rents, and became leaders of society, active politicians, and philanthropists. They were responsible for continuing and enlarging the Astor Library (later consolidated with other collections to form the New York Public Library), which the patriarch had started with $400,000 of the 2 percent of his fortune that he left for the public weal. It is quite easy to follow successive Astor generations, since the head of the family was nearly always named after the founder, as if the old man were ruling from beyond the grave. William married Rebecca Armstrong, a member of the Livingstone-Armstrong clan (then deemed the most aristocratic family in New York), and this union formed the basis of the Astors' great social ascent. Their eldest son, John Jacob III (1822-90), was considered the first aristocratic Astor and indeed looked as if he had long reigned over a great English country estate.

The change in two generations from a squat, square-featured, sharp-eyed German butcher to a suave, full-fledged grandee was astounding. John Jacob III took as his wife the well-born Charlotte Augusta Gibbes, the first of the great Astor ladies. His younger brother William (1830-92) married Caroline Schermerhorn of a distinguished Dutch family. It was she whom many would regard as *the* Mrs. Astor, following her scheme, concocted with the social arbiter Ward McAllister, to establish the "Four Hundred," the exact number of New York's *crème de la crème* who could be entertained in the William Astors' private ballroom. The two brothers split the family fortune, but given that it had quadrupled since the patriarch's death, little damage was done. When John Jacob IV (1864-1912), William's son, inherited from his father in 1892, he was still richer than William K. Vanderbilt, Jay Gould, or newcomer John D. Rockefeller.

HOTEL MADNESS

John Jacob III and his brother William built enormous adjoining town houses on Fifth Avenue and 34th Street. After the death of John Jacob III, William Waldorf (1848-1919), his son and heir,

"Meet me at the Astor" was an invitation to an elegant or interesting evening, since the Astor House or Hotel, in all its successive incarnations, was invariably the political and artistic center of New York. FAR LEFT: The simple, neoclassical façade of the first Astor House in Lower Manhattan. BOTTOM: Some of the prominent men who dined at the first Astor House, including, on the left, Thomas F. Byron, ex-chief of police holding a cup of coffee inscribed with the Astor initials, and, next to him, Judge Joseph H. Choate, later Ambassador to Great Britain. The Astor House had an unusually large number of rooms for the time, its own gas plant, and a big steam system that sent hot water to the rooms as well as to the bathing chambers in the basement. TOP: A symphonic concert (c.1910) in the great ballroom of the first Waldorf-Astoria Hotel, built in 1895-97 on Fifth Avenue at 34th Street, the site of the William B. Astor mansion in New York City.

the United States, and their carriages—as well as those of the merely curious—clogged Fifth Avenue from 59th Street to Washington Square. Walter Damrosch conducted the New York Philharmonic, and Astor's guests strolled through the beautiful glass-enclosed Palm Garden, the white and gold ballroom, and the main hall (copied after a Florentine palazzo), where a costumed Turk served coffee.

William's gamble paid off, for the hotel made a great deal of money, and Caroline moved out. She had Richard Morris Hunt build her a Gothic château on Fifth Avenue and 65th Street, which by then was a far more fashionable neighborhood. Now, after seeing the success of the Waldorf, John Jacob IV (1864-1912), Caroline and William's son, felt compelled to put up *his* hotel on the site of his parents'

decided to knock the family palace down and put up in its place the first Waldorf Hotel, the most ornate, glamorous, and modern hotel in the world at the time. He had several motives besides making money, which was far from guaranteed in an expensively built and run luxury hotel. There was, for instance, the vanity of linking his name to New York's social and business center, which had also been a guiding force in his great-grandfather's decision to build the Astor House. "Meet me at the Waldorf" would be fun to hear in the better clubs, offices, and houses of New York. Then, too, John Jacob III wanted to make a big statement in the United States, now that he had failed in his career as a politician and was spending most of his time more or less idle in Europe. Finally, he hated his Aunt Caroline, who had severely competed with his own wife on the social scenes of New York and Newport, and could think of no better revenge than to throw up a large, noisy public hotel next to the palace from which she still reigned. The hotel, built at a cost of $5 million, first opened its doors in 1895. For the inauguration, 1,500 guests came from all over

RIGHT: The Astor Hotel on Times Square, which reigned as the queen of Broadway and the New York theater district until demolished in the 1960s. For generations, the great Louis XIII palace was one of the most loved and vibrant of American grand hotels, thanks to the actors, musicians, opera singers, and honeymooners who thronged there.
BELOW: The St. Regis on the corner of New York's Fifth Avenue and 55th Street, shortly after this supremely aristocratic hotel opened at the turn of the 20th century.

abandoned headquarters. When William Waldorf heard that his cousin, known as Jack, wanted to call his palace the Schermerhorn in honor of Caroline's family, he announced plans to build New York's largest stable directly opposite. The renowned Philadelphia hotelier George Boldt orchestrated a deal between the cousins: Jack agreed to name his hotel the Astoria on the condition that it be three stories higher than the Waldorf, and Bill went along with this, provided that each hotel could be split off and run separately in case of further quarrels. The hotel, opened in 1897 and operated by Boldt, was demolished a mere thirty years later to make way for the Empire State Building. Simultaneously, in the Depression years 1930-31, the second and even more luxurious Waldorf-Astoria, an Art Deco palace, rose on Park Avenue between 49th and 50th streets, where it thrives today.

The cousins' hotel-building did not stop with the Waldorf-Astoria in 1897. In 1904 William built the Astor Hotel on Longacre Square (renamed Times Square later that year, when the newspaper of that name moved uptown). It would be dominated by New York's theater district for half a century, vastly increasing real estate values in the neighborhood—to the general benefit of the family who owned most of it. This enormous mansard-roofed, red-brick pile was famous for the actors and musicians who made it their home, as well as for the roof garden with its restaurants, café, and hanging gardens lit by Japanese lanterns, where generations of New Yorkers cooled off during the oppressive summer heat. John Jacob's answer to all this was the Knickerbocker Hotel on another corner of

Times Square, and the splendid and luxurious St. Regis Hotel on Fifth Avenue and 55th Street. In the latter, Jack indulged his scientific bent, introducing central heating, air conditioning, and a central vacuuming system throughout all eighteen floors of what was then New York's tallest hotel. (The glorious St. Regis was renovated in 1991 at a cost of $100 million, with the result that Jack's beautiful revolving bronze doors and marble floors shine today as they did for the palace's opening in 1904.)

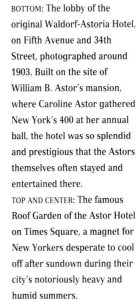

BOTTOM: The lobby of the original Waldorf-Astoria Hotel, on Fifth Avenue and 34th Street, photographed around 1903. Built on the site of William B. Astor's mansion, where Caroline Astor gathered New York's 400 at her annual ball, the hotel was so splendid and prestigious that the Astors themselves often stayed and entertained there.

TOP AND CENTER: The famous Roof Garden of the Astor Hotel on Times Square, a magnet for New Yorkers desperate to cool off after sundown during their city's notoriously heavy and humid summers.

RIGHT: Although successful as the builder and owner of the Waldorf Hotel (the first half of the famous Waldorf-Astoria), William Waldorf Astor failed in politics and decided to seek a more gentlemanly life in England, where he acquired Hever Castle in Kent and eventually both British citizenship and titles, first Baron and then Viscount.
BELOW: A cartoon sending up William Waldorf Astor for his eagerness to become a British citizen and peer.

THE ENGLISH ASTORS

By the turn of the century, the Astor family had effectively been divided in two. The English branch was started by William Waldorf, who had pursued a well-intentioned but ill-fated and eventually humiliating career in the swamps of New York City's politics. In 1890 he fled to England, calling it "a country fit for gentlemen to live in." Nonetheless, he would return occasionally and even take up residence in the Waldorf-Astoria Hotel. His dream was to become an English lord, which necessitated

buying Hever Castle in Kent, giving up his American citizenship, contributing hundreds of thousands of dollars to British charities during World War I, and creating a power platform by purchasing the *Pall Mall Gazette* and the Sunday *Observer*. Major John Jacob Astor, his son, was to buy the London *Times* in 1920, making the family a major force in English journalism and politics. The hidden cost of becoming Lord Astor, however, proved enormous since the English branch of the family would be heavily taxed after World War I, in both Great Britain and the United States, before the creation of a tax treaty between the two nations. This double load decimated the fortune of that half of the family, forcing them to sell a large part of their holdings in the United States. Meanwhile, the American branch was then headed by John Jacob IV, who also fell victim to international life, when he went down with the *Titanic* on April 15, 1912, reportedly standing at attention in full evening dress next to a friend, Major Archie Butt.

THE ASTOR LEGACY

Following the death of John Jacob Astor, the illustrious dynasty he founded belongs as much to the history of society, or of palace- and hotel-building, as to the story of American business. Still, no family have left such an enduring stamp on the urban landscape in which they lived, and their holdings dwarfed those of such important American landowners as Chicago's Potter Palmer and Marshall Field, or retailer Alexander T. Stewart, the founder of Wanamaker's who, with John Jacob Astor and Cornelius Vanderbilt, was one of the three richest men in the United States, or even such old-time New York patricians as the Goelets, Rhinelanders, Beekmans, Lorillards, and Schermerhorns.

BELOW: William Waldorf Astor caricatured as a tweedy, monocled English lord whose American millions promised to be a life-saver for Britannia, which happened to be the name as well of the royal yacht.
ABOVE: The magnificent building designed by Carrère and Hastings for the New York Public Library, an institution founded in large part by a legacy from the original John Jacob Astor, and still nurtured by the Astor Foundation.

In Gilded Age Europe it would be impossible to find anyone who made such a large, new fortune out of land. This was for a simple reason: Most urban property remained in the hands of aristocratic or ruling families totally disinclined to let it go. Large sections of London's West End still belong to the Duke of Westminster, and Bedford and Tavistock Squares confirm feudal origins by their very names. The possible exception to the European rule was Paris during and after Baron Haussmann's renovations, made under Napoleon III's parvenu Second Empire (1852-70), when some disenfranchised aristocrats sold their properties in the rapidly expanding French capital. Yet, no single name stands out in Paris or elsewhere, making the Astors the land kings of modern times.

TRANSPORTATION

The two most prominent families in the United States after the Civil War were the Astors and the Vanderbilts. In New York's social strata, the former considered the latter arrivistes, although the fortune they commanded had come only a few decades earlier. While the Astors got their land largely through the massacre of wildlife, the Vanderbilts accumulated their vast properties—including New York's Grand Central Terminal and large tracts in midtown Manhattan—with the riches they had earned in transportation, first river and ocean shipping but then, overwhelmingly, railroads. Beginning in 1850, the iron rail revolutionized the transport of goods and passengers, giving rise to some of the most colossal fortunes ever assembled. In a ten-year span, 1880-90, the amount of track crisscrossing the United States increased from 115,647 miles to 208,152. New networks of this sort not only wove nations together; they also opened up the enormous natural wealth that had long been unreachable, locked in the great landmasses of North America, Russia, and, to a lesser extent, Europe. Improvements in transportation were at the very heart of the Industrial Revolution and the huge economic expansion that made the Gilded Age possible.

Thanks to ever-larger and more economically run ocean freighters and ever-more extensive webs of iron rail, the cost of transport, an essential component in every economic good, fell dramatically, thereby allowing the doctrine of comparative advantage to take root. If wheat could be more efficiently grown in the fertile soil of the United States, the Argentine pampas, or the Australian outback and shipped inexpensively to Europe, then technological know-how, concentration of capital, and a trained work force would guide the resources of more developed countries toward industrial development. Accordingly, prices would fall and wages increase, humankind would benefit, and the glow of prosperity enter the households of all willing to work at what they were best suited. There would, of course, be dislocations, but labor could migrate easily from places of surfeit to new frontiers begging for hands to till the soil, build homesteads as well as factories, and, ultimately, help forge new societies full of hope and prosperity. That, at least, was the theory. In fact, until shocking abuses were brought under control, the new land and sea routes permitted a few unscrupulous robber barons to compile some of the largest estates of all time, particularly in the United States.

OPPOSITE: Claude Monet (1840-1926), *La Gare Saint-Lazare* (detail), 1877 (Musée d'Orsay, Paris). As a "painter of modern life," Monet took the bold step of executing a series of canvases devoted to that foremost emblem of 19th-century modernism—the train station.
BELOW: Edward Lamson Henry (1841-1919), *The 9:45 Accommodation, Stanford, Connecticut,* 1867 (Metropolitan Museum of Art, New York City). This painting of an early American railroad was commissioned by John Taylor Johnston, president of the New Jersey Central. Passengers arrive in their horse-drawn carriages to catch the new-fangled means of transportation.
OVERLEAF: Albert Bierstadt (1830-1902), *The Rocky Mountains, Lander's Peak* (detail), 1863 (Metropolitan Museum of Art, New York City). Better than any other artist of his time, Bierstadt, an emigrant from Germany, captured both the grandeur and the purity of America's landscape as it had been before the arrival of Europeans. The new Americans would lace it with crisscrossing networks of rails, destroy the aboriginal population, and exploit the land for their own, often rapacious, benefit. Seen here are members of the Shoshone tribe beside the Green River, which flows at the foot of the Wind River Mountains in Wyoming.

RIGHT: Crossing the continent by rail was the great American adventure during the second half of the 19th century. The young girl in this travel picture seems to elicit considerable enthusiasm from her pet dog, which has forgotten its ball in the excitement of a trip on the far-reaching Chicago, Rock Island & Pacific Railway. BELOW: Currier and Ives, the renowned printmakers whose work reflected most aspects of daily life in 19th-century America, entitled this scene *Across the Continent* (1869). The passenger train is simply marked "Through Line: New York to San Francisco," with less fortunate travelers shown heading out in stagecoaches. Almost certainly, the travelers by both means would end up populating the Western wilderness, newly enriched by the Gold Rush of 1849.

By amalgamating, merging, and price-fixing, railroaders could charge fees totally unrelated to costs or any other reality. Large customers could obtain special rates or even rebates in collusion with the owners of the roads, thus freezing out—and finally bankrupting—their smaller competitors. The payoff frequently came in the form of stock issued by newly created monopolies that gave railroaders and financiers material interests in key industries, all to the ultimate detriment of the consumer. Finally, the problem brought the attempted solution of strict controls by such government agencies as the United States Interstate Commerce Commission, established in 1887 in response to the roaring protest of American farmers, Western manufacturers, and shippers against the stranglehold of the railroaders. For many years, however, corrupt senators and congressmen made the ICC a toothless agency, and wholesale abuses seriously abated only with the merging, purging, rationalization, and consolidation effected by, above all, the great banking house of J.P. Morgan and Jacob Schiff's Kuhn, Loeb & Co., which brought order to an exceedingly chaotic industry. J.P. Morgan played much the same role in the railroads that he had in steel, but his potentially dangerous power would be curtailed primarily by the advent of automobiles and trucks running on roads built with public funds for the public benefit. These thoroughfares finally deposed the railway kings, depriving them of the choking grip they had long held on all economic activity.

Owning a railroad that monopolized the carriage of food, oil, ore, or finished products from the source to the consumer proved to be one of the most sublime licenses to steal ever invented, and the struggle to consolidate control of transport in specific areas made up much of the history of finance in the Gilded Age. At the turn of this century, 85 percent of the stocks and bonds traded in the United States represented equity in railroads, and when the Soviet government defaulted on the obligations of the destroyed Czarist Empire after the 1917 revolution, European and American banks and private investors found themselves burdened by enough worthless paper to cover their walls with portraits of Nicholas II, pretty railway cars, and handsomely engraved images of Siberia's mountains and lakes. For many rogue financiers, controlling or owning a railway was little more than an excuse for upsetting financial markets and creating the booms and busts on which they could profit from the stupidity and gullibility of outside investors. Europeans, for instance, lost over $600 million on American railroads. At the same time, however, robber barons could not take their tracks or rolling stock with them to the afterlife, so in the end much of their legacy accrued to the immense benefit of the public at large.

OBTAINING LAND FOR RAILROADS

Modern transport in the Old World developed in a manner essentially different from the way taken in the New World, even though the industry generated tons of new money on both sides of the Atlantic. In much of Europe and in Russia, of course, land belonged to ruling families, the feudal aristocracy, and a few small farmers, while in the United States the young republican government expropriated and forcibly seized the great landmass from its Native American owners. Land grants came from legislators in Washington, D.C., who conceived the notion of making such grants to railroad promoters in exchange for endowing the country with a new system of transport. The scheme left great financial decisions to be made by bureaucrats whose small salaries often rendered them corruptible. As a result, promoters raised money for roads that were never built, railroaders laid new tracks virtually parallel to ones already in place, and fiscally insecure new lines quickly went broke, destroyed existing fare structures, and created total chaos in both the industry and the financial markets. Cornelius Vanderbilt summed it up neatly when—following one of the many stock market panics caused by wild speculation in railroad paper—he said that building train tracks from nowhere to nowhere was not sound business practice.

COMMODORE VANDERBILT

Although neither the first nor the last of the railroad tycoons, Commodore Cornelius Vanderbilt (1794-1877) lost no time once he realized, fairly late in life, that he was uniquely equipped to practice the magic alchemy of transforming railway paper into a money-producing machine beyond compare. The amazing Vanderbilt career involved some of the shadiest operators ever to appear on the financial scene, and the ultimate triumph of the Commodore as one of the richest men in the world is a monument not only to physical courage, brilliant intellect, and moderately ethical behavior within a den of thieves, but also to a single-minded determination to acquire fabulous wealth. If John Jacob Astor became the king of real estate, Commodore Vanderbilt emerged as the absolute titan of modern transport.

Cornelius Van Derbilt, as he spelled his name early in life, was born on May 27, 1794, on Staten Island, New York, where he grew up without receiving much formal education. At the height of his career, this richest of all men still wrote English in a phonetic manner; nevertheless, he possessed such an extraordinary photographic memory that his small desk never had any papers on its clean wooden top or in its small drawer. He concluded most of his great business deals orally, and seemed able to pull out the most esoteric and distant financial information with total recall. Perhaps of all the American tycoons, the Commodore was the most heroic in terms of pure physical strength, love of battle, total commitment to the production of wealth, fearless appetite for risk, and pure killer instinct.

Young Cornelius, who could easily beat his friends in games of strength, developed a taste for the sea. It helped that his father, also called Cornelius, owned a small sailboat that carried his farming produce from Staten Island to Manhattan. At the early age of sixteen, Corneel, as his parents called him, discovered that a small two-masted, flat-bottomed piragua was for sale and could be profitably used to transport passengers between Staten Island and the city. His father agreed to lend him $100—provided he could plant a rocky field with corn before his birthday. Corneel rounded up all his friends and promised them free rides and perhaps a bit of his profit if they helped him move rocks and sow the land. In no time he showed up for the money, and was soon operating his small ferry for 18 cents one way or 25 cents round trip. So skillfully did Vanderbilt sail his craft that watches could be set by his arrivals and departures to and from the small Staten Island dock. To get through calm water, he once poled so vigorously that he ended up piercing his chest to the bone. And seldom did the sea become so

LEFT: The modest house in which Commodore Vanderbilt was born in 1794. The founder of the Vanderbilt fortune, which made him one of the very richest men of his time, could hardly be accused of having come into the world with a silver spoon in his mouth. Growing up on Staten Island, young Cornelius Van Derbilt came to love, and love conquering, the sea. BELOW: Rough, tough, and courageous, the first Cornelius Vanderbilt braved high seas in a rowboat to carry supplies and thus frustrate the British blockade of New York Harbor during the War of 1812.

Henry A. Ogden, *The Clermont* (New York Historical Society). Thomas Fulton (1765-1815)—gunsmith, painter, engineer, inventor—was one of early America's most versatile figures. Popular imagination links him mainly to the development of the steamboat, which he undertook in association with Robert R. Livingston, a rich and prominent landlord along the Hudson River. In this period painting, "Fulton's Folly" is being hailed as "Fulton's Triumph" during the triumphant maiden voyage of the *Clermont* up the Hudson from New York City to Albany. The vessel was described as "a curious looking thing that rolled through the water by her two great arms, resembling the wheels of a Grist Mill." Notwithstanding the skepticism, the inventor's successful passage allowed him and Livingston to obtain a monopoly on Hudson River transport, which the future Commodore Vanderbilt would take upon himself to break.

storm-tossed that he would not brave it, provided there were passengers willing to take the risk and pay the money. After his first season, Corneel could not only repay the $100 loan but also buy two more ships, vessels that proved extremely successful in navigating near the shore during the War of 1812, when the British fleet blockaded New York Harbor.

Meanwhile, the age of steam had arrived—thanks to Robert Fulton's historic run on the Hudson River in 1807 with the paddle steamer *Clermont*. Moreover, Fulton and his partner, Robert R. Livingston, had obtained a monopoly on steam navigation in New York waters, which forced all competitors to pay them a fee. Corneel took a ride on one of Fulton's ferries, studied its machinery, and immediately understood that the era of sailing ships would soon be at an end, except for sport.

Several operators attempted to break the monopoly, notably Thomas Gibbons, a lawyer who later became governor of New Jersey. Gibbons needed a tough and cunning captain for his small side-wheeler, the *Stoudingen*, jokingly referred to as the *Mouse of the Mountain*, and so in 1818 hired Corneel, then a young idealist opposed to monopolies, believing that "no man ever ought to be worth more than $20,000." He would soon modify this attitude quite radically. In 1824 Chief Justice John Marshall pronounced the monopoly illegal, declared the commerce to be intercourse, and expounded the principle of the plenary power of Congress to regulate interstate commerce. Owing to this historic opinion, New York became a free port, and American navigation entered a period of tremendous expansion, an epic development that Vanderbilt would soon lead.

Four years later, at the age of 35, Vanderbilt established his own steamboat routes radiating north and south out of New York, an ever-expanding business that would occupy him for the next twenty years. Whenever contested, he lowered his rates and either bankrupted his competitors or forced them into mergers. It was on the route between New York's Westchester and Putnam counties that Vanderbilt first met up with the slightly younger Daniel Drew (1797-1879), a cattle rustler and horse trader who was to be his partner, rival, and challenger for over forty years in one of the oddest business relationships ever. Drew, who at the height of his career reputedly had more cash ready for speculation than anyone in the United States, and Vanderbilt, who in his railroading days was essentially an ingenious

stock speculator, matched wits and attempted to ruin each other on multiple occasions, seemingly for the mere sport of it. Along the way, they also destroyed the fortunes of small and large investors alike.

Among his contributions to the world of commerce, Drew mastered the trick of depriving his cattle of water until they were close to the door of the slaughterhouse. At that point, he served them slabs of salt, inducing a terrible thirst that drove the beasts to engorge vast amounts of water just prior to being weighed. "Watering cattle" was the early version of "watering stock," a popular technique whereby business owners and their bankers would vastly inflate the price of the equity they issued to the public on the basis of future prospects, put the "water" into their own financial reservoirs, and still maintain controlling interest at the public's expense. On the Hudson, Drew first confronted but then joined Vanderbilt, after which both accepted enormous bribes to keep their ships off certain passages. Soon Vanderbilt boats were plying ever busier routes up the Hudson, down to Philadelphia, and across Long Island Sound, while connecting Manhattan to his birthplace via the Staten Island Ferry. It was time for a move out to sea by the captain now respectfully known in shipping circles as "The Commodore."

TOP: After breaking Fulton's shipping monopoly on the Hudson, Vanderbilt became the king of river travel in the north, whereupon he also gained the trappings of success and wealth. However, he was not without competition, mainly from Daniel Drew (LEFT) with whom the powerful Vanderbilt split up routes to their mutual advantage.

BELOW AND OVERLEAF: The scale and luxury of the paddle steamers run by Vanderbilt and Drew made a sheer delight of journeying on the beautiful Hudson River, between rapidly developing New York Harbor and the state capital in Albany.

RIGHT: The *C. Vanderbilt* weighed over 1,000 tons, traveled at a top speed of 25 miles per hour, and boasted elegantly stuffed rosewood furniture.

BELOW: Commodore Vanderbilt's private yacht, the *North Star*, was the same length as Great Britain's royal yacht *Victoria and Albert*, and it so impressed Europeans that a British journalist declared it high time that "parvenu" be considered a term of praise rather than derision. Not one to waste assets, Vanderbilt turned his yacht into the flagship of a relatively short-lived and unsuccessful transatlantic fleet, launched for the purpose of challenging such established shippers as the Canadian Samuel Cunard and George K. Collins. After selling his Atlantic and Pacific Steamship Company in 1864, Vanderbilt used the proceeds to get into railroads.

THE GOLD RUSH

The Commodore first turned his eyes westward, where the 1849 gold rush was on, attracting vast numbers of fortune hunters from Europe and the Eastern Seaboard. Whoever got there faster stood a better chance of staking a good claim; yet, sailing around South America's Cape Horn was a hazardous adventure that took several months. A shortcut across Nicaragua or Panama could reduce the traveling time to less than a month. Consequently, George Law, one of Vanderbilt's most capable competitors on the rivers, headed for Panama, while the Commodore fixed his sights on Nicaragua. Here the latter foresaw one small canal capable of bringing ships from the Caribbean into the San Juan River and Lake Nicaragua, and another providing a similar linkage between the banks of the lake and the Pacific Ocean a short distance away.

Vanderbilt organized the Accessory Transport Company, which ran exceptionally fast steamships on both sides of the isthmus and transported passengers to and from Lake Nicaragua over land and

across the lake by small ferry, cutting 400 miles and several days from the more difficult Panama passage. Each day might literally mean a gold mine, and soon the Nicaragua adventure was making immense sums of money, despite a price-cutting war that brought rates down by more than half. The British refused to finance the canal, and Vanderbilt lost interest except for the operation of his steamships, which he sold in 1852 at a good profit, while remaining both president of the company and its New York agent. Now worth $11 million, he decided to take a vacation on his *North Star*, the largest private yacht in existence.

THE GREAT RAILROADER

Like John Jacob Astor, dabbling in real estate while cleaning up on furs, Cornelius Vanderbilt had fiddled with railroads as a by-product of maritime transport. Also like Astor, the Commodore would use his initial fortune as a mere springboard to even more colossal riches. Finally, both tycoons started their real careers after the age of seventy. In the case of Vanderbilt, the six-part formula for making money the second time round—now on tracks—was summed up by a contemporary admirer: Buy your line; Stop the stealing that went on under the other man; Improve it in every way within a reasonable expenditure; Consolidate it with other lines for the sake of efficiency; Water its stock; and Make it pay a big dividend.

The first new killing made by Vanderbilt was the Harlem Railroad, whose stock he started to buy at $10 in 1857 upon becoming a director, along with his old friend Daniel Drew. During the panic of that year, Vanderbilt took a large position in Harlem bonds, not a terribly exciting move since the line in all its history had rewarded stockholders with a grand total of 13 percent in dividends. Harlem, however, had franchise rights to operate in New York City, as well as an entrance from the north and east, which theoretically gave it the right to run a streetcar service along the entire length of Manhattan. The directors lobbied as well as bribed city officials—in particular the infamous politician "Boss" Tweed—and the shares started to rise dramatically in anticipation throughout 1862 and 1863. Needless to say, insider trading was rife, and by the time the municipal government opposed Harlem's plan, the stock had risen to $50. The next day it shot up to $70. Meanwhile, George Law, who had given Vanderbilt a run for his money in Panama, lobbied in Albany, the state capital, to get the franchise canceled, and when he failed, the stock soared to $100. Vanderbilt got himself elected president, and the price reached $116. Drew, taken off the executive and finance committees, sold his stock at an immense profit. Almost immediately he turned around in total betrayal and attempted to convince Tweed, then New York's street commissioner, to withdraw the franchise and make a killing, along with him, by shorting Harlem stock. As the news leaked out in June, the shares started sinking back to $73—but the shrewd Vanderbilt refused to be taken in. He and his directors had the funds to buy all shares sold by worried stockholders as well as all the shorts. Even more, they bought up *all* the outstanding equity, thus "cornering" the stock and forcing it to climb, since there was none available for Drew and his friends to cover their short positions. By August, when the short had been covered, the stock was up to $179.

Inevitably, Drew was kicked off the Harlem board, and William Henry Vanderbilt (1821-85), the Commodore's son and heir, took the job of managing the railroad while his exigent father turned to the Hudson River Railroad. This ran parallel to the Harlem line on the other side of the river, which made it Harlem's main rival for both freight and passengers. If the Vanderbilt group could control both services, it would have a near monopolistic position on traffic into New York City. The Commodore, together with Tobin and Jerome, started buying Hudson shares in 1863, at the same time that, triggered by rumor-mongering about an attempt on the part of the state legislature to block the takeover, the bears began to sell the stock short, just as they had Harlem's. Here, too, the Commodore set a trap and caught the big prize. Naturally, he soon bought control of the Hudson, ousted the directors, and put William to work again as he refocused his attention, now on the richest target of all. This was the New York Central Railroad, whose largest shareholders were the shipping magnate Edward Cunard and none other than John Jacob Astor, Jr.

The Central owned, among other properties, nine small railroads between Albany and Buffalo that presented obstacles to the Commodore's scheme of complete monopoly. Their total capital-ization was $25 million, too large even for the Vanderbilt group to control, but a foot in the door might permit them to organize a raid on the management and ultimately merge the Hudson, Harlem, and Central into one of the most powerful railroads in the land. Vanderbilt owned a bridge over the Hudson that the Central used for a fee, and when his targeted rivals made it clear that any takeover attempt

ABOVE: Daniel Drew, who ceased to be the Commodore's partner and became a deadly rival, glowers in this early photograph.

OPPOSITE BELOW: *Ruined: 1869 Panic*. The very title of this engraving, after a drawing by G.C. Bush, says it all in regard to the effect on the investing public of the self-serving manipulations of the securities markets practiced by Gilded Age robber barons.

RIGHT: The first Grand Central Station, on New York's East 42nd Street, was commissioned by Vanderbilt in 1869 and designed by Isaac C. Buckhout. The neo-Baroque, mansarded façade concealed the thrillingly modern train shed behind it (see opposite).

BELOW: In this cartoon, Jay Gould blows Daniel Drew up on Wall Street, while a policeman lurks in the background, ready to arrest him.

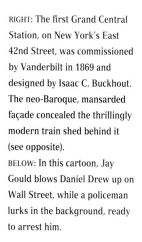

would be repulsed, he forced the Central's passengers to walk over the ice with all their baggage to a train that was waiting on the other shore. This, in addition to lobbying, blackmail, stock purchases, and refusal to let the Central use sections of the Hudson's lines, eventually forced the Central's directors to call a vote, which gave the Vanderbilt group a majority position on the board, with the Commodore as chairman. Under their management, all the lines prospered and finally merged, whereupon Vanderbilt, with financial legerdemain, unloaded $90 million in stock watered by almost $50 million, over $50,000 for each mile of track between New York and Buffalo. Even the most hardened and brilliant financiers were agog at this coup, which encouraged yet more speculation in railroad stock and destructive takeovers.

The Evil Trio

But the tycoon never rests. Now Vanderbilt thought of expanding westward toward Chicago, knowing as he did that the Erie Railroad had the same idea. The Erie, considered "the Scarlet

Woman of Wall Street," had as its treasurer none other than Daniel Drew, who spent most of his time manipulating its stock, an activity that inspired his bankers to compose and chant a jingle:

A "NORTHWESTERN" BLOW.
"When Rogues fall out, will Honest Men have their dues?"

LEFT: The iron and glass, radically modern train shed behind the ornate façade of the first Grand Central Station in New York City. The great barrel vault defined the largest enclosed space in the United States at the time.
BELOW: James Fisk, who conspired with Jay Gould and A.R. Corbin, President Grant's brother-in-law, to corner the gold market in the United States, which triggered the worst panic of the 19th century on Wall Street. By printing ever-more stock in the Erie Railroad, the robber barons defeated Commodore Vanderbilt in his attempt to take over the line.
FAR LEFT: Although Jim Fisk had to go about with bodyguards, owing to his devastating manipulations of the financial markets, he met his end when shot, on the stairs of the Grand Central Hotel, by a jealous rival for his mistress.

Daniel says up—Erie goes up
Daniel says down—Erie goes down
Daniel says wiggle-waggle—it goes both ways.

Drew's associates in the Erie adventure were Jay Gould (1836-92), known as "the Mephistopheles of Wall Street," and James Fisk, who started his business life smuggling cotton during the Civil War. Among the capers these wily traders performed was an attempt to corner the entire gold supply of the United States and therefore the currency it backed. Carried out in cahoots with the lobbyist A.R. Corbin, President Ulysses S. Grant's brother-in-law, the scheme precipitated one of the most devastating of all Black Fridays on Wall Street, September 24, 1869. The havoc that "Jubilee Jim" Fisk and Gould wrought on the financial and commodity markets was such that neither could appear in public without bodyguards, and in 1872 Fisk was shot to death by a rival for his mistress on the steps of the Grand Central Hotel that served as his headquarters. Vanderbilt's takeover campaign lasted a few years and became a cause célèbre, since it was the only defeat the Commodore ever suffered. In its simplest terms, the crooked trio shorted Erie stock all the while that Vanderbilt was buying it for control. Despite his massive purchases, the stock continued to fall because Drew & Co. were illegally printing stock certificates. The more shares the Commodore bought the more they printed, and Jim Fisk proudly announced to the newspapers that "if this printing press don't break down, I'll be damned if I don't give the old hog all he wants of Erie." Vanderbilt got an injunction, and as the police closed in, the trio escaped beyond their jurisdiction to New Jersey—laden with suitcases of cash and the stock book. They holed up with an army of bodyguards in a fortified hotel, where Vanderbilt sent his men to shoot it out. Finally, the Commodore got fed up battling Fisk and Gould. He had lost the fight for the Erie, wanted to settle the score, and invited his nemesis, Drew, to come by and make a deal. Having settled the affair and even recovered some of his losses, he surmised philosophically that it never pays to kick a skunk.

Although approaching eighty, Vanderbilt continued to buy up small railroad companies for consolidation with his major holdings. In 1869 he built the largest rail terminus in the world for the Harlem line—Grand Central Terminal on New York's 42nd Street just east of Fifth Avenue. (This splendid station would be demolished to make way for the present, even more palatial building, which dates from 1913.) The New York Central also owned most of the land in the vicinity, and as it soared in

PURCHASE TICKETS VIA ERIE RAILWAY

RIGHT: A 19th-century poster advertising the Erie Railroad, operated by three of the most notorious speculators in American financial history: Daniel Drew, Jay Gould, and James Fisk.

BELOW: A cartoon satirizing the campaign undertaken by Commodore Vanderbilt, the principal shareholder in the Hudson River and New York Central Railroads, to gain control of Jim Fisk's Erie Railroad and thus access to Chicago. As the cartoon implies, both tycoons increased their power and wealth by watering the stock of the companies they managed.

FAR RIGHT: In this cartoon, an elderly Commodore Vanderbilt professes to be retired from business and speculation even as he vigorously pursues both, almost to the end of his 83 years.

value, Vanderbilt became one of the principal property magnates of the rapidly growing city. In his scarce free time, the Commodore indulged his love of harness racing, which kept him at his horses, whip in hand, practically to the last. In 1869, a year after his wife from the Staten Island era, Sophia Johnson Vanderbilt, died, he married anew, this time to a woman five decades younger than himself. Vanderbilt enjoyed participating in séances and befriended two spinster mediums on Staten Island, Victoria and Tennie Williams, whom he even set up in business with a gift of $7,500. Otherwise, he unfailingly refused any request for personal assistance, explaining: "I am sorry for the distress of people, but if I was to begin that sort of business, my door would be blocked from here to Broadway, and I'd have to call the police to get to my office of mornings." But under the influence of the new Mrs. Vanderbilt, the Commodore gave $50,000 to their

clergyman to buy a church and $500,000 to Central University in Nashville, Tennessee, which would become Vanderbilt University.

The Commodore died quietly on January 4, 1877, at the ripe age of 83, leaving an estate of $100 million, 60 percent of which was stock in the New York Central and Hudson River railroads. His heirs—primarily his sons and four grandsons—knew how to spend the money, but primogeniture would keep the fortune intact.

THE CALIFORNIA QUARTET

That building railroads was a mandate to steal could find no better confirmation than in the careers of California's famous "Big Four": Charles Crocker, Mark Hopkins, Collis P. Huntington, and Leland Stanford. Crocker is immortalized by his bank, Hopkins by one of San Francisco's grandest drawn the elephant." Still, the grant was linked to progress, and the associates had to raise the money to get going. Turned down by San Francisco's conservative bankers, they had no choice but to sell their own bonds to the public, eventually raising a total of $27 million. Simultaneously, Governor Stanford started to wheedle money out of the cities along the planned route. When, for example, the Southern Pacific threatened to bypass Los Angeles—then a small town—the citizenry were forced to turn over to the railroad the proceeds of a bond issue equivalent to 5 percent of the entire assessed land value of the county. William Z. Ripley, an authority on the subject, estimated that govern-

FAR LEFT: Seen clockwise are the famous "California Quartet": Mark Hopkins (1802-87), Leland Stanford (1824-93), Charles Crocker (1854-97), and Collis P. Huntington (1821-1900). Their Central Pacific Railroad, once linked to the Union Pacific (LEFT), became one of the greatest undertakings in American industrial history.

hotels, Stanford by his university, and Huntington—albeit indirectly—by the Henry E. Huntington Library, named after his nephew, associate, and principal heir. Huntington, together with his Eastern-born partner Hopkins, had become rich in a hardware store, Stanford had practiced law and, from 1861 to 1863, served as governor of California (a useful vantage point from which to exploit his constituency), and Crocker had begun as an ironmonger and gold miner. In order to invest jointly in schemes that would be to their mutual profit, the four successful friends formed Pacific Associates. Theodor Dehone Judah, a local engineer, fired up their imagination with his description of a transcontinental railroad, setting out a possible itinerary through the mountainous landscape of the Rockies and Sierra Nevada. They rode out on horseback and quickly realized the fortune to be made by bringing the riches of the forty-niners to the West Coast.

Pacific Associates had a total purse of $200,000, which Huntington put in his trunk and took to Washington in 1861, along with a set of plans. He claimed to be head of the Central Pacific Railroad capitalized at $8.5 million—not a penny of which had been paid in. Thanks to the skillful lobbying of Huntington and others, the Pacific Railway Act was passed in 1862, giving to Pacific Associates a federal charter to build the Central Pacific Railroad from the sea eastward. The bill required the Central Pacific to meet the equally embryonic Union Pacific Railroad of Thomas Durant and the Ames brothers, a line that was to start building westward from the Missouri River. The Union Pacific received 12 million acres and $27 million in 6 percent thirty-year bonds as a first mortgage, the Central Pacific 9 million acres and $24 million. Nobody could accuse Huntington of having misused the $200,000 stake of his group, for as he cabled Stanford: "We have

Building the Western railroads entailed tremendous risk and challenge.

RIGHT: A construction crew, near the Green River on the western slope of the Cascade Mountains, stops for a rest after building a trestle across a gorge prior to tackling the Stampede Tunnel. Note the heavily scarfed Chinese laborer seated on the left.

FAR RIGHT: Giant wheels used to transport tree trunks near Redding, California.

BELOW: An Irish laborer shot full of arrows by Indians who are riding away in the distance.

OPPOSITE: A famous photograph by William H. Jackson shows human creation dwarfed by nature. Crossing Colorado's Rocky Mountains was clearly a Herculean challenge.

ment underwrote 60 percent of the cost of the railroad's construction, and that much of this public money went directly into the pockets of the entrepreneurs. Counties and towns paid up as the track got closer, thereby financing most of the large building. Work began on January 8, 1863, and involved 3,000 Irishmen and 10,000 Chinese, the latter brought over specially from China and paid $1 per day, while the Irish received $2. The road went through the Summit Valley and rose to nearly 7,000 feet in the central Sierras, running through mining country near Carson City, Nevada, and across that state toward Salt Lake City, Utah. Mountains were knocked down or drilled through and gorges spanned with shaky bridges. Meanwhile, laborers who helped work these miracles died in avalanches of rock and snow, flash floods, and Indian attacks, as well as from dynamite explosions and disease. Money seemed no object, and, according to later government reports, waste exceeded that in normal construction by 75 percent. There was, however, a logic in this, owing to a scheme invented by the Central Pacific.

The California quartet organized a construction company, the Credit and Finance Corporation, which contracted for the building of the road with the Central Pacific, an enterprise that belonged to them as well. The railroad paid approximately $79 million to the builders out of the monies received from stock- and bond-holders and the government.

It appears that nearly half of this disappeared, or at least could not be accounted for; thus, the missing funds clearly went right to the shareholders. No one ever found out the truth, the records having been destroyed by a fire in the railroad's main office. In 1867 the Union Pacific's con-

struction company was impressively baptized the Crédit Mobilier, a title designed to cash in on the solidity of France during the Second Empire, and it pocketed approximately $10 million in the same way. The shareholders of the Crédit Mobilier included a large section of the nation's cabinet, as well as several congressmen and senators. Trading in the shares by unscrupulous speculators, as well as revelations of bribery, did much to bring on the

crash of 1873, the nineteenth-century equivalent of Black Tuesday, 1929. When investigated and exposed, the government's role in the financing of railroads became a national scandal, which had a severely negative impact on the market for railroad paper. By that time, however, the entrepreneurs were as rich as Croesus. The Union Pacific's 20,000 workers continued pushing their way forward, as did the Central Pacific crew, despite constant attacks and terrible suffering from desert heat. Troops were called in to protect both companies' workers, who lived in ramshackle villages thrown up for short periods and filled with prostitutes, gamblers, and swindlers. The two lines feverishly raced one another to the finish, since the subsidies grew in proportion to the land covered by track. In

BELOW: Henry Villard, an old-timer in the railroads, concentrated on bringing settlers from Europe to populate the wilderness that he and his associates had obtained as land grants in return for a promise to network the nation with tracks. The land Villard sold or developed provided part of the funds needed to finance the ongoing work of building tracks. The rest came from bond issues (which could not always be floated) as well as from municipal authorities paying blackmail money to keep their towns or cities from being bypassed.
LEFT: Hopeful settlers crossed the country in covered wagons, since train transport was often not yet in place. Moreover, emigrants came massively laden with tools, clothes, and large families. Dust flies as one of many long caravans crosses the Great Plains.
OPPOSITE: Frederic Remington, *The Old Stage Coach of the Plains*, 1901 (Amon Carter Museum, Fort Worth).

1869 the Central Pacific met the Union Pacific at Promontory, Utah, the historic linkage marked by a morning ceremony during which a golden spike was driven into the track.

THE BANANA BELT

Meanwhile, other grand schemes were cooked up. A group of Pennsylvania financiers, including the steel king Andrew Carnegie, won a charter for the Texas & Pacific Railroad, and the banker Jay Cooke obtained the charter for the Northern Pacific, including 47 million acres of land. This was intended to be no less than a second transcontinental railroad that would go from Duluth, Minnesota, to the mouth of the Columbia River, opening up vast tracts of land in the Dakota territory, Idaho, Washington, and Oregon.

The United States government believed its land grant to Cooke generous enough that no other financial subsidy would be necessary. Officials in Washington probably figured that the super-salesman would peddle bonds, which indeed he attempted to do to the tune of $100 million. German, British, and Dutch bankers were entertained in his palace and shipped off to inspect the rich land ready for exploitation. Cooke used his influence to promote the project through all the major newspapers of the country, regaling and even bribing the press. He hired a journalistic genius, Sam Wilkenson, who described the natural wonders along the northern Pacific in such ecstatic terms that many began to visualize the territory as a world of vast orange groves and banana plantations, complete with monkeys and other exotic fauna. The looping circuit of the planned road did resemble a banana, and "Jay Cooke's Banana Belt"—most of it under snow a good part of the year—became Wall Street's epithet for promotional nonsense. Still, the propaganda helped Cooke bring thousands of settlers from Europe to develop his land. He proceeded building the road but

rapidly ran into serious trouble. Cost overruns were enormous, the engineering was shoddy to the point that a large section of track sank into a lake, and, worst of all, the market for the bonds dried up following the Crédit Mobilier scandal.

Concurrently, John Pierpont Morgan, the great financier, had joined forces with Anthony Drexel, Philadelphia's runner-up in bank circles, to form Drexel, Morgan and Company. Now they decided to ruin Cooke in order to appropriate his near monopoly on government loans. Cooke was counting on the profit from $300 million of refinanced federal debt to bridge the gap in his railroad activity, and, to defeat this goal, Drexel, Morgan initiated a press campaign through the Philadelphia *Public Ledger* to prove that the banana belt was on its way toward becoming another South Sea Bubble. With this, Jay Cooke collapsed, and when his all-important bank closed on September 18, 1873, it almost closed the entire financial world as well. Thirty-seven banks and brokerage houses in New York City shut down that afternoon, trading on the New York Stock Exchange ceased, the public staged a run on the banks, and—needless to say—construction on the Northern Pacific, as well as every other railroad in the country, came to a screeching halt. It took the nation several years to recover. Eventually, in 1883, the Northern Pacific was completed, albeit by Henry Villard, Cooke's old employee, who had once peopled the northwest territory with refugees and would now do so again, this time on behalf of his German bondholders. Villard sent hundreds of agents through Europe, again recruiting hordes of immigrants to populate the American frontier. In one period of a few days, 6,000 wagons filled with settlers crossed the Rockies. To celebrate the completion of the railroad, Villard brought west in his private train President Ulysses S. Grant and most of the cabinet to watch him drive in the last spike—this one made of gold. Chief Sitting Bull, the Sioux hero,

BELOW: The Philadelphia banker Jay Cooke helped settle the West by using such exotic imagery to promote his railroad investment that many pioneers and immigrants envisioned a tropical paradise rather than the wintry wilderness they actually found upon arrival. Although Cooke's Banana Belt and the Atchison Topeka Banana Line had nothing in common, tempting fruit clearly whetted the public's appetite for travel on the railroads.

RIGHT: James Jerome Hill (*fifth from right*) poses with fellow railroaders in front of one of the first locomotives of the Great Northern Railroad. Hill was as important to the development of Western Canada's railway network as Commodore Vanderbilt was to that of the Eastern Seaboard of the United States.

FAR RIGHT: Edward Henry Harriman, who made his fortune during the stock-market panic of 1869, was one of the greatest of all the railroad assemblers. By the end of the century, the Harriman lines included the Central Pacific and the Southern Pacific, which were agglomerations of several other enormous combines.

was released from jail for the occasion, and a group of Native Americans who had virtually relinquished all rights to their land also participated in the ceremony. The same year the overextended Villard went broke and retired to his luxurious New York City mansion, presently incorporated into the Helmsley Palace Hotel.

BATTLE OF TITANS

Another great railroader was James Jerome Hill (1838-1916), a genius known as the "Commodore Vanderbilt of the West." From his adopted base in St. Paul, Minnesota, this one-eyed Canadian formed a partnership with two of his fellow countrymen, Lord Strathmore and Lord Mount Stephen, to create the Great Northern Railroad. Operating between St. Paul and far-off Puget Sound, the line often ran parallel with the Northern Pacific, upon which its new owners waged a constant rate war. The year Hill reached Puget Sound both the Union Pacific and the Northern Pacific went belly up. Helped by J.P. Morgan, the Canadian group bought up large amounts of Northern Pacific's stock with the intention of turning the line into an auxiliary of the Great Northern, which had survived the crash. The two railroads would be known as the Hill Lines. Now, just as Commodore Vanderbilt had looked west and run afoul of Daniel Drew, Hill looked east and tangled with Edward Henry Harriman (1848-1909).

In him Hill met a formidable opponent, and the "Hill-Harriman War" that ensued became the last great railroad donnybrook. Harriman left an estate estimated at $75-$100 million, while Hill's was in the mid-fifties, both fortunes far more than their heirs could spend for the next several generations. It was thanks to the founders' protean ambitions that vast areas of the country were developed. When the railroad pirates died, the heroic period of their industry came to a close, but the main players—Vanderbilt, Drew, Gould, Fisk, Hill, the California quartet, and Harriman—had set an example for daring, shrewdness, and greed that remain fundamental to ongoing American history.

EUROPEAN RAILROADERS

Monarchs gave out railroad concessions in Europe, and it was inevitable that their favorite bankers, the Rothschilds, would get a piece of the action. In London, however, the normally astute Nathan Rothschild failed to see the potential of the new transport technology, which had actually originated in Great Britain. Indeed, he figured among the terrified majority convinced that traveling at such speed would cause devastating damage to both mental and physical health. As a consequence, Nathan missed the boat, or rather the train, to one of the most lucrative of all new industries, leaving it to be instantly dominated by more visionary entrepreneurs. The same could not be said of the other Rothschild brothers, who enjoyed the advantage of having witnessed the success of the English experi-

Italy. In Naples, brother Carl Rothschild lent large sums to the Pope, who hoped that a railroad through his states would bring his people together and prevent revolution, while in Frankfurt the eldest brother, Amschel, financed hundreds of miles of German track. All these operations were paid for by stock issues, underwritten and peddled internationally by the Rothschild family bank. Railroad stocks became nearly as hot in Europe as in the United States, and when Salomon's railroad opened in 1839 the price of its equity shares tripled the next day.

ment in railroading while the Continent remained virgin territory, so to speak. Nathan urged them on, and by the 1840s the Rothschilds had become the railway tycoons of Europe south of the Channel.

Dozens of private companies were created in anticipation of making a large profit, and in 1835 Vienna's Salomon de Rothschild applied to the Emperor of Austria for the right to build a railway designed to freight coal and salt from Polish Galicia to Vienna. Thanks to intervention by Chancellor Metternich, the railroad, tactfully called the Kaiser Ferdinand Nordbahn, was constructed, becoming the first link in a vast chain of tracks that would crisscross the immense and rich Austro-Hungarian Empire, all the way through the Brenner Pass to

In Paris, James de Rothschild (who had anglicized his original name, Jacob) made a major mark in the history of French transport, beginning in 1837, when he undertook to build the first rail line between Paris and St. Germain. At its inauguration, staged to great hoopla, Baron James's friends King Louis-Philippe and Queen Amélie took a ride and declared themselves well pleased, thereby launching railroad mania *à la française*. Baron James followed in 1839 with another small railroad between Paris and Versailles, which had to compete with a parallel line on the other side of the Seine built by his bitter rival, the banker Achille Fould. (The two Jewish financiers were called the chief rabbis of the Rive Gauche and the Rive Droite.) A year later, Baron James asked Napoleon III to grant him a truly major concession, this time for a railway running between Paris and northern France, the site of the nation's heavy industry and its most important farmland. The new railroad, known as the Chemin de Fer du Nord, proved immensely profitable. In fact, James entered the big time with the very sort of monopoly that Vanderbilt dreamed of and took nearly two decades to achieve. Driven by rumors and speculations, Nord shares rose and fell, prompting James to observe, with his usual dry

LEFT: An early scene satirizing the gauge change on British railroads in the 1880s. Such problems discouraged several entrepreneurs from investing in the new means of transport.
FAR LEFT: The line from Paris to St. Germain, financed by Baron James de Rothschild in 1837, was the Family's first major undertaking in the new industry, for which they became financiers, owners, and underwriters.

BELOW: An 1890 *Vanity Fair* (London) caricature of Maurice de Hirsch, the Bavarian railroad broker. Baron de Hirsch became so involved in his vast project to build a line from Vienna to Istanbul that he often dressed in Turkish pantaloons and a fez while smoking a narghileh. Called "Türkenhirsh" once he had become rich, Baron de Hirsch found himself brought into Edward VII's "Jewish Court." He padded the monarch's pockets, organized lavish shoots, and, in general, played the role of an extraordinary personage.

RIGHT ABOVE AND BELOW: Prior to the great Balkan adventure, the Hirsch family had been active in railroads only to the extent of building a short line in Russia and joining the Rothschilds to help finance Germany's railroads.

wisdom, that as long as people were kept busy trying to make money, they would not be hatching plots against the government.

Despite their clearly dominant position, the Rothschilds could not be considered railroaders by profession, like Vanderbilt, Hill, or Harriman. The nearest European counterpart to the American tycoons was Baron Maurice de Hirsch (1831-96), who belonged to the third generation of a prosperous Jewish family of court bankers in Bavaria. His father had successfully dabbled in railroads, building the line from Moscow to Ryazan, and had founded the East Bavarian line with the Frankfurt Rothschilds. At a young age, Maurice was sent off to be apprenticed at the Bischoffsheim and Goldschmidt bank in Brussels, where he had the good sense to marry the boss's daughter, Clara Bischoffsheim, which led most people to assume he was

extremely rich. However, the firm did not offer him a partnership or permanent employment, and so Hirsch joined with a Belgian adventurer, André Langrand-Dumonceau, to found an insurance company in Vienna. This soon expanded into a catastrophic land development scheme in Hungary and Spain, which acquired somewhat tenuous concessions to build railways in Holland, Belgium, and the Balkans. With Bischoffsheim's backing, Hirsch also obtained, with the Anglo-Austrian Bank as partners, a concession for an East Hungarian railway. In 1868 he came up with a concession to link Vienna with Constantinople by rail. The distance to be covered was some 1,000 miles, making this the longest track yet laid. It took incredible determination, cunning, and patience to battle through the intrigues of the Ottoman Sultans; the Russians, who were intent on creating chaos in the hope of gaining a warm-water port on the Black Sea; Britain, eager to keep the Sultan's empire intact for the sake of maintaining avenues open to India; and Austria-Hungary, which was protecting backposts of its empire. In addition, Europeans had long since come to believe, with some justification, that law and order took a rest the moment one entered the bandit-infested and violence-prone Balkans.

The Ottoman concession was the only one that Hirsch decided seriously to undertake. He was helped by the Austrians, who wanted to develop trade in what was contingent territory (the Turks, after all, had come as far as Vienna during their doomed attempt at world conquest) and to stop the Russian advance. In addition, Hirsch enjoyed the support of several Sultans, including Abdul Aziz, who when forced to abdicate committed suicide by cutting his veins with scissors; Murad, the dead Sultan's nephew, who was declared insane three months after his accession; and Murad's brother, Abdul Hamid, known as Abdul the Damned for his great Armenian massacre and the liquidation of all potential family challengers to his rule. It also helped that Baron de Hirsch had mastered the technique of bribery, the *baksheesh* so appreciated in the Orient, and his munificence toward the Sultan's ministers assured him of both government finance (for what it was worth in the decrepit, crumbling, and bankrupt Ottoman Empire) and local support. The railroad progressed fitfully for twenty years before it was completed, and several times the Baron lost his fortune, and even his concession, but always seemed to spring back. When the line reached Constantinople, the Sultan gave its builder the Grand Cordon of the Osmanje Order, the highest recognition available to a foreigner. (The Bavarian Baron was popularly referred to as "Türkenhirsch.") In 1890, after becoming fed up with the whole enterprise, Hirsch sold out to a group led by Deutsche Bank and went off with a profit thought to be around £7-10 million. True to his origins, his munificence toward oppressed and suffering Oriental Jews was extraordinary, and, true to his snobbism, he dropped millions into the ready pockets of Edward VII to become part of his Jewish court of rich financiers. Indisputably, this banker-railroader gave the Gilded Age one of its most colorful and international characters.

LEFT: The world at the end of the pioneer railway that Baron de Hirsch built from Vienna across the bandit-infested Balkans to Istanbul. Few things captured the imagination of 19th-century Europeans more than the mysterious Middle East, here depicted by Count Amadeo Preziosi in a view over the Golden Horn and the Bosphoros from the terrace of a Turkish house in Galta, on the eastern bank of the Golden Horn.

DISCOVERERS, CONSOLIDATORS, AND MONOPOLISTS

—

Monopoly was the title of the game in the Gilded Age. From oil wells to gold mines, from steel to diamonds, the magic formula consisted of gaining near total control over an economic necessity. By eliminating competition, the monopolists could dominate production and distribution and thus fix prices and maximize profits. Because of its obvious potential for abuse, monopoly is generally considered to be a pernicious activity detrimental to public welfare. Consequently, from the beginning of the twentieth century, the United States Congress has enacted massive legislation designed to break up the trusts organized at the end of the previous century. Still, the early monopolists played a distinctly beneficial role in developing sources of raw materials, in rationalizing their exploitation, and in laying the foundations of modern industry. Along the way, they also created gigantic personal and financial empires. There is not sufficient space here to deal with any more than a few of the great monopolists of modern times. Among these, the place of honor must go to John D. Rockefeller, whose very name is synonymous with monopoly. Modern history abounds in merchant princes, tycoons, moguls, and robber barons, but the Rockefellers have always managed to remain above the melée, auraed in near-royal mystery and power. In practically any corner of the globe, the mere mention of their name arouses immediate visions of money beyond measure. While other nouveaux riches flaunted their good fortune, the Rockefellers maintained a Waspish discretion, to such a degree that they always seemed to inhabit a world of pressed dark-gray flannel rather than plush velvet. The accumulated wealth of the family dwarfed anything created privately, and since 1937, the year the patriarch, John D., died, his heirs have been impelled by a desire to give away the bounty he took out of the ground.

JOHN D. ROCKEFELLER

John Davison Rockefeller, the creator of the business trust and shaper of modern monopolistic practice, was born in Richford, New York, on July 8, 1839, the son of a quack doctor. In 1859 John D. founded Clark & Rockefeller, a small commission firm in Cleveland. At the end of his first year in business, the parsimonious, modest, and religious Rockefeller was grossing the not inconsiderable sum of $500,000. Shortly a group of businessmen asked him to inspect some new oil fields in Pennsylvania with a view to investing in the black goo, a natural resource then arousing the same excitement that the gold fields of California had a decade earlier. At the time, oil was employed as a lubricant or refined for indoor lamps as well as for such byproducts as paraffin and naphtha. Its industrial use, particularly as an automobile propellant, would not come for another several decades. Rockefeller recommended that the group avoid the production of oil but consider the possibility of refining it. In 1864 he opted for the latter himself, by cashing in part of his interest in Clark & Rockefeller and buying, together with his associate, an interest in a small refinery belonging to a local engineer, Samuel Andrews, for a few thousand dollars. A short time later, he sold the rest of his Clark & Rockefeller shares to his partner, bought out Clark's interest in the refinery, and devoted himself entirely to oil. Andrews's methods for refining oil surpassed those of the competition, and Rockefeller had enough capital to set up his business on a larger scale than his grab-bag rivals. His next move was to harness the capital and abilities of a former client of Clark &

BELOW: The oil industry in its infancy, with a Texaco peddler selling cans of kerosene for indoor lamps. Gasoline, at the time, burned off in the refining process, while petroleum served only for lubrication and lighting fuel. OPPOSITE: Once industrialists had laid the groundwork, bankers assumed a leading role in knitting together their giant trusts and eventually selling them to the public. The great master of the process was, of course, J.P. Morgan, who created the first billion-dollar corporation, United States Steel, and boldly undertook to consolidate the transportation industry on both land and sea. Here the powerful banker is seen exhorting nothing less than the sun, moon, and other planets to get together on light. Morgan shouts through his megaphone: "Say, if I could get you guys together on the light business, there ought to be a bunch of money in it for all of us, see!"

RIGHT: Early oil wells in West Virginia.

BELOW: A *Vanity Fair* (April 20, 1861) cartoon showing a grand ball given by whales to celebrate the discovery of fossil oil in Pennsylvania. Despite the gradual replacement of blubber by petroleum, the slaughter of whales continues even today, mostly for precious ambergris used in perfume. The banner reading "Oils well that ends well" proved to be overly optimistic.

Rockefeller, Henry Morrison Flagler, who had married a niece of Stephen V. Harkness, a rich Ohio whiskey distiller. After much arm-twisting, Harkness reluctantly succumbed and coughed up $100,000. The new firm of Rockefeller, Andrews & Flagler was now underway—and the oil business changed forever.

The neat and meticulous John D. hated disorder, cut every corner, counted every penny, and nurtured a grand vision. Oil was a brand-new industry. The sources of supply belonged to a constantly quarreling group of wildcatters, and small refineries had sprung up without any unified strategy. As a result, the market was chaotic, a situation that John

D. hoped to supplant with a single monopoly controlling the production, refining, and sale of oil products throughout the world. On January 10, 1870, Rockefeller and his partners incorporated the Standard Oil Company of Ohio with a capital of $1 million. Rockefeller traded on the tremendous respect he enjoyed in Cleveland, his brother William charmed politicians and bankers, and Flagler worked like a demon. (Even in old age, possessed of a colossal oil fortune, Flagler was busily launching a railroad across the Florida Keys, the most astonishing engineering achievement of its day.)

One by one, the best refineries of Cleveland joined Rockefeller's group, pulled in by a Machiavellian scheme. Rockefeller convinced the Lake Shore Railroad, which brought the Pennsylvania crude along its tracks to the Cleveland refineries, that he could offer the company far larger shipping contracts than anybody else if it granted him a substantial—and secret—rebate on freight charges. Given that shipping constituted a large part of the raw material cost, this meant that non-Rockefeller refineries would be paying far more for their oil and thus rendered uncompetitive. The 50-cent discount per barrel left Rockefeller with a 25-percent advantage over his rivals. Small refineries either had to join the cartel or close. The scheme worked in Cleveland, whereupon Flagler formed the South Improvement Company, which made similar deals with the Erie, Pennsylvania, and New York Central railroads. Even worse, these deals also allowed Standard a slightly different rebate on all the ship-

Among the many gifts of John D. Rockefeller, the greatest may have been his genius for choosing brilliant associates and harnessing their talents to both his advantage and theirs.

thing from varnish to medicine. If an independent supplier tried to step out of line, the Rockefeller alliance refused him delivery and let his oil spill on the ground. When a group tried to subvert the Rockefeller-controlled railroad transport by building a pipeline over the land and hills of Pennsylvania to the New Jersey refineries, John D. beat them to it with his own pipeline system—gaining, in the bargain, a certain independence of the railroads while also consuming his adversary. He now had the power to set the price on any business related to the production, refinement, or sale of oil that fit his master plan. Once Rockefeller set his laser-like eye on something, the sputtering owner faced a choice of bankruptcy or sale, and the price fixed was one that would create an ally rather than a foe, if the manager was Rockefeller material.

ABOVE FAR LEFT: Henry Rogers was a partner of Charles Pratt, an extremely important independent petroleum refiner who attempted to put together a syndicate that would destroy Rockefeller's monopoly by shipping oil through a pipeline rather than on the rails. Rockefeller built an even longer pipeline, broke Pratt Oil's back, and absorbed the company into his monopoly along with Rogers, who became one of the most faithful of the Rockefeller lieutenants. Here, the bronze (or gold) effigy of Rogers is being worshiped by Uncle Sam.

LEFT: Henry Morrison Flagler (*fourth from left*) was Rockefeller's first partner in what would become Standard Oil. Using the fortune he made in oil, Flagler went on to build railroads in Florida, put up fantastic luxury hotels in St. Augustine, and almost single-handedly make Palm Beach and Miami into popular resorts.
ABOVE: Operated from its enormous headquarters in New York, Standard Oil became the world's largest monopoly.

ments of independent producers as well as information on their production. With this arrangement in hand, the major refineries of Pittsburgh, New York, and Philadelphia had to join Standard as well.

By 1878 the 39-year-old John D. controlled 95 percent of the pipelines and refineries in the United States, which made him as well as his numerous partners colossally rich. Standard Oil managed the market in such a manner that only the most minimal play could occur in the supply and price of what had become an essential commodity, one that lit up the great majority of houses and workplaces of the nation. Gasoline, the staple product of the oil industry, soon poured out of refineries to slake the thirst of an increasingly motorized and energy-starved world, as did benzine, fuel petroleum, and lubrication oil, which were later used for every-

In 1881, the forty companies controlled by John D. and his partners were linked together by complicated interchanges of stock. Samuel C.T. Dodd, Rockefeller's attorney, conceived the notion of a trust whereby the 37 stockholders who made up the alliance turned over their shares "in trust" to nine trustees in exchange for "trust certificates," while the trustees controlling the majority shares became stockholders of all the alliance's component companies. Now endowed with overwhelming power, the trustees had the freedom to reorganize the trust in the best interests of its shareholders; moreover, they formed a united council that gave direction to the management of their entire industry.

The creation of the Rockefeller Trust was an historic event in American business, serving as both a

RIGHT: It was John D. Rockefeller's vision that brought the world oil industry into being, an industry that made vast fortunes for those who joined the Rockefeller trust. The great monopolist was fond of saying: "I am harnessed to a cart in which people ride. I must work for the rest." However, his passengers—that is, his partners—had little choice, since the alternative to traveling on his wagon was being eaten alive.

BELOW: Rockefeller lived in extreme quietude, remained always impeccably turned out, attended church regularly, and liked to be seen distributing dimes to little children.

FAR RIGHT: One of J.D.R.'s few real enjoyments, besides amassing millions, was playing golf on his private course at the Rockefeller estate in Pocantico Hills, New York.

model and an inspiration to all industries seeking to wrest unity from chaos. The papers were so brilliantly drafted that the cottonseed-oil industrialists paid $250,000 just to have a look at them. Very soon, there were trusts involving everything from linseed oil to steel, thanks to the groundwork laid by Rockefeller and his lawyers. The object of hatred, envy, and admiration, Rockefeller's achievement may have received its greatest tribute from William Vanderbilt: "There is no question about it but these men are smarter than I am by a great deal... I never came in contact with any class of men as smart and alert as they are in their business."

John D. grew old gracefully and even elegantly, surrounded by his family, lionized by all he had made rich, and detested by the many he had ruined. He retired from active management of Standard Oil in 1896 to an estate he had built—Pocantico Hills in New York's Westchester County, which is still in the family's possession—and concentrated on increasing his fortune for the next 41 years. The patriarch also knocked about a golf ball on his own eighteen-hole course and told a Sunday School class that "it is wrong to assume that men of immense wealth are always happy." At his retirement, John D. was worth an enormous $200 million and his associates' joint fortunes easily matched that. Fourteen years later, when the internal combustion engine caused a rapidly accelerating demand for gasoline, the Rockefeller hoard approached the billion-dollar mark. It increased substantially thereafter as the family trust branched out into real estate and mines, and bought up major holdings in the great American corporations that followed and influenced the nation's growth. Such is the prestige of the Rockefeller name that when

the clan sold an interest in Rockefeller Center to the Japanese in the late 1980s, the transaction was considered a betrayal of America's pride. Actually, the decision to sell turned out to be a brilliant one, for soon thereafter the New York City real estate market crashed.

ROYAL DUTCH SHELL

Consolidating all of America's wildcatters was a Herculean task. Bringing together those of the Near East, the Orient, and Russia might have daunted even Hercules; indeed, it required the combined efforts of not one great entrepreneur but several. Essentially, there were three important groups. The monopoly of oil production in Baku, part of Russia's Caucasus, originally belonged to the Mirzoieff brothers, Armenians who by 1871 were producing a mere 24,000 tons. Their franchise was broken in 1875 by the Swede Robert Nobel, from one of the world's outstanding families of industrialists, financiers, and inventors. His father had been primarily responsible for creating the torpedo boat, and one brother invented dynamite, before establishing the Nobel prizes, while two other siblings built the St. Petersburg dockyards. By 1885 the Baku fields were producing 2.5 million tons, thanks largely to the imagination and dynamism of the Nobels, who owned 70 percent of immensely rich wells that produced nearly half as much petroleum as the United States did at the time. The only oil men in Russia to cap their shafts

Express, hiding his son Nubar in a rolled-up Turkish carpet. Although focused on Turkey and Iraq, Gulbenkian always turned up with a boutonniere in his lapel whenever an oil deal was in the offing and regularly cleared a commission. Known as "Mr. 5 Percent," Gulbenkian made sure to be included in the greatest oil amalgamation since Rockefeller's.

Standard Oil had begun to throw its weight around the world, and the European oil companies risked falling victim to its predation if they continued to undercut each other. The only logical solution lay in their merging into a giant cartel powerful enough to challenge Standard Oil. In 1903, Deterding paid a visit to Frederick Lane, the mas-

in the American manner, the Nobels also built pipelines and reservoir tanks and introduced the first oil tankers.

The second giant, the Royal Dutch Company, was founded in 1890 for the purpose of extracting petroleum in the Dutch East Indies. Its guiding light as of 1896 was Hendrik W.A. Deterding, who had worked in the Netherlands Trading Society, a merchant bank dedicated to developing Holland's South Sea outposts. Then there was the Shell Transport and Trading Company, established in 1897 as a brainchild of Marcus Samuel, later Viscount Bearstead, who started as a small shell dealer in London, built ships, and later focused on wildcatting oil in Borneo and shipping it to Japan. The English Rothschilds helped him develop exponentially in the Far East, while their French cousins went into the oil business in Russia.

As for the Germans, they had taken interests in Mesopotamian oil fields as an offshoot of their control of the Anatolian Railways. Finally, there was that extremely colorful figure, Calouste Gulbenkian, who seemed to be in the middle of myriad business transactions. He escaped from Abdul Hamid's Armenian massacre in the luxury of the Orient

termind of all the Rothschild oil interests and the founder of the Europaische Petroleum Union, which marketed Rothschild, Nobel, and German oil under the Shell umbrella. Deterding took out his gold pencil and drew a straight line across a piece of paper. As he wrote in his memoir: "I told [Lane], 'that line represents a price level, firm and steady as it should be among all sound and decent oil traders.' Then, rushing my pencil up and down—sometimes above the line, but more often below it, I said 'That represents prices as they are today, constantly shooting up and down, so nobody knows where he is. Should we continue these cut-throat methods for another twenty years, those who survive—even the most powerful—will be in the same impasse as we are today.'"

Basically, Deterding was proposing a merger to fix prices to everybody's mutual benefit; to unify production, transport, and selling so that each market could be supplied by the nearest source at a steady price; to eliminate waste and overlapping; and to rationalize the infant industry exactly as Rockefeller had done in the United States. With capital of £2 million, the two titans formed the Asiatic Petroleum Company, which was, in effect, the

LEFT: The Nobel brothers' refinery was in Russian Baku, the richest deposit of petroleum outside the United States before the discovery of the immense oil fields of the Arabian peninsula. Located on the west coast of the Caspian Sea, and once a vassal state of the Persian shahs, this capital of Azerbaijan was the chief petroleum center of the Soviet Union until World War II.
ABOVE: Baku also constituted the principal building block in the great Royal Dutch Shell Trust assembled by the genial banker Sir Hendrik Deterding (1865-1939), seen here below an early Royal Dutch Shell stock certificate.

BELOW LEFT: The Shell of Royal Dutch Shell was brought in by Marcus Samuel, a small London mollusk merchant who proved to be one of the sharpest wheeler-dealers in the Far East, with shipping and trading interests in Southeast Asia, particularly in Borneo and Java, where important oil fields were discovered.
ABOVE: The interior of a Samuel-owned drilling rig at work in 1898 on the island of Sumatra in the Dutch East Indies. Once he had become a full-fledged tycoon, Samuel was elevated to the peerage, becoming Viscount Bearstead.
BELOW RIGHT: Following on the heels of oil, the next great monopoly occurred in steel, a 19th-century alloy of iron with a far higher tensile strength, greater malleability, and lower carbon content. In John Ferguson Weir's masterpiece *Forging the Shaft* (1874-77), now in the Metropolitan Museum of Art, one feels the heat and strength needed to pull an iron cylinder from an early blast furnace.

holding company for the first step in the Royal Dutch/Shell merger. This consolidated organization became the sole European enterprise with a worldwide system for exploring, producing, refining, and marketing oil. Gulbenkian undertook to bring in the non-Rothschild Russian oil interests, large producers that could have caused serious problems with the monopoly. Four years after the founding of Asiatic Petroleum, Lane, Gulbenkian, Marcus, and Deterding formed a production company in The Hague and a transport, storage, and distribution company in London—both owned 60 percent by Royal Dutch and 40 percent by Shell—thus putting the final touches on the merger.

It was now time to take on Standard Oil, a visionary project planned by Deterding and Lane but largely executed by Gulbenkian. If Royal Dutch/Shell did not establish worldwide production and sales, Standard Oil could dump oil in their territories at a loss and make up the difference on its own monopolized home turf. To counter this possibility, Gulbenkian put forward the bold idea of

raising capital from American banks and doing business right under Rockefeller's nose. Soon thereafter Royal Dutch/Shell became a major retailer in the United States.

As new fields came on line and demand increased, the European and American oil companies alike took big positions in the petroleum reserves of Egypt, Mexico, Venezuela, Argentina, and, of course, Saudi Arabia, the Emirates, and Persia. The United States government eventually forced Standard Oil to break up into several different companies. Even so, the giant combines remained just that. Later known as the "Seven Sisters," they would loom large in every aspect of modern history, while also allowing the tycoons who created them to amass stupendous fortunes.

MEN OF STEEL

The prime ambition of any developing country is to be self-sufficient in the production of steel, considered the basic building block of industry. Iron, a metal dating back to ancient times, is made from iron ore, coke, and limestone, while steel—a nineteenth-century invention—is basically refined iron. The burgeoning railroads initially needed hundreds of thousands of tons of iron for their tracks, all of which would be replaced with the far longer-lasting and tougher steel once its production was rationalized. As the shipping industry switched from wooden vessels to steam liners and iron riggers, it demanded vast amounts of hard metal, giving birth to sea craft that combined the elegance of the great age of sail with the scale and solidity of modern times. Very shortly, the first skyscrapers added to the demand, as did industry's growing appetite for pipes, tubes, wire, and other metal products.

The undoubted iron and steel king of the New World was Andrew Carnegie (1835-1919), who with his parents had emigrated from Scotland to Allegheny, Pennsylvania, near Pittsburgh, in 1848. At the age of fourteen Carnegie started working twelve-hour days in a local cloth mill, before moving on to a telegraph office, where the new technology fired his imagination. Thomas A. Scott, the entrepreneur whose Empire Transportation challenged the Rockefeller interests, was the Pittsburgh-based

superintendent of the Pennsylvania Railroad when he read in a local paper of an honest telegraph boy who had found a $500 draft on the street and brought it to the proper authorities. Already on the lookout for someone to run his own telegraph machine, Scott hired Carnegie, after which he soon made his "white-haired Scotch devil" a personal

assistant. At the same time that Carnegie quickly rose to become superintendent of the railroad's Pittsburgh branch, he also kept his ears open when bright professionals were around the office. Tipped off about American Express, he mortgaged his mother's house and then used the proceeds to buy AmEx shares on margin. The stock rapidly multiplied, whereupon Carnegie paid back the bank and then used the balance to purchase $127 of shares in the Woodruff Palace Car Company, which in two years would be paying him $5,000 in dividends.

Before long Carnegie realized that he should not be in the employ of others, for hardly had he taken a stab at oil prospecting when he hit a gusher. This gave him a small stake that he leveraged to buy into a local plant owned by Pittsburgh's Kloman Brothers, which made the best railroad car axles on the market. In this venture the budding tycoon was joined by his brother Tom and two friends, Tom Miller and Henry Phipps. Carnegie also had borrowed to acquire a small firm that built iron bridges, which he merged with the onetime Kloman works to form the Union Iron Mills. The small, wiry Scotsman possessed a genius for sales, while Miller was a railroad purchasing agent. Between the silvery tongue of one owner and the other's conflicts of interest, the new company very soon had more orders than it could fill. The enterprise expanded and prospered, making it possible for Carnegie to turn toward New York and further opportunities in 1867. There he opened an office on Broad Street and hung out a sign that read, simply: "Andrew Carnegie, Investments." By 1868, with an income of $50,000 per year, he could contemplate a gentleman's life of learning and public service.

FAR LEFT: **Andrew Carnegie was born in this small cottage in Dunfermline, Scotland, in 1835. At the age of thirteen, he emigrated with his parents to the United States, where he would gradually forge the world's most important industrial giant, the first billion-dollar corporation, United States Steel.**
BELOW: **A rough group of workers at Jones and Laughlin Steel in 1891. Carnegie discovered his real genius in finance, which left him with scant interest in the work conditions or general welfare of his numerous employees.**

Successful emigrants liked nothing better than returning to Europe covered in glory and showing off their success to the less fortunate who had stayed at home.

RIGHT: A triumphant, nattily dressed Andrew Carnegie arrives in Scotland conveyed in an elegant coach and four with liveried footmen, who have descended so that their magnifico can pose—perhaps symbolically—with reins in hand. Carnegie built an immense pile in Scotland, Skibo Castle, from which he ran his empire largely by letter or Marconigram.

BELOW: Carnegie dreamed of becoming a philanthropist, and so, after selling his interests to J.P. Morgan in 1900, for a reported $492 million, which made him the richest man in the world, he happily gave most of it to cultural causes.

FAR RIGHT: Carnegie in apotheosis behind his desk in an astonishingly modest Pittsburgh office. Most early tycoons, unlike today's, had no interest in spending money uselessly on opulent working quarters.

Until 1872, Andrew Carnegie had been a solid success, a crack money-maker in stocks, bonds, oil, and iron products. So far, however, he had done nothing of such epic significance as to launch him into the really big time. During a trip to London that year he met Henry Bessemer, who in 1856 had come upon a ten-minute process for making steel out of pig iron in a special, high-heat converter. The superiority of steel's tensile strength meant new rails capable of carrying more tonnage, heavier locomotives, and stronger bridges, all resulting in lower freight rates and many fewer repairs. The possibilities were vast, especially in a United States market protected from imports of British steel by a tariff of $28 per ton.

Andrew Carnegie and his remaining partners at Union Mills (Miller had been eased out in the early stages after he introduced his customers, and Kloman was dropped in the panic of 1873) now pushed ahead with the steel plant at Braddock, a Pittsburgh suburb, and named it after their largest potential customer, J. Edgar Thomson, president of the Pennsylvania Railroad. Running the operation was the legendary Captain Bill Jones, arguably the most brilliant steel man of his day, whose many inventions and innovations advanced the industry beyond measure. Carnegie was lucky to have him, given that he seldom visited his plant and had a complete lack of interest in anything technical. The Scotsman did, however, possess a sixth sense about people and an X-ray eye for figures, as well as the grit to be dissatisfied no matter what results were achieved. Within four years of the plant's opening, Carnegie Brothers & Company were producing 10,000 tons of steel per month and earning

$1.6 million for the year. With Jones in charge, Carnegie's production cost fell far below that of the competition. The mill quickly became the finest in the world, the sheer scale of its activity such that Carnegie could buy and ship his raw materials cheaper than anyone else. Like Rockefeller, moreover, he got secret rebates from the railroads. During the next 25 years, the expansion of Carnegie's steel operations was equalled only by that of Standard Oil.

THE COKE KING

Again like Rockefeller, Carnegie wanted control over his raw materials, which included thousands of tons of coke a year. Coke is coal baked for 24 hours until it turns into gray lumps, and Connellsville coke, the finest available, was 80 per-

BELOW: Although born well-off, Henry Clay Frick was a large, tough, hands-on industrialist, who parlayed his family's small coal holdings into a major stake in United States Steel.

cent owned by Henry Clay Frick (1849-1919), a mogul in his own right and one of the rare robber barons born with a silver spoon in his mouth. (J.P. Morgan was another.) His grandfather had been a whiskey distiller whose Pennsylvania plant sat on a great seam of bituminous coal, an asset the family enlarged by buying up substantial coal acreage as an investment. Young Frick leveraged to the hilt to buy more coal mines in the Connellsville area. Then, at the age of 21, he borrowed $10,000 from Pittsburgh's Mellon Bank to acquire coke ovens.

In addition to slaving over his coke business, the young Frick cleared $50,000 as a middleman selling a railroad, which helped his business through hard times. Confident of himself and the future, he borrowed from Mellon even at the depths of depressions and ruthlessly bought out suffering competitors until he was running a medium-sized monopoly and could gouge the market. Frick was renowned for his uncommunicative manner, both in public and in private, and even in the middle of a monetary crisis he was at a loss when asked by a desperate financial reporter for a statement. His response came in written form:

> The USA is a great and growing country.
> (Signed) Henry Clay Frick
> P.S. This information is confidential and not for publication.

Frick had difficulty getting through the great crash of 1873, but by 1878 H.C. Frick and Company had held on long enough to be the main supplier of coke to the steel industry, which suddenly found itself flooded with orders from the newly consolidated railroads. Pittsburgh desperately needed coke to fuel its ovens, and when its agents came to Connellsville, they found that one firm controlled 80 percent of the fuel. The price Frick charged rapidly escalated from 90 cents a ton to $2, then up to $3, $4, and $5, of which 60 percent was pure profit. By 1879 the thirty-year-old millionaire had 1,000 employees and the admiration of his largest customer. Carnegie decided to try amalgamating his business, and in 1883 he and Frick merged their companies in one of the most important vertical integrations yet accomplished.

In 1892 came the historic strike at Carnegie's Homestead, Pennsylvania, steelworks, resulting in one of the bloodiest contests ever staged between capital and labor. Three hundred armed guards

ABOVE LEFT: A miner emerges with his coal-filled van from one of Frick's rich deposits (BOTTOM). Frick baked the coal into coke, an essential element for steel-making, and as Carnegie's main supplier, he was eventually absorbed into the Scot's industrial interests. Without Frick, Carnegie would have been unable to manage his vast empire, but the two titans eventually disagreed on how to allocate profits from their common enterprises.

RIGHT: The Homestead Mill, the epicenter of what was to become United States Steel, on the Monangahela River in Pittsburgh, c. 1892.
BELOW: It was J.P. Morgan who brought together warring giants in the largest merger of the Gilded Age. The notorious gambler John W. Gates ("Bet-a-Million Gates") had parlayed a small barbed-wire business in Texas into the Federal Steel Company, his own conglomerate of iron and steel companies, thanks to J.P. Morgan's financial wizardry and the legal genius of an Illinois Judge, Elbert H. Gary. Meanwhile, Morgan's competitor, George F. Baker, created a trust for tinplate, steel hoops, and endless other metal products in association with the Moore brothers, a pair of smart Wall Street operators. Baker and Morgan then ganged up to destroy Carnegie and Frick, who retaliated with a massive plan to kill the competitors in turn. Wall Street trembled, but finally J.P. Morgan saved the day, even if "floating" the shares to form U.S. Steel involved some work, as the cartoon indicates.

WAITING FOR THE BALLOO ' ASCENSION.
A dernier Hape a Sudden Fund . Hot Da: Load os a Kmt

from the Pinkerton Detective Agency confronted the striking employees of the plant, which had been prohibited from hiring union members. In a pitched battle on land and even on barges in the Monongahela River, fourteen men lost their lives and 163 suffered serious wounds. The scandal provoked a fierce public outcry, as well as an attempt on the life of the ruthless Frick by a Polish-Russian immigrant, Alexander Berkman. A self-declared anarchist, as well as "a violent and destructive opponent of all government," the 25-year-old Berkman shot Frick in the neck and ear, then stabbed him several times as the tycoon wrestled his would-be assassin on the floor of his Pittsburgh office. In this he was joined by his vice-chairman, with whom he had been working at the time. Eventually, after a brute struggle, Frick pinioned Berkman to the ground and flung himself on the attacker's body until shouts attracted help from outside the office. A deputy sheriff rushed into the room and prepared to shoot. "Leave him to the law," said Frick, "but raise his head and let me see his face." Noticing the culprit move his jaw as if he were chewing something, Frick and the sheriff forced his mouth open and extracted a capsule containing enough fulminate of mercury to blow up everyone in the room.

That night, from his home, Frick proclaimed: "I do not think I shall die, but whether I do or not, the Carnegie Company will pursue the same policy and it will win." To Carnegie he cabled: "Was shot twice but not dangerously. There is no necessity to come home. I am still in shape to fight the battle out." The coke king was clearly made of steel, and the Homestead Mill kept the unions out for decades. A grateful Carnegie wrote: "If his health be spared, I predict that no man who ever lived in Pittsburgh and managed businesses here will be better liked or more admired than my friend and partner Henry Clay Frick."

THE BILLION-DOLLAR COMPANY

Carnegie and Frick's steel and coke were the basis of the largest conglomerate yet, United States Steel, the first billion-dollar corporation. The assemblage of this gargantuan concern was really the work of J.P. Morgan, and it provides a near-perfect demonstration of the techniques the great banker employed, the influence he could wield, the power that emanated from his offices on Broad Street, and the control of investment banking over the fabric of American industry and commerce.

On April 1, 1901, the formation of United States Steel, with 168,000 workers and a capital of $1,402 billion, was announced. Its tangible assets were about half of that dollar amount, and the syndicators' total take came to about $150 million. Morgan received a fee of $12.5 million, but his true reward was the driver's seat of the world's largest corporation. The company chieftains who had been bought out were all sitting on millions. Many even had trouble figuring out their net worth, and most headed for Wall Street, thereby vastly inflating a speculative bubble that would lead to more panics and crashes. Old foxes like Frick and Henry Phipps quietly sold the bonds and shares they had received in exchange for their interests. They were smart enough to know the difference between steel and water. Carnegie quipped that he would probably get his company back by foreclosure, since he owned a large part of its first mortgage bonds. In the end, he too opted for cash. The irony, of course, is that had they all held on through the various crashes ahead, their heirs would probably have been still richer. Andrew Carnegie died in 1919, after enjoying many years in his magnificent castle in Scotland, and spending $350 million of his immense fortune on 2,811 libraries (in Britain and Ireland, British colonies, and the United States), Carnegie Hall, Carnegie Tech, and other philanthropic enterprises.

THE KRUPPS, MERCHANTS OF DEATH

In the second half of the nineteenth century the rising demand for steel—to be used in railroads, steamships, skyscraper frames, and, especially, cannons and other armament—spurred the growth of important steelworks throughout the world. The creators of the resulting conglomerates—Krupp and Thyssen in Germany, Schneider in France, and Skoda in Czechoslovakia, among others—became the monarchs of their respective nations' industries, where they provided support for both commercial and military expansion. All prospered from wars, and the burgeoning trade in armament seems to have overshadowed the peaceful uses of their vast productive capacity, thanks to such shadowy figures as Sir Basil Zaharoff, the Russian-born merchant of death who purportedly gained a guinea on every soldier killed during World War I. Zaharoff, like his suppliers, suffered no qualms about selling arms to both sides in any struggle, carrying on the longtime policy of the largest armament complex of all, Friedrich Krupp of Essen. Business was above politics, and to be *unpolitisch* was a license for maximizing profits.

The ideas of Friedrich Krupp were, in many ways, premature, since the scale required for the vast enterprise he envisaged was unattainable in a divided Germany. His son Alfred (1812-87) would be the first to flourish in the steel business, thanks to the German Customs Union of 1834. In one year, Alfred tripled his staff so as to process orders from all parts of the new trade confederation. He also created the firm's logo of three railway tires, in which many would later see the interlocking muzzles of cannons. The firm remained a purely German phenomenon until 1851, when, at London's Great Exhibition, Alfred displayed a single block of cast steel weighing 4,300 pounds, a technological wonder of the time, together with a group of six-pound field guns on a base of ashwood. Krupp won the Grand Prix, beating Britain on its own turf, and was soon processing important orders from Kaiser Wilhelm I as well as from other major governments, including those of Russia, the Netherlands, England, Switzerland, Spain, and Austria. The "Cannon King" had been launched. Quite appropriately, United States Steel exhibited a plowshare at the London show.

The 1860s saw the arrival of two important inventions for heavy industry: Sir Henry Bessemer's method of casting steel from liquid iron in converters rather than in closed furnaces, and Sir William Siemens's process of casting steel from iron ore and scrap, a superior technology whose patent Krupp bought. The Krupp firm grew at an extraordinary rate—from seven people in 1826 to 1,500 in 1859, 2,000 in 1861, 4,000 in 1863, and 8,000 in 1865—and this was only the beginning. Like Carnegie, Krupp quickly took possession of essential raw materials, thanks to the assistance of Chancellor Bismarck and the Kaiser, and made a killing during the Franco-Prussian War of 1870-71. For the artillery Krupp sold to France, Napoleon III made him an officer of the Légion d'Honneur; meanwhile, the cannons that Krupp sold to the Kaiser utterly destroyed the forts of Metz and Sedan and punctured the balloons with which an encircled Paris attempted to remain in touch with the rest of France. Having now humbled its main obstacle to European domination, the freshly proclaimed German Empire prepared for *Deutschland über Alles*, with Alfred Krupp at the head of the nation's industrial might. This leader would prove almost monomaniacal in his obsession with the Krupp works,

ABOVE: Alfred Krupp, while not the first family member in the steel business, was responsible for its great period of growth. The Krupps bought coal mines in French Lorraine, Luxembourg, and Germany, acquired iron fields in Spain and Sweden, after which the Friedrich Alfred Forge quickly became Europe's largest ironworks.

LEFT: The Krupps, of course, specialized in armaments. Indeed, their munitions works, seen here in December 1917, produced cannons of all sizes, the most famous being "Big Bertha," which caused absolute terror in the bloody conflict of World War I.

For the Krupps, the armaments industry proved to be an inexhaustible gold mine. As soon as they had peddled a line of killing instruments, they invented superior weapons that could destroy whatever had been manufactured. Through stock manipulations, Fritz Krupp purchased the large Grussonwerke arms factory in Magdeburg and the Germanenwerft shipyard on the North Sea coast, where the Kaiser led the race to beat Great Britain in building dreadnought battleships.
ABOVE: Krupp also manufactured the deadly submarines that would change naval warfare forever and not always to Germany's advantage (see opposite).
BELOW: Gustav Krupp von Bohlen und Halbach and his managers follow the coffins of their workers killed in an industrial disaster at Krupp's Essen factory. April 1923.

virtually excluding all private life, to the despair of his wife Bertha and son Fritz.

Doctors described the anxiety suffered by Krupp and his constant complaints as "hypochondria bordering on insanity." To satisfy his chronic restlessness, the industrialist continually wandered about Germany and the rest of Europe, directing his empire by means of written communications, 30,000 of which have survived. Krupp ran the vast firm dictatorially, and in order to control it even from beyond the grave, he put together a sort of Magna Carta for the House of Krupp, the 22-page *Generalregulativ*, which prescribed every stage of the work—and the private lives as well—of the *Kruppianers*. These became little more than slaves to the goals of an autocratic owner and the *Vaterland* embodied in Krupp's largest customer, His Imperial Majesty the Kaiser.

On the positive side, the longer the Krupp employees stayed, the better they performed their jobs, and the better were the results for the firm. In this, Alfred Krupp anticipated the highly successful work ethic, lifetime employment, and industrial success of postwar Japan. Under his stern paternalism, the Kruppianers were in fact quite well taken care of, which had the desired effect of making them fiercely devoted to their firm and its leader, as well as demonically efficient in turning out steel cylinders, axles, railroad-car wheels, and thousands of miles of tracks for the growing American railroads. Alas, they were equally effective in producing an ever-larger supply of arms for whatever quarreling European powers could marshal the means to pay for them.

Quite appropriately, Alfred's son Fritz (Friedrich Alfred, 1854-1902) took over the reins of the firm in 1888, the same fateful year that Queen Victoria's first grandson became Kaiser Wilhelm II. With a militaristic program of facing down Britain on the high seas, humbling France, and dominating Europe by brute force, "Willy" knew that his future would be bound up with the industrial might of the Kruppianers. Their mutual interests were so at one as to become two sides of the same coin, and the firm expanded exponentially. Fritz Krupp increased his personal fortune from 119 million marks in 1895 to 187 million in 1902, but he lost his reputation as a serious industrialist, and appropriate partner to the austere Kaiser, following scandalous revelations of orgies with olive-skinned boys on the Isle of Capri. Fritz returned *persona non grata* to Germany and consigned his long-suffering wife Marga to an insane asylum. Shortly thereafter he was found unconscious in bed, the victim of a cerebral hemorrhage, according to the official explanation. More likely, he committed suicide. Forty-three thousand Kruppianers and the Kaiser attended the funeral.

Failing a male heir, the reins of the Krupp empire passed to Fritz's daughter, Bertha, after a relatively long regency under Marga, the latter released from the asylum to prepare her daughter for power. In Rome, during a reception at the Royal Prussian Embassy, Bertha met a good-looking young attaché, Gustav von Bohlen und Halbach, whose family had emigrated to the United States and then returned to Germany. Bertha and Gustav were married in the presence of the Kaiser at Villa Hügel, where, in his wedding speech, Willy exhorted Bohlen "to keep supplying our German fatherland with those *Schutz- und Trutzwaffen* ['defensive and offensive weapons'], whose production cannot be attained by any other nation."

The apotheosis of the Krupp works came in 1914. Early in the century, the firm had gradually devoted two-thirds of its production to the domestic market rather than to export. During World War I, the military essentially took control, and the entire output of Europe's largest industrial combine served nothing but the bellicose needs of *das Vaterland*. No longer could the firm supply armaments for all parties in the conflict, despite its previous policy of leasing patents on shell fuses to Vickers. Later, Krupp even asked the British arms merchant to pay 123 million shillings in royalties on the bullets used by British soldiers to kill their German enemies. Krupp was quite prepared for war with a labor force of 82,000, nine steel plants, and thousands of major machines. Contrary to the Kaiser's predictions, the German army did not achieve instant success; quite the contrary, hostilities of the grossest, most genocidal sort dragged on for more than three years, as did the escalating demand for matériel, exceeding anything ever

imagined. By the end, Krupp's personnel had expanded to 170,000 and its per-month production to 14,000 tons of explosives, 9 million artillery shells, and 3,000 field pieces, in addition to submarines, battleships, and armor plate.

When the conflict finally ended, the Allied powers completely dismantled all of Krupp's war capacity, while prohibiting Germany from any and all military activity. However, by the time Hitler sought revenge for the humiliations of the Versailles Treaty, the Kruppianers had recovered and were first in line to support his cause.

THE GUGGENHEIMS

The great industrial surge during the Gilded Age, as well as many new inventions, created enormous demand for metals other than steel, among them zinc, tin, copper, and lead. Large fortunes were made by prospectors, mine owners, and smelters in North and South America alike. Outside the booming world of steel, no one made money from base metals more successfully than the Guggenheims, a family of Jewish immigrants from Aargau in German-speaking Switzerland whose background was similar to that of the great immigrant bankers described in the next chapter. In 1848, at the late age of 55, Meyer Guggenheim, the family patriarch, arrived in Philadelphia with his twelve children. There he peddled household goods while his son Meyer (1828-1905) sold them in the countryside to the Pennsylvania Dutch.

The Guggenheims' real start came about largely by accident. In 1881, Meyer—like everybody else—dipped his little toe into metal speculation, by purchasing a third interest in two lead and silver mines for $5,000. Soon, in his black frock coat, he was peering down a flooded black hole in Leadville, Colorado. To pump the water from the mine would cost $25,000, which only Meyer had at his disposal;

BELOW LEFT: The Kaiser's *Scharnhorst* and *Gneisenau* foundering in 1914, as conceived by the painter William Lionel Wyllie (National Maritime Museum, London).

ABOVE: Meyer Guggenheim, the family patriarch, made his first real money manufacturing a stove polish that would not dirty a housewife's hands, following which he went on to sell coffee and wholesale spices, manufacture lye, and import lace from his native Switzerland before making a colossal fortune in mining. By 1879, at the age of 51, Meyer had almost gained millionaire status, after 32 years of hard work in the promised land of the United States. He also had seven sons, all of whom were active in the business.

Meyer Guggenheim (*seated at center*) sits in the firm's boardroom surrounded by his sons. When the boys were young, the patriarch assembled them and gave each a stick to break. He then put together seven sticks that nobody could even bend, emphasizing that individually each was fragile but together they were invincible. Benjamin (*far left*) was the first to go into mining, but eventually he retired to a life of pleasure that would be dramatically terminated when he went down with the *Titanic* in 1912. Benjamin was the father of that great patroness of modern art, Peggy Guggenheim. Murray (*second from left*), with a remarkable mind for figures, formed a vast trust to monopolize Chile's large nitrate deposit. Isaac (*third from left*), Meyer's firstborn, was eventually overshadowed by his brothers. His major achievement lay in building the largest of the Guggenheim houses on Long Island. Daniel (*fourth from right*) was a business genius and diplomat, whose first commercial accomplishment was convincing President Porfirio Diáz to allow the Guggenheims to explore and exploit any mine they wanted in Mexico, a deal that generated a stupefying fortune for the investors. Daniel even got the better of Rockefeller in the ASARCO trust, whose chairman he became, before going on to pioneer in rocketry. Solomon (*third from right*) founded the Solomon R. Guggenheim Museum in New York, the result of the interest he developed in art rather late in life. Simon (*second from right*) was in charge of the family's large silver interests in Colorado, where he served as state senator for several years. Finally, William (*far right*) became an elegant expatriate after working in the family mines.

thus, he bought out one partner, gained control, and returned to Philadelphia. A while later, he received a telegram: "Rich strike, fifteen ounces silver sixty percent lead." This happened to be the highest silver content of any mine in the whole rich area. Soon the lode was paying Meyer $17,000 per month, and before the mines were depleted they had enriched the Guggenheims by some $15 million, which was only the start of their vast fortune. Meanwhile, after he realized that the Holden Smelter in Denver was taking a large part of his profit, Meyer invested $500,000 to open his own plant in the same city

It was time to expand abroad, and the Guggenheims headed for Mexico, where mines were incredibly cheap, labor plentiful as well as low-cost, and capital short. Daniel went down in 1890 to get concessions from the renowned dictator Porfirio Díaz, who had taken an important part in overthrowing the short-lived experiment at European rule in Mexico under the ill-fated Emperor Maximilian and his Empress Carlotta, who, as a consequence, spent most of her life in a madhouse. Díaz, always prepared to be cut into a good deal by the right people, allowed the Guggenheims to build two smelters at Monterrey and Aguascalientes and to "undertake the exploration and exploitation of any mine they want to lease or buy in Mexico." All equipment could be imported duty free, and any money spent on the smelter would remain free of tax. By 1895, the yield from the smelters came to $1 million per year, which made the family the principal mining force in Mexico. The pleased Meyer informed his sons that it was now time to gain control of all smelting interests in North America.

In 1889 the Guggenheims formed the Guggenheim Exploration Company, known as Guggenex, part of which was floated on the New York Stock Exchange. Their competition was the United Metals Selling Company, a trust formed by William Rockefeller, son of the great monopolist John D., his partner Henry Rogers, and the Lewisohn brothers. The Rockefeller group brought in the Amalgamated Copper Company (later Anaconda), and the Lewisohns contributed their large accumulation of copper interests. This led to the formation of the even larger ASARCO (American Smelting and Refining Company), which combined 23 different smelters in an attempt to defeat the Guggenheims and absorb all their interests. The scenario practically repeated the great steel war that ended in the formation of United States Steel, with the Wall Street mafia once again mobilized. To work out their strategy and financing, the Guggenheims recruited a pair of brilliant Wall Street speculators, Thomas Fortune Ryan and William Whitney, bringing them in as full partners. As before, the family got lucky, this time when the ASARCO workers went out on strike for two full months in 1900. Having convinced mine owners to sell him their ore, Daniel increased production dramatically in Mexico, dumped metals throughout the world, and started buying ASARCO shares at distress prices. The Rockefeller gang offered to buy out the enemy for $45 million, to which the Guggenheims agreed, provided all the *mischpoche* went on the board of the merged giant and owned a 51 percent controlling interest. An immigrant family of stove-polish and lace sellers had succeeded in controlling worldwide an industry still in its infancy. Hardly pausing for breath, the

Guggenheims now married into the cream of New York's Jewish banking and retailing community and started to live life at the top.

After Meyer's death in 1905, Daniel became head of the tribe and proved himself entirely the equal of his driven, ambitious father. In a brilliant move, he hired one of the world's most gifted mining engineers, John Hays Hammond, for the then colossal salary of $250,000 per year plus 25 percent of any mine he brought in. Worth every penny of it, Hammond led the Guggenheims to riches beyond their wildest imagination. Today, the Guggenheim name immediately brings copper to mind, because of the Bonanza Lode above Kennecot Creek in Alaska, a large, bare greenish mountain lost in the northern wilderness whose ore proved to be 70-75 percent pure, in contrast to the 2-3 percent yielded in Utah and Nevada. Hammond had literally found a copper mountain, and to bring out its ore, he needed the sort of financing that only J.P. Morgan and Jacob Schiff, the emperors of Wall Street, could provide. The new capital made it possible to organize railroads, span rivers with metal bridges, build harbors, and launch steamship lines. It was as if the rigors of the Trans-Siberian railroad had been brought to the wilderness that Russia had sold for an amount no greater than the monthly earnings of this great enterprise. The first cargo to leave in 1911 generated $500,000, whereupon the Guggenheims decided that everything in Alaska, above or under ground, should belong to them.

Their worldwide strategy was quite simple and also ruthless: always buy during depressed markets, exploit cheap foreign labor to bring wages down at home, go solely for the main chance, and be vertically integrated. Keeping to this course, the Guggenheims went on to conquer Chile as well as the metal wealth of the Congo and Angola in partnership with Thomas Fortune Ryan and King Leopold of the Belgians. When the guns of August began firing in 1914, the family controlled 75-80 percent of the world's silver, copper, and lead, and could fix output and prices at will. They were the undisputed monarchs of metal.

The Lure of Gold

Despite the enormous fortunes made in other natural resources, nothing has ever so caught the popular imagination as gold, the eternal and international repository and symbol of wealth. The metal has the advantage of being rare and malleable, bright, colorful, and tarnish-free, as well as light and easily transportable. By virtue of all these qualities, gold lends itself to decorative objects of great beauty that confer instant status upon their owners—the rich and powerful. While gold has been found in most parts of the world, either as nuggets in riverbeds or veins in ore-bearing rock, its greatest concentrations—in the American West and on the very tip of the African landmass—came to light only in the second half of the nineteenth century.

Prior to 1848, California had been an unpromising northern appendage of Mexico, which ceded the region to the Union in that year. During the same *annus mirabilis* a German-Swiss settler, John Augustus Sutter, discovered gold on his property in the Sacramento Valley. After much wandering, all the way to the Hawaiian Islands, Sutter had arrived in California in 1839 and talked the Mexican governor, Juan Batista Alvarado, into granting him 50,000 acres of land at the confluence of the Sacramento and American rivers. He hired some Indians, built a sawmill, and started farming with considerable success. Eventually, he developed 3,500 acres of grain, planted hundreds more in fruit trees, and built a herd of livestock several thousand strong. When his partner in the sawmill business dredged the first nuggets from the Sacramento River, Sutter found little reason to rejoice: "I knew

The discovery of gold in California caused a great migration from the East Coast to the Far West. Hopeful prospectors headed out in droves—on land, over the sea, or by a combination of the two means. No single event so concentrated shipowners' attention on the fastest, cheapest, and most efficient way to cut across the narrow Central American isthmus that frustratingly blocked the shortest route from the Caribbean to the Pacific Ocean. BELOW: The *Hartford-Captain LeFèvre* steams toward California from New York City in 1849. Endless studies were made for building canals across Nicaragua and Panama in order to avoid the long and hazardous voyage around the Cape Horn. Meanwhile, passengers were dropped by sailing packets on one coast, transported overland through the Central American jungles, swamps, and lakes by train, mule, canoe, or paddle steamer, eventually to be picked up on the western coast by other packets bound for San Francisco. ABOVE: A poster beckons prospectors to book passage on the fast-sailing *Josephine*. In many cases the captain and crew were so eager to join the Forty-Niners that they all jumped ship in San Francisco, leaving many a vessel to be turned into a hotel for returning miners.

Tooling up for the Gold Rush was an expensive procedure, and anything forgotten would have to be purchased from gouging merchants in the goldfields at astronomic expense.

BELOW: A contemporary caricature shows a hopeful prospector equipped with not only a shovel but also sausages, teapot, and bedwarmer.

FAR RIGHT: George W. Northrup, on the eve of his departure, poses for a last portrait with pickaxe, pistols, and a full bag of nuggets, optimistically marked "Gold. $90,000." Like most of his friends, he probably spent all his savings and settled down to farming. California was only one of the many places where gold was eventually discovered.

ABOVE: Charles M. Russell, *Pay Dirt* (Gilcrease Museum, Tulsa). This picture could have been painted anywhere in the Far West during the second half of the 19th century.

OPPOSITE ABOVE: A gold mine in Alaska characterized by the primitive and amateur conditions in which the precious metal was extracted.

OPPOSITE BELOW: Three rather old and grimy prospectors wash and pan gold in Rockerville, Dakota.

nothing of the extent of the discovery but I was satisfied that it would greatly interfere with my plans." Soon headlines shouted: "The whole country resounds to the sound of gold. GOLD, GOLD, GOLD." The rush was on, starting with $25,000 of the nuggets culled in 1848 by a few locals. Caravans headed West while sailing clippers risked the terrors of Cape Horn. At the rush's height in 1852, 100,000 hopefuls were shoveling away mountains or sieving rivers through their pans to extract gold dust and nuggets worth $81 million. In less than a decade, gold amounting to $345 million was spent just in San Francisco, which, as a result, grew from a tiny outpost called Yerba Buena into a boomtown of banks, saloons, and brothels.

To real money-makers, however, gold constituted a sideshow—and for several reasons. First of all, California gold was so easily available and so heavily concentrated that anybody with a shovel or a pan could get at it. Most miners simply took the cream off their claims before moving on and thus never really got rich. Too, gold's price was fixed by the government, which eliminated the need for amalgamations or mergers to control supply and demand. The gold rush was really a free-for-all in which poor immigrants sought instant riches and the fulfillment of their dreams. For most of them, it meant an arduous trip out, weeks or months of disappointment, sickness or even death, and a humiliating return home. The call of gold, however, had an element of machismo and promised a splendid adventure to many a young man working in a grim factory.

The real money was made "fleecing the Golden Fleecers," and in a climate of easy-come-easy-go, the sky posed the only limit to what gougers could charge for food, drink, mining equipment, and other necessities of life. One merchant purchased 1,500 dozen eggs off a coastal schooner and sold them, at a nice profit, for 37 cents per dozen, only to find them for resale at ten times his price. A San Francisco lady of the night cleared $50,000 a month from sex-starved miners determined to spend all they had earned, their assumption being that the nearby hills contained an endless supply of gold. Although California's tycoons made their fortunes in railroads, finance, and real estate, their first stake came from exploiting the dreamers. The Gold Rush did give a shot in the arm to the whole nation, but its true achievement was in attracting people to the West. Many a miner settled down, raised a family, and so laid a cornerstone in the foundation of the American dream.

SILVER AND GOLD: THE COMSTOCK LODE

If California gold did not directly produce many huge fortunes, the same cannot be said of silver, thanks to the incredibly rich mines discovered in the shadow of the Sun Mountain of the Gold Canyon in the barren Washoe Valley near Virginia City, Nevada. Most of the forty-niners passed through the Gold Cañon on the way to what they believed were greater riches in California, although they did pluck nuggets out of rocks with their knives and mined some gold from the hills. But the gold dust intermingled with a blue ore that choked their rockers and carried away the quicksilver that otherwise easily separated the gold residue from ore. One day, as the disgusted miners were discarding the blue residue, an astonished Mexican miner shouted, "*Bueno, bueno. Mucha plata, mucha plata,*" as he pointed to the Sun Mountain, but nobody listened.

In the spring of 1851, two brothers, Allen and Hosea Grosch, acted on a hunch, assayed the blue ore, and nearly fainted. It was almost pure silver. They kept silent for over four years while attempting to dig up enough gold to take out serious claims and have the capital necessary to exploit them. In 1857 Hosea died of gangrene after puncturing his foot with a pickaxe, and Allen set out westward to dig for more gold. In his log cabin, he left behind a locked box containing his ore samples as well as a survey with the silver mines located on it. Before departing, Allen Grosch signed an agreement with another miner, George Comstock, that he would

give him a 25 percent interest in his claims if Comstock guarded the cabin and black box until he returned. Alas, the desert winter claimed Allen, and as soon as Comstock heard of his death he broke open the black box but failed to decipher the survey. Shortly thereafter, an extremely rich find was made and called the Gold Hill. Comstock matched it up to the black box's documents, figured which were the other mines the Grosches had pinpointed, and staked his own claims.

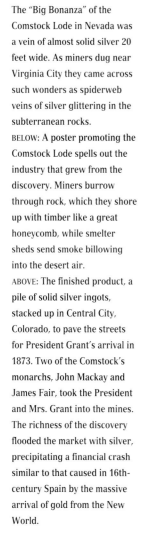

The "Big Bonanza" of the Comstock Lode in Nevada was a vein of almost solid silver 20 feet wide. As miners dug near Virginia City they came across such wonders as spiderweb veins of silver glittering in the subterranean rocks.

BELOW: A poster promoting the Comstock Lode spells out the industry that grew from the discovery. Miners burrow through rock, which they shore up with timber like a great honeycomb, while smelter sheds send smoke billowing into the desert air.

ABOVE: The finished product, a pile of solid silver ingots, stacked up in Central City, Colorado, to pave the streets for President Grant's arrival in 1873. Two of the Comstock's monarchs, John Mackay and James Fair, took the President and Mrs. Grant into the mines. The richness of the discovery flooded the market with silver, precipitating a financial crash similar to that caused in 16th-century Spain by the massive arrival of gold from the New World.

Comstock started mining but still failed to grasp that the real value of his claim lay in silver rather than in gold. A passerby took a sample of the blue stuff to a nearby assayer, who replied that "the ore was $4,791 to the ton, $3,196 in silver, the rest in gold. It's almost solid silver." The Comstock Lode became the greatest bonanza of the West and transformed Virginia City into a mythical arena of whoring, gambling, high life, and shoot-outs. Among those who profited most were two Golden Fleecers from Dublin, John W. Mackay and James G. Fair, who teamed up with two Frisco stockbrokers, James C. Flood and William S. O'Brien, to buy control of existing mines through securities manipulations. They also hit a 20-foot vein of nearly pure silver, the Big Bonanza, which was by far the most important strike of precious metal in history. While Fair became a United States Senator from Nevada, Mackay went on to the telegraph business and the pinnacle of New York society. Flood and O'Brien, the other newly rich magnates, quickly built great palaces on Nob Hill and emerged as San Francisco's most distinguished citizens. If California gold was responsible for populating the West, Nevada silver brought it civilization as well as an elegant and cultivated society.

All that Glitters Is Not Gold

In 1867 a Boer farmer, Schalk Jacobus van Niekerk, visited a neighbor on land near the Orange River. The host's son was playing five-stones with pebbles, and van Niekerk jokingly remarked that one of them would make a pretty stone for a woman's brooch. A few months later, a geologist in Colesberg identified the stone as a 21.25-carat diamond. The story does not reveal whether the little boy got a tip, but two years later a shepherd who knew better brought a fine white diamond of 83.5 carats to van Niekerk, who paid him with 500 sheep and 10 oxen. Richard Southey, the Lieutenant-Governor of the Cape colony, announced to the Cape Assembly that this was the stone on which the future of South Africa would be built. The diamond, known as the Star of Africa, was eventually sold to the Earl of Dudley for £30,000, after which van Niekerk retired, but diamond fever would now start in earnest.

The first diggers were the Boers, and the trickle of a few farmers soon increased to over 10,000. Prospectors, many from the American Gold Rush, set sail for Africa, and as the word got out, hopefuls poured in from Britain, Ireland, Germany, and Russia as well. Soon, diamonds were being found over a vast area in the yellowish topsoil, which the prospectors eagerly dug out and pan-washed in the nearby river. So plentiful were the stones that anything less than one carat was allowed to be sluiced away. The diggers emptied the remaining stones on a sorting table, where they separated rocks from diamonds and cheered loudly whenev-

er a big, cloudy white stone made its appearance. Little did these pioneers know, as they laid claim to or purchased pieces of land, that what they were excavating was merely the capricious droppings of the hillocks that once crowned the great pipes nearby.

Bulfontein and Dutoitspan

As the diggers wandered in search of more stones, they found hospitality at two Boer farms, Bultfontein and Dutoitspan, totally unaware that these sat right on top of one of four large pipes choked with hundreds of thousands of carats of diamonds in every size, color, and shape. Adriaan van Wyk, the owner of Dutoitspan (named for his predecessor), asked for a royalty equal to a quarter of the value of diamonds found on his property once systematic digging began in 1870. Soon, however, he decided to sell—for £2,600! Mining settlements quickly dotted the river, and digging got underway at nearby Bultfontein. In 1871, a pipe was discovered at Vooruitzigt, 2.5 miles distant, on a farm called De Beers after its owner, and only 2,000 yards away diggers from Colesberg stumbled upon yet another pipe. First named the Colesberg

Kopje (Dutch for "hillock"), it became known as New Rush for the speed with which its first sixty feet had been excavated, producing every month diamonds worth close to £5,000. The picking was incredibly easy in the light surface soil of decomposed yellow ground that washed away in the rain and left diamonds visible to the naked eye. After a while, the miners hit blue Kimberlite and thought the game was over. But as they broke up this friable rock, they found that it held an even greater

The fantastic wealth of South Africa's mine owners would have been impossible without the cheap labor provided by underpaid and exploited Africans. From as far away as Basutoland, Zululand, Mozambique, and territories to the north, natives arrived at both the diamond mines and later the goldfields of the Witwatersrand, the largest deposit of gold in the world, which would become the site of Johannesburg. African miners—housed in large camps, known as townships or locations, poorly fed and clothed—drowned their sadness in rotgut provided by willing white dealers. Instead of returning to their villages, with a little capital to show for the years they spent in misery, many died from overexposure and alcohol poisoning. Black workers were known to their employers as "Kaffirs," a term cynically applied as well to the South African financial paper then traded throughout the world. At the end of a day in the Kimberley diamond mines, the two naked natives seen here have had their hands placed in large leather mitts chained to their wrists as a brutal precaution against theft.

BELOW: Barney Barnato, caricatured in an 1895 issue of *Vanity Fair* (London). A onetime English music-hall performer, Barnato made a vast fortune first dealing in diamonds mined in Kimberley, after which he consolidated his holdings into what became the De Beers diamond monopoly.

TOP: An extremely rare photograph of the Big Hole at the Kimberley Diamond Mine in 1879 shows the adobe-like mounds of the various claims. The spiderweb threads were used to haul up leather buckets of diamond ore, and the entire scene perfectly reflects the abject confusion before the establishment of the De Beers monopoly.

FAR RIGHT ABOVE: The friable stone was brought up in a haulage bucket to be washed by stark-naked natives in one of the first rotary washing machines, made in 1874.

FAR RIGHT BELOW: Washed diamonds would then be sorted for both size and quality.

concentration of diamonds, which simply increased the farther down they went.

Hundreds of claims were made in these mines, each the size of a squash court. Over them swarmed the Africans in heat of 100°F, a fine red dust powdering their bodies, clogging their eyes, and filling their nostrils and mouths. At the end of the day, the mine inspector searched their hair, their orifices, and even their open wounds before purging them with heavy doses of castor oil to make certain they stole no diamonds. At night, everyone returned to nearby settlements—Beaconsfield on the north side of the Dutoitspan and Bultfontein mines and Kimberley a few miles away. Echoing the Wild West, the white miners drank, whored, and gambled. Meanwhile, the black slaves sang, chanted, danced, and carried on tribal rivalries and blood feuds. From time to time, the miners took their clean and sorted stones to the local post office and—there being no registered mail—trusted to luck that one day the merchants in Hopetown would send them back a check, provided the packages had not fallen off the coach along the way.

Clearly, some order had to be brought out of this chaos. The first problem was oversupply. Inevitably, the price of diamonds began to fall, filling prospectors with the fear that perhaps there would be no end to these once rare and priceless gems, which, as a consequence, would shortly have the value and attraction of topaz. Also, as the adobe-like claims were sunk deeper into the ground, one started to collapse onto the other, claims crossed, and people resorted to murder in a blind and greedy rage. In other words, mining became far too difficult and expensive for a band of small entrepreneurs. Diamond mining in the 1880s resembled the American oil business before John

D. Rockefeller came along to organize a disparate group of small independent producers into a powerful monopoly that served everybody's best interest. The Gilded Age did not want for potential monopolists, but those who emerged in South Africa were exceptionally colorful.

RHODES AND BARNATO

The son of a vicar educated at Harrow and Trinity College, Cambridge, Cecil Rhodes (1853-1902) was born in a small town in Hertfordshire. As a boy, he appeared to be tubercular (the real problem was from attending school. In 1870, the seventeen-year-old Cecil joined his brother Herbert, who had left—like John Buchan's David Crawford—for Natal to make his way growing cotton. Before long, however, Herbert caught diamond fever, as did Cecil in 1871, when he too left the farm and found his way to the Colesberg Kopje. There, the fickle Herbert turned the three claims he had acquired over to his younger brother and returned to the relative comfort of Natal. Although a somewhat nervous, uncommunicative young man, Cecil had a way of creating admirers devoted enough almost to kill for him. Among these was the young Charles Dunell Rudd, with whom Rhodes dug. Together, they expanded their operation to include pumping water out of the enormous hole that New Rush had become and selling ice made by a machine brought up from the Cape in a mule wagon. The ice profits alone came to £1,500, not bad considering that the partners had sold a slightly off-color 17-carat diamond for £150. With the ice money they bought into a large claim on the De Beers mine, and for the next decade Rhodes commuted between Oxford, where he enjoyed his life as a scholar, and Kimberley, where he and Rudd vastly increased their fortunes. It was probably at Oxford that Rhodes evolved his odd theory of uniting most of the world, including the United States, in an immense British-dominated federation, a sort of Imperial nightmare with fascist overtones. His first step would have been to seize control of all Africa by building a largely British-owned railroad from Cape Town to Cairo.

Very different was Barnett Isaacs, a London cockney born in 1852, a year before Cecil Rhodes. The grandson of a rabbi and son of an Aldgate shopkeeper, Isaacs worked at a pub with his brother Harry. They both adored the English music hall, where Harry got a part-time job, playing the stooge to Barnett (known as Barney), the unpaid straight man. When Harry took his curtain calls, the manager used to call out "Barney too," which is how Barnett Isaacs became Barney Barnato, one of the strangest figures ever to populate Britain's Gilded Age. David Harris, one of the Isaacs brothers' many cousins, had left for South Africa whence he wrote home about its immense possibilities. Soon Harry was on his way to the "dark continent," where by 1872 he was performing as "Signor Barnato, the

LEFT: Diamonds come in all sizes, shapes, and colors, and sorting them is a task that needs considerable skill as well as patience. Here, at Kimberley, the job is being carefully done around the turn of the century. Diamonds are the end product of deep carbon deposits squeezed by immense pressure and baked by intense heat more than 60 miles below the earth's crust. When igneous activity cracked the earth's surface in prehistoric times, diamond-containing volcanic material spewed upward, scattering some stones on the surface and forming conelike "pipes" below. Over the eons, wind and rain propelled stones into rivers, and only those without flaws arrived uncracked near the ocean.

BELOW: The person most immediately associated with South Africa's gold and diamonds was Cecil Rhodes, here caricatured as a colonialist in a 1900 issue of *L'Assiette au beurre.*

Greatest Wizard Known," while also making some extra change as a prizefighter. He played in New Rush and shortly set himself up there as a "kopje-walloper," one of the small dealers who bought stones from the diggers (many people wondered whether the "wizard" might be dealing in stolen gems). The next year, Barney arrived in South Africa with a little cash and forty boxes of cheap cigars. With these modest assets, plus a wealth of nerve, as their stake, the "Barnato Brothers, Dealers in Diamonds and Brokers in Mining Property" were in business by 1874. The Barnato brothers never found acceptance in the diamond clique. Nevertheless, it was they who first realized that the mines needed "cartelization."

Wernher, Beit & Company

Two other key figures in the eventual diamond cartel were Alfred Beit and Julius Wernher, who subsequently teamed up to form one of the most powerful financial organizations of its time, Wernher, Beit & Company. Wernher started his business life as the South African representative of Paris's Jules Porgès, the son of a Prague jeweler who had become Europe's largest diamond merchant. The direct interest of European *diamantaires* in the South African mines was a crucial development. First of all, a colossal profit margin lay between the price of the raw diamond sold by a prospector to a "kopje-walloper" and the price of the cut and polished stone once set in a Cartier necklace. Moreover, European dealers had access to large pools of capital and possessed the financial know-how to fine-tune the rough music then coming out of Africa. Simply put, they could summon the alchemy of big business. In 1873 the nearly 21-year-old Julius Wernher—a massive, muscular, heavily bearded Prussian dragoon from Darmstadt—left for the Cape.

Alfred Beit, Wernher's soon-to-be partner, was the son of a German-Jewish silk merchant from Hamburg. His first job had been with a relative, the merchant David Lippert, in whose Amsterdam office Beit studied the diamond trade. (Amsterdam and Antwerp were Europe's centers of the Jewish-dominated business of diamond cutting and polishing.) Once a shy, unprepossessing, and even lethargic young man, Beit changed abruptly after arriving at Kimberley in 1875. Right away, he grasped the importance of matching the expertise of the diamond cutter and merchant with the raw material coming out of the mine. "I saw at once," he later wrote, "that some of the Cape stones were as good as any in the world, and I saw, too, that the buyers protected themselves against their own ignorance by offering generally one-tenth part of what each stone was worth in Europe. It was plain that if one had a little money there was a fortune to be made."

Beit became the South African representative of the new Wernher-Porgès amalgamation, since

Both Julius Wernher (ABOVE) and Alfred Beit (RIGHT BELOW) were German Jews associated with Europe's largest diamond merchant, Jules Porgès, whose South African headquarters in Kimberley are seen here in 1870 (RIGHT ABOVE). Wernher, Beit, and Porgès all became wealthy in the diamond rush, after which they invested their huge fortunes in Johannesburg's rich goldfields. And so did later German-Jewish settlers, in particular Sigismund Neuman and Herman Eckstein, whose "Corner House" became the center of the enormous gold empire of the central and east Rand. Eighty percent of this enterprise's profits went to Wernher, Beit & Company, and its turnover in 1912 was more than the gross national product of South Africa's two largest provinces. "Corner House" produced 3 million ounces of gold per year, plus untold carats of diamonds, making Wernher the richest man in Britain. He lived to see his son marry the niece of Russia's Czar Nicolas II.

Wernher spent most of his time in London keeping order in the Syndicate. By the late 1870s, a few big fish in the mine fields had eaten up the smaller ones. Barney Barnato was probably the richest individual at the mines, and in 1876 he bought six more claims in the Kimberley for the substantial sum of £30,000. Four years later the cockney left for London and, in modern parlance, "went public," floating four new mining companies that reported a staggering quarterly production of 10,328 carats. Other flotations followed, and within a year there were 71 more stock issues. Instead of going at each other with pickaxes, South Africa's mine owners had clearly decided to slug it out on the stock exchange and in the boardrooms of the City, although the chaos that ensued was none the more attractive. It did, however, put the match in the court of those Randlords with financial acumen and access to such great bankers as the Rothschilds, Schröders, and Barings. Thanks to a series of takeovers and mergers led by Porgès, Barnato, Rhodes, and the Wernher-Beit axis (Beit was now dealing with both Rhodes and Porgès), there were by 1883 only 46 companies and 56 private holdings in the four great mines. Still, the problems of overproduction remained endemic. Two years later, only seven companies and three private holdings controlled the Kimberley, while eleven and eight dominated De Beers. The battle had essentially been reduced to an all-powerful Barnato in the Kimberley corner and Rhodes triumphant in the De Beers corner.

Barnato, a onetime prizefighter, would not give up easily, and so he dramatically increased production in order to reduce the price of diamonds and thus squeeze the already-strapped Rhodes. The joker in the pack was Porgès's French Company, which both Barnato and Rhodes desperately wanted, and the former made it his game to deprive the latter of the means to take it over. However, Beit saved the day by getting Rhodes £1 million from the London Rothschilds. After a 24-hour meeting in South Africa, Rhodes and Barnato came to terms, and, beginning in 1889, all of South Africa's diamonds would be controlled by a cartel that fixed production and sold as a single syndicate to the trade, solely under the De Beers name. Output was cut by 40 percent, the price of diamonds immediately rose by 50 percent, and it has been kept on a steady uphill curve ever since. All the leading players became unbelievably wealthy, after which Porgès retired, Wernher and Beit launched their bank, Barnato became a London celebrity, and Rhodes spent most of his fortune in futile colonial adventures. Even today nobody really knows the value of the stones underground or hidden in De Beers safes.

Cecil Rhodes, and his old diamond partner, Charles Rudd, made an almost incalculable amount of money in South African metal. Rhodes then spent most of his wealth attempting to colonize Zambia to the north (later named Rhodesia in his honor). He also became Premier of the Cape, as well as the instigator of the odd and ill-fated Jameson Raid, an attempt by a small group to destroy the power of the Boers, remove President Kruger, and surreptitiously bring all South Africa into the British Empire. This rash play disgraced some of the most respected figures in South Africa, caused immense embarrassment in Britain, and created deep and lasting enmity between Queen Victoria and her grandson, Kaiser Wilhelm II, whose open defense of Kruger hastened Rhodes's death. This came in 1902, when the 48-year-old tycoon uttered the famous words: "So much to be done, so little time." Beit was so distressed by both the Jameson Raid and the loss of his old friend and partner that he suffered a stroke in Johannesburg shortly afterward, surviving for two years as an invalid before dying at the age of 53 in his country house in Hertfordshire. Barnato went on living it up in London, showing off his racehorses and mistresses and doing vaudeville skits. At the age of 45, he met a death similar to that of the late Robert Maxwell. He apparently jumped or was pushed off a ship taking him from the Cape to London on the way to Queen Victoria's Diamond Jubilee in 1897. Julius Wernher enjoyed a somewhat longer life, holding court in his magnificent, custom-built offices at 1 London Wall, in an art-filled mansion originally owned by the Marquess of Bath next to the Ritz, and at Luton Hoo, one of England's most beautiful

Adam houses, with gardens designed by Capability Brown.

In addition to diamonds, enormous fortunes were also made in the gold mines on the Witwatersrand, which would become the site of Johannesburg. Many of those who gained wealth in diamonds went on to the gold fields, and for Britain, the Randlords were the equivalent of America's railroaders, and their fortunes often just as large. Many took active part in South Africa's politics, and most received knighthoods from their sovereign, the notable exception being Barney Barnato. The despised Robinson, a south African who had lost his ground-floor position at Kimberley but then made a gigantic fortune on the Rand, was offered a peerage, but the established Lords made such a fuss that he turned it down. In 1917, Ernest Oppenheimer secured a controlling interest in the giant De Beers gold and diamond interests, which he passed on to his son Harry, a longtime supporter of freeing South Africa from apartheid—an institution that, in so many ways, was the creation of the first Randlords.

H. Macbeth-Raeburn, *Queen Mary*, 1910 (House of Lords, Westminster, London). In this state portrait the consort of George V is seen in her diamonds, most of which came from South Africa's mines. The 3,025-carat Cullinan diamond, the largest stone ever discovered (named after South Africa's Sir Thomas Cullinan) was presented to Queen Mary's father-in-law, King Edward VII, and two of the largest gems cut from it are in the Imperial State Crown and the Royal Sceptre.

BANKERS

A worldwide survey of modern banking could easily fill several volumes, and the profiles of the giants that follow should perhaps be viewed as more an exercise in nostalgia than a history of finance. Nonetheless, it is hoped that the sketches may give some indication of both the power wielded by the great money men of the Gilded Age and their contribution to modern society.

The tradition of large-scale mercantile banking goes back to the Renaissance. The most celebrated of all the early financiers were, of course, the Medici, the great Florentine family who dealt in wool and quickly became bankers to much of Europe. In Venice, it was the importers of riches from the Orient who created important financial institutions, while the wealth of Genoa's merchant princes came out of shipping first and then banking. In Germany, the Fuggers of Augsburg began as weavers but then made prodigious fortunes based on a monopoly in the mining and trading of silver. With few exceptions, the merchant bankers traded first in goods and then in money, eventually leaving the commodities to others while devoting themselves entirely to finance. No transaction went through without documents, and those who generated them often found it a far cleaner and more profitable business to buy and sell the paper rather than the bulky, perishable, variably priced merchandise that stood behind it.

Nearly all of today's important bankers descend from seventeenth-century Continental entrepreneurs, many of them Jewish. During the nineteenth century, London's City (the financial center of the British Empire) saw the arrival of the Barings and the Rothschilds from Frankfurt, the Lazards from Alsace, the Hambros from Denmark, and the de la Rues from Genoa. The nineteenth century proved to be a golden age for Jewish bankers, who, from the Middle Ages onward, had served as the money-changers of Europe, a trade left open to them by Christian disapproval of lending and its attendant usury. Long barred from most professions in Europe, locked up at night in ghettos, and viewed as Shylocks in the popular imagination, the descendants of the Israelites had been forced into a pro-

fession with which they became almost totally identified and in which, over time, they developed particular skills. It was Jewish money-changers on Germany's busy trade routes who became bankers of princes and then princes of bankers, once the many restrictions on their lifestyle, education, and movement had been lifted or at least curtailed.

Many German Jews found freedom and prosperity in the New World, at the same time that others left for Britain, a country untouched by the official segregation practiced elsewhere in Europe and in Russia. Those who remained on the Continent came into their own during the second half of the nineteenth century, thanks largely to the immense clout gained by the Rothschilds as a consequence of their success in underwriting the wars and ambitions of Europe's monarchs and governments. It also helped that "our crowd" in New York City and *la haute juiverie* in Europe coalesced into a tightly integrated force, one that carried tremendous weight in the life of international finance. Working together by day with tycoons and bankers of other faiths or cultures, they returned after business hours to their own. The outstanding

BELOW: Less than a century separates this representation of a lady changing money for a soldier on a European country trade route and (OPPOSITE) the scene painted by James Cafferty and Charles Rosenberg in *Wall Street, half past two o'clock, October 13, 1857*. During this short period both the scope and the sophistication of financial markets had grown enormously. In the Gilded Age, bankers became staggeringly rich from the expansion of trade and industry to an international scale. They and their clients, however, often came to grief when hit by one of the many bubbles and bursts that buffeted the financial world. The painting is ironic, representing as it does the calm before the storm—the moment when the worst "panic" in twenty years began.

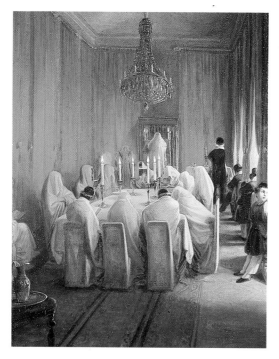

exceptions to this rule were the Rothschilds, who early on grew into pillars of international society, even while insisting upon their original identity, and finally found themselves cultivated by the grandest ruling families of Europe. But Christian or Jewish, it was the leading merchant bankers who controlled much of the world economy during the Gilded Age.

THE ROTHSCHILDS

The legendary fortune of the Rothschilds helped save many a monarchy and government, stem financial panics, and give the Family (the clan always used a capital F) power unlike any other in the world of money and banking. At the peak of

their influence, from 1850 to 1900, the Rothschilds' combined net worth was estimated at over £400 million, or about $20 billion in today's terms, a phenomenal achievement considering that it took John D. Rockefeller several decades to arrive at one-tenth of that sum nearly half a century later.

Such was the Family's impact on the fate of nations that when a worried neighbor queried the matriarch Gutele Rothschild (who continued to live in the Frankfurt ghetto despite her sons' enormous wealth) if there would be war between two major European powers, she authoritatively replied: "War? Nonsense, my boys won't give them the money." She was not far wrong, since the "boys" financed sovereigns and regimes, armies, trade, the Suez Canal, Wellington, the railroads, and any other individual, group, or project that promised to make masses of money through the Family's banks in London, Paris, Vienna, Frankfurt, and, for a short time, even Naples. In fact, before the advent of radio or telephone, the Rothschilds kept themselves so fully abreast of world events, via their own international network of couriers and carrier pigeons, that governments depended on these superior communications to run their nations. The deadly weapon of timely information allowed the Rothschilds to manipulate financial markets and reap unheard-of gains, often at the expense of others. The most famous example was advance knowledge of Wellington's victory over Napoleon at Waterloo, which they received by carrier pigeon dispatched by their secret spy, craftily deployed at the scene of battle. Pretending that Wellington had lost, the Rothschilds started to flood the London exchange with orders to sell consols, the government securities of Great Britain. Having thus set off a trading panic, they re-entered the market secretly at a frac-

Beginning in the Middle Ages, banking had become largely a specialty of Jews in Europe, where they were allowed to do little more than traffic in "filthy lucre," traditionally disdained by Christians for its association with the sin of usury. Despite pressures to convert, Israelites of all classes maintained their identity and religion.
ABOVE: The Rothschild family at prayer, as portrayed in c. 1800 by Moritz Daniel Oppenheim.
RIGHT: William Callow (1812-1908), *Market Place, Frankfurt* (Victoria & Albert Museum, London). Many Jews lived in important German towns, such as Frankfurt, whose attractive streets and markets they could not frequent after dark.

tion of their receipts. By the time the triumphant news of the battle filtered into the exchange, the Rothschilds held practically all the consols, which now soared in value.

The Family have inspired numerous books, a musical comedy, and a movie, as well as individual characters in works by Heinrich Heine and Honoré de Balzac. Their splendid eighteenth-century French furniture and opulent interiors—often referred to as *le style Rothschild*—gave the Gilded Age its quintessential look. Rothschild horses raced and won against those of Edward VII, among other British monarchs, and they still dominate the track at Ascot, Longchamps, and Deauville, where their jockeys ride in the Family colors, yellow with blue polka dots. The Rothschilds were the first Jews to be ennobled, by the Emperor of Austria, and the first to be received by the great aristocratic families of Europe, who, in turn, coveted invitations to the Family's elaborate dinners, hunts, and balls. When the first Jewish peer, Nathaniel, Lord Rothschild, appeared at an East End synagogue in London, a rumor went buzzing about the temple that the Lord had arrived, prompting a few worshipers to prostrate themselves in the belief that the Messiah had indeed come. In a way, they were not mistaken, since the Balfour Declaration of 1917, officially recognizing the establishment of a national home for the Jewish people in Palestine, was addressed to the second Lord Rothschild at his office in New Court. During the decade that followed, his cousin Baron Edmond supported Palestine almost single-handedly. Of all the Gilded Age parvenus, the Rothschilds were the most flamboyant, the most outrageous, and, in less than fifty years, the most spectacularly successful in achieving everything that money could buy: power, influence, status, respect, and even fear, magnificent houses, furniture, and art, beautiful women and fine horses. Yet, to this day, they have preserved both their work ethic and their links to the patriarchal past.

MAYER AMSCHEL—THE FIRST ROTHSCHILD

Mayer Amschel (1743-1812), the patriarch, was born in the shabby, overcrowded, malodorous Frankfurt ghetto. Here, about the only trades available to Jews were peddling and money-changing, a situation that helped Mayer decide to study at a Yeshiva near Nuremberg in the hope of becoming a rabbi. But when the death of his parents left him penniless, he became an apprentice in the Jewish banking house of Oppenheimer at Hannover, a city where coreligionists received better treatment than in Frankfurt, which locked them in the ghetto after dark and taunted them during the day with shouts of "Jew, do your duty." With this, the victims had to step into the gutter, doff their hats, and bow. Jews could not even take a name for themselves; thus, Rothschild derived from the house with the "red shield" in which the family once lived.

Having completed his apprenticeship, Mayer Amschel left Oppenheimer to return to the squalid Rothschild quarters in Frankfurt, where his two brothers ran a secondhand shop. Aided by his knowledge of ancient history, he started buying old coins for resale to aristocratic families around Germany. The young speculator found his most important client in the immensely rich Landgrave William of Hesse-Cassel, to whom he reputedly sold a few pieces at a small loss in order to curry

The "House of the Red Shield" in the Frankfurt ghetto, where the enterprising Rothschilds acquired their name. The family patriarch, Mayer Amschel, moved here from a smaller house in the ghetto after making a reasonable fortune from his early banking activities with the Landgrave of Hesse-Cassel. The house served both as home and office, while the basement constituted a veritable rabbit warren of secret hiding places for documents, cash, and coins. The Rothschild heirs built vast and elaborate palaces around Europe as their fortunes increased (see pages 124-129), but the family matriarch, Gutele, refused ever to live anywhere other than in the House of the Red Shield.

favor. This was the first of many transactions between a Rothschild and a head of state. Prince William could boast a royal lineage far grander than his modest realm would suggest. Indeed, he was a grandson of George II of England, a nephew of the King of Denmark, and a brother-in-law of the King of Sweden, all of whom owed him money for the sale of his male subjects as soldiers of fortune. "The Hessians" not only fought in Europe; they also kept peace in the American Colonies. When one of his mercenaries died, William got a compensation bonus, all the while that he also took the lion's share of the troops' wages.

Thanks to this near-slave trade in soldiers, William became the richest sovereign in Europe. The person to whom he assigned the management of his complicated financial life was a bastard offspring, Carl Buderus, who liked not only the subservient manner wisely adopted by Mayer Amschel but also the bribe in old coins given in the hope of gaining regular access to the Prince. In a short time, Mayer Amschel was cashing some of the drafts drawn on London in payment of William's mercenaries, and by the 1780s he could add on to the family shop a tiny counting house. Here he installed an intricate safe, a trapdoor leading to a hidden cellar, and a near-undetectable cavern.

Soon this safe haven would contain secret documents relating to many of the financial transactions of the increasingly affluent Landgrave William, who remained unaware of how closely his great fortune was being linked to the ghetto peddler through the corrupted Buderus.

THE FIVE SONS OF MAYER AMSCHEL

Mayer Amschel had five sons whom he would assign like Roman pro-consuls to various parts of Europe. Amschel (1773-1855) was to stay on in Frankfurt, Salomon (1774-1855) to be sent to Vienna, Nathan (1777-1836) to London, Jacob (James, 1792-1868) to Paris, and Kalmon (Carl, 1788-1855) to Naples. Meanwhile, the boys began to travel about the German principalities developing their father's nascent banking business, hawking Hesse's financial paper, and handling the bonds in which Landgrave William invested his tremendous fortune. Buderus became a full partner in their small bank, which soon was competing with such distinguished Gentile firms as Frankfurt's Bethmann brothers and Rüppell & Harnier, from whom they took such important business as the big loan agree-

ABOVE: Three of the sons of Mayer Amschel Rothschild (*from left*): Salomon, head of the Viennese branch; Amschel Mayer, who continued to run the Frankfurt business after the patriarch's death; and Carl, who made a beachhead in Naples. Not seen in this engraving were two other brothers, in fact the true geniuses of the Family: Nathan (RIGHT), with his wife after arriving to set up the Family bank in London; and Jacob (OPPOSITE), who anglicized his name to James and founded the all-powerful French dynasty. Dispatched to their respective outposts all over Europe, the brothers became known as the "Five Arrows," for the missiles that make up the Family's coat of arms.
ABOVE RIGHT: The Landgrave William of Hesse-Cassel entrusting his treasure to Mayer Amschel Rothschild after being exiled by Napoleon in 1807. The Rothschild patriarch strikes an appropriately servile pose, but the confidence placed in him launched one of the most dazzling of all financial sagas, since the Rothschilds made a fortune trading with the royal funds entrusted to them.

ments between William and his uncle, the King of Denmark.

Shortly before the Napoleonic occupation of Hesse, Nathan Rothschild left for Manchester and started dealing in cloth. Bonaparte declared that he would "remove the house of Hesse-Cassel from rulership and... strike it out of the list of powers." While William sought exile in Denmark, the Rothschilds hid most of his jewels in their cellars. They also took over a large part of his financial affairs, becoming the conduit through which much of the vast Hessian income was collected and accounted for, all in contravention of Napoleon. This meant secret codes in Yiddish, stagecoaches with false bottoms, and, long before electronic banking had ever been imagined, the transfer of dividends across borders without trace. It was important that William have no record or control of the massive financial skullduggery, or any knowledge of how it was done, a situation the Rothschilds refrained from exploiting at their client's expense. On the other hand, they did not rush to pay, for with the Hessian funds available to them from the time of receipt to the time of delivery, the secret agents (the family menbers) made a fortune trading in cotton, cloth, gold, and other commodities for their own account. Thanks to Napoleon's siege of the Continent, Britain became the world's financial capital, which persuaded Nathan to move from Manchester to London, where he would henceforth deal only in money—mainly William's. Millions flowed through the headquarters he established in New Court, and by 1810 Nathan could boast of having multiplied his original stake 2,500 times. This Rothschild had emerged as one of the richest men in England, his fortune estimated to be even larger than that of the German Prince who had been the launching pad for the world's greatest bankers.

Meanwhile, brother Jacob, who adopted the more elegant name of James, moved to Paris, where Napoleon's secret police correctly suspected him of being at the center of a great money-smuggling

scheme. To pay for the Iberian campaign against the French, Nathan, on behalf of the British government, bought up all the gold of the East India Company and sent it to the Duke of Wellington in Portugal. The huge, top-secret transfer of assets, conducted largely by James, succeeded brilliantly. Had it failed, Napoleon's forces might well have crushed Wellington, conquered Britain, and thus changed the entire course of European affairs. Altogether, the British delivered to their Continental allies some £30 million in gold, over half of which passed through the hands of Nathan Rothschild, whose bank reportedly cleared a profit of £1 million.

Next, the Family started to cultivate Prince Metternich, the leading Austrian statesman and key to the riches of Central Europe, who was in the process of raising one of the largest loans in history—1 billion francs—so that France could indemnify Napoleon's victors. Originally squeezed out of the deal by the older and more powerful Barings, the Rothschilds quietly bought up a large portion of the paper and beared the market, pushing many of Europe's leading bankers and statesmen to the brink of financial disaster. Never again would the Frankfurt upstarts be left out.

Between 1817 and 1824 Nathan alone underwrote £5 million in loans for the Prussians, £12 million for Great Britain, £4 million for the Kingdom of Two Sicilies, £3 million for Russia, and the same for Austria. Among his great innovations was paying interest or dividends in British pounds regardless of the currency in which the loan had been emitted. He never touched Latin America, which defaulted on all its loans in 1824, nearly gutting the Bank of

LEFT ABOVE: After becoming rich in several major financial transactions, Baron James de Rothschild moved to the extremely grand Hôtel Fouché at 19 Rue Laffitte in the heart of Paris's financial quarter.
LEFT: In the Hôtel Fouché, Baron James lived in high style, entertaining artists and statesmen who found themselves fed by the greatest chef of all time, Antoine Carême. Not only serenaded by Frédéric Chopin, Carême also inspired praise from such literary lights as Heine and Balzac.

ABOVE: Prince Metternich, the leading statesman of Austria during the first half of the 19th century, practiced realpolitik in persuading the reactionary Hapsburg Emperor to ennoble the Rothschilds, thereby acknowledging the Family's successful efforts to solve the financial problems of the Austrian Empire. In this way, the Rothschilds, as Barons, became the first Jews ever to add an aristocratic particle—von or de—to their name.
FAR LEFT: Baron James de Rothschild, the founder of the French branch of the famous banking family.

England, which the Family saved by an emergency transfer of gold from James in Paris. Nathan, together with his rich brother-in-law Moses Montefiore, also founded the Alliance, one of the world's largest insurance companies. To all effects and purposes, he had now replaced his father, Mayer Amschel, as the Family leader. It was Nathan, for instance, who sent his elder brother Salomon to Vienna. Here he founded a Family bank that became so successful that Metternich had the Austrian Emperor bestow the title of baron upon all the Rothschilds, who, as a consequence, are grandly refered to even today by their first names: Baron Edmond, Baroness Liliane, Baron James, Baroness Betty, etc. Only the British Rothschilds disdained the Austrian patents of nobility, preferring to wait for elevation to the House of Lords, on condition that they swear allegiance on an Old Testament—no mean achievement in a Christian nation.

In 1821 Carl moved to Naples, after which Rothschild money would soon be financing most of Italy, from Tuscany to the Papal States. "Rothschild has just kissed the Pope's hand and at his departure expressed his satisfaction with the successor of St. Peter in the most gracious terms," quipped a jealous observer. Amschel, the eldest of Mayer Amschel's five sons, busied himself in Frankfurt, where he became treasurer to the German confederation and one of Europe's pioneer backers of railways, roads, and factories. Amschel also kept up with the descendants of Buderus and the Landgrave of Hesse-Cassel, although by then the Family were far more important than their original benefactors. Had there been a sixth brother, a Rothschild might have gone to the United States and changed the history of finance, but the Family found quite enough to do in Europe without taming

the Wild West. The brothers, symbolized by five arrows in the Rothschild coat of arms, proved to be the practitioners of *mischpoche* par excellence, linking themselves into one indivisible financial institution, whose combined power and wealth made anything possible.

THE THIRD GENERATION OF ROTHSCHILDS

After Nathan died in 1836, his son Lionel firmly grasped the reins and, helped by brothers Mayer, Anthony, and Nathaniel, floated over £1 billion in foreign loans during his tenure. The most famous transaction came in 1875, when Lionel was supping at his Piccadilly mansion with an old friend, Prime Minister Benjamin Disraeli. The butler brought a telegram from the Paris office announcing that the nearly bankrupt Khedive of Egypt wanted to sell his controlling shares in the Suez Canal. Britain could scarcely have been more interested, since possessing the shares would severely diminish the

BELOW: A caricature of Mayer Amschel de Rothschild from an 1871 issue of *Vanity Fair* (London).
BELOW RIGHT: Port Said and the southern entrance to the Suez Canal. When even the Bank of England could not meet the challenge, Lionel Rothschild (FAR RIGHT) and his far-flung *mischpoche* or Family produced the funds that Prime Minister Benjamin Disraeli needed to purchase for Britain the Khedive of Egypt's controlling shares in the Suez Canal, that 19th-century lifeline, built by France, between Europe and Asia.

power of France, which had built the Canal, on the African continent. Parliament were in recess, and, in any event, the Bank of England could not have mustered 100 million francs overnight. Only the mighty Family could. As Disraeli wrote to Queen Victoria on November 24: "It is just settled! You have it, Madame. The French Government has been out-generalled. There was only one firm that could do it—Rothschild's." Not only did Britain now control the lifeline between Europe and Asia, but, in addition, the Queen of England made a

spectacular investment. (In 1936 alone, Suez paid a dividend of 56 1/2 percent on the original shares.) Needless to say, the Family took their usually large cut on the deal.

For the most part, the third generation of Rothschilds had the same drive as their forebears. Alphonse in Paris, Anselm in Vienna, and Mayer Carl in Frankfurt continued to dominate European finance, together with cousin Lionel defeating the most important challenge ever made to the Family. It came from Émile Péreire, a former associate of Baron James, and Achille Fould, Napoleon III's minister of finance, who combined forces to create the Crédit Mobilier, the first true people's bank, or Volksbank, under the auspices of London's mighty Baring Brothers (the latter still hostile towards the Rothschilds for having muscled their way into government loans), Hamburg's banking Heines, the powerful Duchesse de Galliéra, and the Duchess of Leuchtenberg, daughter of Czar Nicholas I. Fould and Péreire damaged Salomon's transport concessions by buying up the Austrian State Railways, took Rothschild's French underwriting business away, and financed the rebuilding of Paris under Baron Haussmann. Paying a 47 percent dividend on capital in their first year of business, the Crédit Mobilier seemed on the verge of eliminating all competition until Baron Anselm in Vienna created the Kreditanstalt, a near clone of the competition under the equally powerful and social auspices of the Princesses Fürstenberg, Schwarzenberg, and Auersperg, in whose veins coursed the bluest blood of the Austro-Hungarian Empire. Despite the palaces, balls, titles, public emulation, and philanthropy, the Rothschilds had not lost their killer instinct, and the value of their bank's shares doubled in a week, while those of the Crédit Mobilier (which they had secretly beared) fell by 50 percent.

In 1862, after looking at his partners with a jaundiced eye, Achille Fould arranged a financial reconciliation between Napoleon III and James de Rothschild at the latter's immense new Château de Ferrières southeast of Paris. During the day, 1,231 head of game were killed, while in the evening the orchestra and choir of the Paris Opéra serenaded the royals and bankers with music composed especially for the occasion by Rossini. By the time the luxury-loving Emperor returned to Paris, along a special torch-lit railway line, the winds had shifted. In 1864, Napoleon III gave the Crédit Mobilier the dubious privilege of raising a mammoth loan to place the ill-fated Archduke Maximilian on the throne of Mexico. By 1866 the bank would show a loss of 8 million francs, and in 1867 it went into liquidation. Vienna's Kreditanstalt, on the other hand, remained the dominant bank in Central Europe until 1930, when the Austrian government begged Vienna's Baron Louis to use its large reserves to bail out a group of smaller banks tottering under the impact of the Great Depression. Against his better judg-

BOTTOM LEFT: Hippolyte Flandrin (1809-64), *Napoleon III* (Musée de Versailles). In his ambition to restore the French Empire, Napoleon III gave unstinting support to the great bankers of the day—the Rothschilds, the Péreire brothers, and Achille Fould, among others—who in turn helped underwrite the vast economic and overseas expansion that France experienced in the years 1850-70.

LEFT ABOVE: Émile Péreire (1800-75), a former Rothschild associate, joined with Achille Fould (ABOVE), to form the Crédit Mobilier. For a while, this first "people's bank" competed regularly with the Rothschilds in the business of financing government, railway construction, and the massive rebuilding of Paris.

ABOVE: Achille Fould (1800-67), French Finance Minister under Napoleon III, nurtured the flowering of the Third Empire by helping to organize the Crédit Mobilier and by pursuing a policy of free trade. Thanks to the wealth this generated, Baron Haussmann had the means to rebuild Paris in the spectacular form it has today.

ment, Louis agreed, even while warning Austria's Chancellor that the results would probably be disastrous. When the inevitable happened and the Rothschild bank in Vienna crumbled, Austrian industry and economy went into yet steeper decline. This, in turn, detonated a long-simmering anti-Semitic rage that brought the arrest of Baron Louis by the Nazis' Heinrich Himmler, who held the Jewish banker for the largest ransom ever paid.

THE ROTHSCHILDS' LEGACY AND INFLUENCE: LA HAUTE JUIVERIE

Disraeli, Bismarck, Edward VII, Hitler, Napoleon III, Queen Victoria, Metternich, cabinet ministers, poets, painters, rabbinical scholars, philanthropists, great collections, railroads, steel mills, palaces, kibbutzes, society balls, and banquets prepared by the great chef Carême are but a few rich threads in the colorful tapestry woven in less than 150 years by the extraordinary Rothschild family. To the Gilded Age they were as the Medici had been to the Florentine Renaissance, and their breathtaking rise from the ghetto to international prominence proved to be unique for the ability of the Family to preserve both capital and identity. They were also an inspiration to what Europeans call *la haute juiverie*, the powerful Jewish bankers of London, Frankfurt, Paris, Vienna, and St. Petersburg. Nearly all these financiers started like the Rothschilds as small money-changers or bankers to princes, and most had interlinked interests with the Family. They did deals together, made joint underwritings, sometimes acted as local representatives or advisers, and often intermarried and emulated

the Rothschild lifestyle. Great town houses filled with art treasures and *le style* Rothschild provided a common denominator, as did philanthropy to oppressed or underprivileged coreligionists and a great interest in the cultural life of the cities in which they lived and worked.

In Berlin, the most famous members of *la haute juiverie* were the Mendelssohns (who spawned the great Romantic composer Felix), the Bischoffsheims, and Gerson von Bleichröder, who virtually alone masterminded all financial aspects of the rise of Bismarck's Prussia. In Frankfurt there were the Goldschmidts, one of whose members, Maximilian, married a Rothschild daughter and perpetuated the Family name as Baron von Goldschmidt-Rothschild. In Paris reigned the Foulds, Sterns, Péreires, Lazards (who became famous through the American firm Lazard Frères), and Kahns; Henri Deutsch de la Meurthe, who started as a kerosene peddler and became an oil tycoon; the aristocratic Cahen

FAR RIGHT AND BELOW: Well after they had been ennobled by the Austrian Emperor, the Rothschilds joined the landed aristocracy when Baron James purchased Château Lafite, an ancient domain near Bordeaux that still produces one of the three original *grands crus* wines of France. Even in the little château itself, *le style Rothschild* prevails, but on a suitably modest scale for comfortable, country living. Another branch of the Family purchased the neighboring Mouton vineyard, whose superior wine—Château Mouton-Rothschild Pauillac— became the region's fourth *grand cru* in 1973.

FAR LEFT: Baron and Baroness Édouard de Rothschild beam at the side of their winning horse. The Family have long glittered in horse breeding and racing just as in high finance, art collecting, philanthropy, and *le beau monde*.
LEFT ABOVE: Anders Zorn (1860-1920), *Sir Ernest Cassel*. Leaving his native Germany for London, Ernest Cassel succeeded as an investment banker almost as brilliantly as the Rothschilds.

d'Anvers; and the de Gunzburgs, French cousins of St. Petersburg's renowned philanthropists and bankers. London had always been open to Jews, and among early arrivals were the shipping Hambros from Denmark; the Sassoons from Baghdad, where they had made a fortune mainly in the opium trade; and Sir Ernest Cassel, the Ansbachers,

and railroader Baron de Hirsch from Germany. Although no more than the tip of an iceberg, these brilliant entrepreneurs had a major impact on the financial and social scene, and despite the Holocaust, which came largely in reaction to their success, many of their descendants remain a significant force in business today.

"OUR CROWD" IN NEW YORK

In New York City, many of the leading bankers had started life as German-Jewish immigrants. This group, immortalized by Stephen Birmingham in his 1967 book *Our Crowd*, made up the cultivated and well-mannered Jewish society of the metropolis. Its princes were named Seligman, Lehman, Guggenheim, Goldman, Schiff, Sachs, Kuhn, Lewisohn, and Loeb. They intermarried, worked, and socialized together, at the same time that they also enjoyed greater esteem among their European colleagues than such seemingly rough parvenu Christian tycoons as the Astors and Vanderbilts.

In the early nineteenth century, Jews emigrated to the United States by deliberate choice, since America offered an unparalleled chance for personal success and wealth. Another, relatively less adventurous wave of German-Jewish immigration flowed toward England, the Netherlands, and France. Most German Jews, however, joined the famished Irish, surviving Armenians, persecuted Russians, and other beleaguered groups on the rugged voyage across the Atlantic, sleeping on vermin-infested straw mattresses, eating slop twice daily, and finally passing through Ellis Island on their way to the New World and a new life. New York, being the center of trade and commerce, was the ultimate destination for any banker, but Our Crowd generally started as peddlers and traders in other parts of the country. Whether the family patriarch had set out on foot or in a wagon became a much-discussed topic once the descendants started to enjoy their affluence.

THE SELIGMANS

The Seligmans—later known as the "American Rothschilds"—began on foot, but within 25 years Joseph Seligman was serving as a financial advisor to the President of the United States. David, his father, had lived in the Judengasse of Baiersdorf, a tiny town on the banks of the Pegnitz River near

Nuremberg, and produced eight sons and three daughters—a large responsibility for a village weaver. His wife Fanny had brought as a dowry a stock of dry goods, including ribbon, lace, and sheets, which her husband used to supplement their small income by selling them and similar items in a shop on the ground floor of their house. Joseph, the first-born son, helped out in the store and, as a sideline, changed money for travelers passing through the village. (The first Rothschilds practiced the same trade, which needed a quick mind to sort out the many currencies circulating among the crazy-quilt principalities of the Holy Roman Empire.) In the 1830s, when the Industrial Revolution was putting small Bavarian weavers out of business, Fanny Seligman decided to stake the family's future on her eldest son. Using her life's savings, which consisted of a small bag of gold and silver coins hidden behind a stack of linens, she sent Joseph to the University of Erlangen. There he studied literature and the classics, delivering his farewell oration in Greek. Ferociously studious, Joseph dreamed only of going to America. His father fought to keep him in Baiersdorf, but in 1837, at the age of seventeen, with $100 sewn by Fanny into the seat of his pants, Joseph departed, along with eighteen other boys from the village, for Bremen and the vast continent beyond the Atlantic.

Arriving in New York in the middle of the 1837 Panic, Joseph Seligman walked some 100 miles to see his mother's cousin in the small town of Mauch Chunk, Pennsylvania. Here he met Asa Packer, the Puritan owner of a small shipyard that made coal barges, who gave the young immigrant a job as cashier-clerk at a salary of 8 dollars per week. Packer had quickly spotted a talented young man, and both would attain great heights, Seligman in banking and Packer as a multimillionaire railroader, United States Congressman, and founder of Lehigh

University. The American Puritans had a particular respect for Jews, seeing their own emigration to the New World as a parallel to the Israelites' search for the Promised Land. They gave their children Old Testament names, spoke of the God of Israel and the God of Jacob, and even referred to a pious and industrious coreligionist as "a good Jew." Packer, consequently, took a deep, personal interest in the well-being of his young charge, who must have been amazed at the difference between Christian behavior in America and that in Europe.

After a year, Packer wanted to give Joseph a raise, but the ambitious youth preferred to strike out on his own. Having saved $200, he invested it in some cutlery, watches, and rings and began peddling them through the Pennsylvania countryside. Before long, he had accumulated another $500 and paid the passage for his next eldest brothers across the Atlantic. Now, Joseph, William, and James Seligman were trudging together through the muddy countryside, selling anything they could make a profit on, from needles to cloth, napkins to spectacles.

When Pennsylvania got too crowded with peddlers, James suggested investing in a horse and wagon to make the store mobile and shortly left for the South, a region in the throes of a major cotton boom. Before long he returned with a $1,000 profit, and in the fall of 1841, all the brothers set out by ship, via New York, for Mobile, Alabama, with $5,000 worth of dry goods. In the South they first set up shop under tents or in the open air. Soon, however, they opened dry-goods stores in three small towns near Selma, Alabama, hired staff, and in no time owned a small chain. In 1842 Fanny Seligman died in Germany, whereupon the brothers brought over the rest of the *mischpoche* and settled them on New York's Lower East Side. The sisters went to work making pants, handkerchiefs, and shirts for the brothers to sell. In 1846 James

OPPOSITE: **During the great wave of immigration from Eastern and Southern Europe, which began in the mid-19th century and ended only with the outbreak of World War I, New York City's Lower East side teamed with impoverished Jews, Italians, and Chinese, among other ethnic groups eager for a fresh lease of life in the New World.**
ABOVE: **The great German-Jewish Wall Street bankers known as "Our Crowd"—the Seligmans, Lehmans, Goldmans, Sachses, Kuhns, Loebs, Schiffs, Lewisohns—all began in America very much in the manner of these two Jewish peddlars on the dilapidated, immigrant-packed streets of Manhattan's Lower East Side.**
LEFT: **William Tylee Ranney,** *Crossing the Ferry*, **1846 (Thomas Gilcrease Institute, Tulsa). When the Lower East Side got too crowded for ambitious Jewish peddlars, they took off for the countryside, first in Pennsylvania and then in the South before moving West. Along the way, their presence became essential to the economy and well-being of rural or even frontier America. By the time of the Civil War, the Seligmans, for example, had moved from a small-town ghetto in Germany to peddling in America, then to the role of trusted advisors and financiers to the Union government—all within 25 years.**

inaugurated J. Seligman & Brothers, Merchants, on a corner of New York's William Street, within spitting distance of Wall Street.

The Seligmans did well. When the sisters married, their husbands became partners and set up other stores, allowing the whole clan to live quite comfortably. In 1860 they bought an undershirt and pants factory, the fourteenth largest such plant in the United States. When the Civil War broke out, the Seligmans rushed down to Washington, wangled their way into the White House, and convinced President Lincoln that they could make wonderful uniforms for his soldiers. Soon a nearly broke Union government owed them $1,437,486.61, a large part of which the suppliers had to take in three-year Treasury bonds yielding 7.30 percent. To pay the factory help, Joseph Seligman needed to sell the bonds and thus quickly left for Europe, where the high yield on the securities proved more attractive to investors than European paper. Having succeeded quite handsomely, Joseph went to the government for more paper and soon found that he had become a banker upon whom the Union effort actually depended. Joseph sold abroad United States government debt issues worth over $60 million, which finally placed the Seligmans in the big time.

At the end of the war, the Seligmans emulated the Rothschilds by setting up a multi-brother, worldwide banking network, with William in Paris, Henry in Frankfurt, and Isaac in London. Joseph, the eldest, with James and Jesse, kept shop in New York while Abraham and Leopold left for San Francisco, a city still aglow from the Gold Rush. During their brilliant careers, the Seligmans arranged Jay Gould's financing of the Erie Railroad as well as his disastrous attempt to corner the gold market, helped underwrite the Union Pacific Railroad, floated billions of dollars of bonds in association with the great J.P. Morgan and August Belmont, the Rothschilds' New York agent, and finally emerged as the leading Jewish bankers of the New World.

THE LEHMANS, GOLDMAN, SACHS, KUHN, LOEB

Like the Seligmans, Henry Lehman, who emigrated from Bavaria, commenced as a peddler. In 1844, he drove his wagon into Mobile, Alabama, and worked his way to Montgomery, where he rented a small building on Commerce Street and spread out his wares—mostly crockery, tools, dry goods, and seeds. The state's capital city was a miserable place, with sewers running down the main street, nocturnal rats prowling the planked or muddy, unpaved roads. Malaria, spread by mosquitoes, posed a constant danger to the entire population of 4,000 white people and 2,000 black slaves. Nonetheless, Montgomery was an active trading and shipping center linked by the Alabama River to the ports of Mobile and New Orleans, and it would quickly become a focal point of the boom in cotton, a commodity sold throughout the world. Henry Lehman saw the immense possibilities and sent to Germany for his brothers Mayer and Emmanuel, creating Lehman Brothers, whose specialty was trading in cotton.

Edgar Degas (1834-1917), *Portraits dans un bureau*, 1873 (Musée des Beaux-Arts, Pau). Like Degas's relatives in New Orleans, whom the artist visited in 1872-73, the Lehman brothers traded cotton in the Old South. Soon they would be trading the paper for such transactions rather than the commodity itself, which in turn led them into Wall Street investment banking.

LEFT: The great trading hall of the New York Stock Exchange, as photographed in 1899. This was the scene of many a rally and rout in the paper value of 19th-century American industry.

ABOVE: After immigrating to New York from Germany, Abe Kuhn joined with Solomon Loeb to found Kuhn, Loeb & Company, a premier investment banking house that specialized in underwriting railroads, the fastest-growing industry in 19th-century America.

In Dixie, cotton was king, and it made the Lehmans very rich indeed. Their customers were mainly in northern American cities and in Great Britain, and they paid in time drafts on New York or London banks. Since these bills were actively traded, the Lehmans naturally found their way into banking, just as Joseph Seligman became a financier through his uniform factory. New York being the financial center of the Southern economy, Emmanuel spent time there while Henry and Mayer worked in Montgomery until the former's death from yellow fever in 1855. By 1858 Emmanuel had opened a permanent office in Manhattan at 119 Liberty Street near the Seligmans, and his affairs went splendidly until President Lincoln imposed the 1861 blockade. Suddenly, this deprived the Northern manufacturers of their access to Southern cotton and left the brothers separated in two different warring camps. Following hostilities, the Lehmans revived their business and added a branch in New Orleans, which served the cotton trade in the Mississippi-Louisiana area and provided the main shipping port for the raw material. Expanding beyond cotton, they began trading in minerals and oil, which soon placed the Lehmans among the richest men in the United States.

Another Bavarian, Marcus Goldman, arrived in New York in 1848 and took up peddling in Philadelphia. As soon as he made a little money, Goldman rented a cellar room next to a coal chute in Lower Manhattan, employing a part-time bookkeeper. Every morning he visited his friends, mostly wholesale jewelers and leather merchants, and bought their notes at a discount, tucking them into an elastic band inside his hat. In the afternoon Goldman and his swollen hat went uptown, where he sold the notes at a slight profit, thanks to the lower rate of interest warranted by his larger volume. Although the individual notes ranged merely from $2,500 to $5,000, he traded about $5 million worth per year. Among their close friends, Marcus and Bertha Goldman counted Joseph Sachs, a schoolteacher and rabbi, and his far richer wife Sophie. Many of New York's prosperous Jews studied at the Sachs Collegiate Institute, run by the Sachs's son Julius, who would marry the Goldmans' daughter Rosa, while another Sachs son, Sam, wed another Goldman daughter, Louise. Goldman asked Sam Sachs, a small dry-goods merchant, to become his partner, and in this simple way was born Goldman, Sachs & Co., a firm specializing in commercial paper and one of the most successful of its kind on Wall Street.

Although Lehman prospered in commodities and Goldman in financial paper, the firms grew truly significant, beginning in the early part of this century, only when they began underwriting. It was as issuers of and dealers in corporate paper that both companies became famous and powerful. European bankers, particularly the Rothschilds and the Barings, had dealt extensively in government obligations, underwriting wars and national debts, but in the United States, it was the creation of the great trusts that opened up a virtually limitless market for the paper of industrial combines, whose need for funds often exceeded that of a

RIGHT: A marriage within "Our Crowd" reflects the new prosperity of successful American Jewish financiers and professionals, who became extremely active in the artistic and intellectual life of New York City. There were, however, strict social barriers between Christians and Jews after working hours, as well as between German Jews and Polish or Russian coreligionists whom Our Crowd considered inferior.

BELOW: Otto Kahn, a key partner in the investment banking firm of Kuhn, Loeb & Company gave "Our Crowd" and New York in general one of their most vivid and indispensable members. Astute in business and elegant in his Old World manner, the German-born Kahn loved life, lived it in grand style (see page 134), and did much to bring the golden age of singing to the Metropolitan Opera.

small European power. From 1898 to 1904, over $4 billion of such securities came on the American market, and the number of trusts grew from a dozen to 318.

Underwriting the railroads, which created great fortunes, became the specialty of Kuhn, Loeb & Company. The investment bank's founders, Solomon Loeb and Abe Kuhn—German Jews like their competitors—commenced in a dry-goods shop and later operated a small Cincinnati factory for men's and boys' pants. Kuhn was passionate about textiles and Loeb obsessed with money, and as soon as they had almost made their first $1 million, they left for the big time in New York City and opened a small bank. The homesick Kuhn soon went back to Frankfurt, while Loeb remained active in the American financial capital. The latter became so absorbed in his business that on one occasion he absent-mindedly signed a letter to his young son, "Your loving Kuhn, Loeb & Company," and attributed his success to invariably saying no first. "You can always change your mind and say yes. But once you have said yes, you are committed."

In Germany, Kuhn met Jacob Schiff, a friend of the Warburgs, Frankfurt's famous bankers, who so impressed him with his ambition that he suggested the young man seek a job with Loeb. From this connection, Kuhn, Loeb & Company would be sparked into financial gianthood. Working closely with railroad tycoons, particularly Edward Harriman, Schiff became the ultimate railroader's financier at a time when billions of dollars' worth of transport paper came onto the market and commissions on a deal could get up to 10 percent.

Schiff attained a stature among New York's smart Jewish bankers equaled only by Joseph Seligman. He was the only member of "Our Crowd" whom J.P. Morgan treated as a peer. But Otto Kahn gave the firm its most colorful partner, noted for his Prussian military posture and elegant Savile Row suits embellished with an orchid boutonniere. For several years, Kahn almost single-handedly supported the Metropolitan Opera, which made him known among European impresarios as "The Great Ottokhan." Thanks to Kahn, Schiff had to endure the distraction of endless visits to the partners' room by hysterical divas and tenors, not to speak of the beautiful actresses whose careers Kahn sponsored in return for their favors.

JOHN PIERPONT MORGAN

In the lawless epoch of the robber barons, J.P. Morgan came to represent order. The United States Congress had yet to enact the first antitrust legislation or authorize the Federal Reserve system or the Securities and Exchange Commission. Absent these safeguards, it was J.P. Morgan, with his universally acknowledged steadfastness, credit, and credibility, that stemmed panics and calmed the financial waters. Not only did the great banker do much to stabilize the stock, bond, and commodity markets; he also worked effectively towards rationalizing several sectors of a chaotic and rapidly growing world economy. The previously described "Morganization" of United States Steel was only one chapter in a life of similar achievement. Morgan played a key role in the reorganization of banking and railroads in the United States, and he fell just short of creating a worldwide shipping empire, one that would have had liners sailing the Atlantic, trains crossing the United States, and freighters plying the Pacific. One Morgan bill of lading would have taken

goods from London to Tokyo at a price nobody could beat. Nothing was too grand for the vision of this larger-than-life tycoon, whose uniform consisted of a black suit and bowler hat, and whose matching coal-dark eyes struck many as having the strength of locomotive lights in a dark tunnel.

Unlike a great many of the modern world's super-rich, J.P. Morgan was born with a silver spoon in his mouth, placed there by God-fearing Yankee traders from Hartford, Connecticut. In 1851 his father Junius had left for Boston to open a dry-goods store with a partner. Junius's son, John Pierpont, was born in 1837, and although not a particularly brilliant student, he could favor his father, during the latter's business trips abroad, with long letters filled with political news and insights. Prior to opening his Boston store, the senior Morgan went to London, then the world's financial center, to establish relationships with Barings as well as with George Peabody, a Boston trader who had become one of London's leading merchant bankers. For Peabody, the secret key to financial

In 1868, John Pierpont Morgan, the shy, thoughtful, European-educated son of a Wall Street banker, was just beginning to make a reputation for himself as a partner in Anthony Drexel's prestigious Philadelphia bank. At the age of 31, his handsome face had not been touched by the nervous disorder that would eventually disfigure it.

RIGHT: The intersection of
Broad and Wall Streets in
Manhattan witnessed not only
the inauguration of George
Washington as the first
President of the United States
but also the development of the
world's most powerful system
of public and private finance, a
world in which "Our Crowd"
and J.P. Morgan flourished.
In the building on the right,
immediately opposite the New
York Stock Exchange (not
shown), J.P. Morgan reigned as
one of the greatest bankers of
all time. He was a force for
steady, rational, efficient
progress at a time when the
explosive American economy
regularly fell prey to the violent
swings caused by excessive
speculation in the financial
markets.
RIGHT: The London
headquarters of J.P. Morgan
and Company, where the great
banker was as much at home
and almost as active as in New
York.

success lay in forming a conduit between the vast
economic potential of the New World and the vast
financial resources of Great Britain. To fulfill this
promise, he joined with Barings's Joshua Bates in
London and New York's August Belmont.
Impressed with Junius Morgan, the aging Peabody
offered him a partnership in 1854, together with the
possibility of eventually leading the bank. Morgan
accepted, establishing the basis for the Anglo-
American character of his son Pierpont, who would
find himself as much at home in the City as on Wall
Street. Junius took the young man out of his Connecticut boarding school, sent him to a Swiss fin-
ishing academy, and then to study at the University
of Göttingen. Soon after, Pierpont did a short stint
at Peabody's bank and observed his first panic, set
off by the failure of Ohio Life and Trust, which
nearly bankrupted the firm. It was a lesson he
would not forget.

Returning to the United States in 1857, the
younger Morgan acted as his father's eyes and ears
in New York, where, in fact, he lived in Junius's
shadow until he was fifty. For one of the toughest
bankers of all time, Pierpont was unusually shy and
reserved, largely as a result of the severe disfigurement of his nose brought about by a rare nervous
disease. (Official portraits were always retouched.)
He married early in life, only for his wife to die a
year later, leaving him with deep psychological
scars. Like his rich friends, Pierpont skipped fight-
ing in the Civil War, and he profited by arranging
loans for the Union on the London market, financ-

ing arms, and speculating in gold, an experience
with violent markets that would serve him well at a
later date. In 1864, as the Civil War ended, Peabody
retired, and his firm became J.S. Morgan & Company. At the same time, Pierpont, with his former
accountant, founded Dabney, Morgan & Company
to specialize in railroad stocks. As a result, Morgan
Jr. floated many of the railroad issues that Morgan
Sr. sold, and shortly thereafter Junius put up
$75,000 to make Pierpont a partner in Anthony
Drexel's highly respected Philadelphia bank.

ORDER ON THE RAILS

Until the end of the nineteenth century, Pierpont Morgan fought against the disorder of the railroad industry. His technique for reorganizing railroads was relatively simple. He and his partners would put troubled lines on a profitable basis by eliminating waste, squeezing water out of the stock, issuing new bonds at a rate the line could afford, and assessing the stockholders for more capital. Then he would either buy a controlling interest or have shareholders hand over their voting rights. As a result, Morgan sat on ten major railroad boards, while his partners spread themselves across another fifty, so that together they had an overview of interlocking interests and the consequent ability to form a master plan. For restructuring a troubled road Morgan never charged less than $500,000, but the real price paid by the railroaders was loss of control. When challenged by these angry entrepreneurs, Morgan would sharply remind them that *their* lines belonged to *his* customers. By 1898 he had majority voting rights in every line on the South Atlantic

J. PIERPONT MORGAN, UNLIKE ALEXANDER THE GREAT, HAS MORE WORLDS TO CONQUER.

seaboard, dominated the Erie & Reading, controlled the Northern Pacific, held major interests in nearly everything else from the Baltimore & Ohio to the Central of Georgia, and served as Vanderbilt's main financier. J.P. Morgan commanded 49,000 miles of track, which left the balance of 36,000 miles mostly to Edward Harriman but also, in bits and pieces, to Jay Gould.

STEMMING THE PANICS

J.P. Morgan and his partners cross-linked banks, trusts, and insurance companies into immense pools of capital. Into these they drew additional funds by creating holding companies and trusts with new stock issues. From such activity came General Electric and, as we saw earlier, United States Steel. By 1902 two large groups controlled the finance and industry of the United States. One team included Morgan, George Baker's First National Bank, the New York Life Insurance Company, and James J. Hill, while the other comprised the Rockefellers, James Stillman's National City Bank, Edward Harriman, and Jacob Schiff's

Kuhn, Loeb. But J.P. Morgan was the dominating force, as he made clear in two panics.

The first of these crises came in 1894, when the firm had changed its name to J. Pierpont Morgan. The United States, like most other countries at the time, held to the gold standard, which obliged the American Treasury to redeem its currency in gold at whatever price speculators fixed. Owing to the immense amount of silver mined at the Comstock Lode, in Mexico, and elsewhere, the nation's silver coins became worth far less than face value and

people began turning them in. As the Treasury took back the paper and coins, its gold reserves fell below the $100 million legal requirement. When the government issued gold bonds, speculators bought and then redeemed them, thus worsening the drain. Meanwhile, in January of that year, American securities sold by nervous Europeans caused large amounts of gold to leave New York in the bellies of the great liners. The government found itself confronted with having either to go off the gold standard and thus lose its credit abroad (a decision that President Nixon took in 1971, causing a serious devaluation of the dollar and its eventual erosion as the world's most serious currency) or to issue more gold certificates. August Belmont went to Washington in the hope of convincing the authorities to pursue the latter course, as a means of bringing gold back to the United States from Europe. However, the paper would have to bear a high interest rate, and the recently formed Populist Party took this as yet another scheme for the enrichment of goldbugs. The Secretary of the Treasury decided instead to issue bonds to the American public, despite the previous failure of similar attempts.

Morgan, worried that the government might go broke, tried to persuade President Grover Cleveland and the Secretary of the Treasury that *he* should be allowed to control the international gold market. If they refused, he pointed out, a check for $10 million

BELOW: A 50-year debenture certificate issued in 1906 by the New York, New Haven, and Hartford Railroad. It was through the issuance and sale of paper like this—stocks, bonds, debentures, etc.—that American industry and its bankers financed their extraordinary growth throughout the Gilded Age.

BELOW AND LEFT: As the giant of American banking, the ever sober, dignified J.P. Morgan had to endure the consequences of his high public profile. These included the heavy-handed humor of tabloid caricaturists.

about to be presented in New York for gold would bounce, which would then trigger a panic. If they accepted his proposal, on the other hand, he would provide $100 million of gold at 4 percent. They agreed, and, with the announcement that Morgan controlled the market, confidence returned, as did some $18 million of the yellow metal already in the holds of liners waiting to take it to Europe. Morgan then cabled his European contacts to send over additional bullion, at the same time that he offered American bankers a higher price than they could get for the metal abroad. The Treasury reserve soon rose beyond the legal limit, and the bonds Morgan forced the government to issue at 104.5 (and which he sold to subscribers at 112) quickly rose several points. The great banker liked saying that he was not on Wall Street for his health, and in saving the nation's credit and gold reserve, his syndicate cleared a profit of over $7 million.

Here an artist has depicted one of the many "panics" that struck the financial markets during the Gilded Age, when American industry and banking were struggling to master the volatile effects of unprecedented growth and speculation.

Morgan performed another act of panic control in 1907. The scenario was very similar to that of today's savings-and-loan mess, except that Morgan acted in the place of the Federal Deposit Insurance Corporation, which did not yet exist. In the two years prior to 1907, bumper crops led to overspeculation, which frightened foreign investors and caused them to start pulling out of the American stock market and British bankers to demand repayment of their American loans. Huge new issues of watered railroad stock found no buyers among the disgusted public, a reality that encouraged President Theodore Roosevelt to launch a public campaign against robber barons, thereby scaring

investors and bearing markets still further. During the summer, several bankruptcies, including Westinghouse Electric, the New York streetcar line, and Charles W. Morse's Eastern Seaboard Trust, caused additional selling. Symptomatic of the situation was the controlling interest that Morse had acquired in a series of trust companies, each of them collateralized by the stock of the other companies. As the crisis deepened, depositors withdrew $3 billion from the banks and markets during the next three months. Once again, the banking world approached the abyss, and this time Morgan had departed on a rented luxury train with a convention of Episcopal bishops. Rushing back to New York along the nation's tracks—which mostly belonged to him—he holed up in his library, rather than his office, in order to operate more discreetly.

On a Thursday night Morgan had all the nation's financial might gathered in the East Room of his library, where, surrounded by illuminated manuscripts and Bibles, he told them to come up with a solution while he played solitaire in the West Room. One by one, they submitted proposals, only to be told: "No, that will not work." Finally, a less than thrilled Morgan accepted to have the Clearing House issue certificates in lieu of cash to the weaker banks, which meant that his rivals could use mere script money to compete unfairly with his own cash-rich institution. But in what was a rare moment during the Gilded Age, Morgan allowed the national interest to supersede personal profit. On Friday morning the panic roared on, and as the weekend approached, Morgan's friends assessed themselves a further $15 million.

Come Sunday morning, clergymen told their congregations to remain calm and have faith, while President Roosevelt announced that prosperity lay straight ahead. Simultaneously, Morgan and Stillman called in $11 million in gold from Britain. (Bankers and Treasury officials tended to use weekends, when markets and banks were closed, to cook up diabolical schemes.) On Monday depositors at savings banks learned that they had to give sixty days' notice before withdrawing their money, which permitted things to calm down considerably while the Thursday plan went into effect. Now, however, the City of New York informed Morgan that *they* were going broke to the tune of $30 million and expected him to find a solution for them, even though he could not count on the banking syndicate. It took him all of 48 hours to resolve the city's problem, but he still had to contend with the trust companies, which needed a last infusion of $25 million. Thus, on the following Saturday night their presidents again made a command appearance in the library, where they heard from Morgan that he had had enough and would leave the ball in their court. After wrangling and worrying until dawn, the much-humbled presidents came into Morgan's office. Meanwhile, his staff had calculated how much each could contribute and had IOUs ready for every single one of them. "There's the place," he said kindly, "and here's the pen." They all signed, which brought the run on the banks to an end.

In this last great adventure, Morgan saved the banks and markets, forced the American President to eat humble pie, and pulled out a very ripe plum for himself. Ironically, his new power earned him the reputation of being the most dangerous of all tycoons, this despite the extraordinary services he

had rendered to both the financial community and the nation. A series of humiliating investigations ensued, and in 1913 America's greatest banker died a bitter, disappointed man. To everyone's astonishment, his personal estate ended up worth a surprisingly modest $75 million. More than half was in books, manuscripts, and works of art, a good part of which would enrich the cultural life of New York City, thanks to the collector's generous legacy.

ANDREW MELLON

Although J.P. Morgan bestrode American finance like a colossus, he had solid competition from many other major banking dynasties. As seen in the previous chapter, the Mellons of Pittsburgh faithfully financed the expansion of Henry Clay Frick, their close relationship with him typifying the Mellon philosophy. Quietly and discreetly, the Mellons helped entrepreneurs in whom they believed, taking positions in their businesses as well as extending loans. As Frank R. Denton, their director, described it, they were "a sort of revolving fund for the promotion of enterprises," and they stayed away from the speculations and stock-floating activities of their more flamboyant New York colleagues. Judge Thomas Mellon, founder of T. Mellon & Sons Bank in 1870, was a successful lawyer of Irish stock who had bought up mortgages and liens and engaged in standard commercial banking. All eight of his sons entered the business, the most brilliant being Andrew (1855-1937),

LEFT: "Panic, as a health officer, sweeping the garbage out of Wall Street" is the title of this cartoon satirizing the devastation in the American financial markets caused mainly by the speculators who had gained a large foothold in the railroad industry. Note that the "health officer" has one foot firmly planted at the door of Drexel & Co., which would soon change its name to that of one of its principal partners, J.P. Morgan. Equally notable, the one name cited in the detritus being swept away is that of Jay Gould, the most notorious of the railroad speculators, often referred to as "the Mephistopheles of Wall Street." BELOW: William H. Beard, *The Bulls and Bears in the Market* (New York Historical Society). It is difficult to tell who is winning this battle—the pessimistic bears or the optimistic bulls—but, as in all market panics, confusion reigns and blood will be spilled in front of the stock exchange.

RIGHT: Always shy and reticent, thanks in part to the disfigurement of his nose, J.P. Morgan did not like to be photographed, except for carefully controlled, formal portraits, and could deal harshly with tabloid photographers, as here.
BELOW: With its marble columns, dome-vaulted and frescoed ceiling, bronze busts, and della Robbia lunettes, the original entrance hall to the Morgan Library received visitors in something like Roman Imperial splendor—thanks to the architects McKim, Mead & White and their munificent patron, J.P. Morgan. The great banker preferred to spend his immense earnings for the enrichment of American culture rather than on a personal lifestyle of egregious consumption.

to whom he turned over the bank in 1886, by which time it had become one of the most important in the country. Three years later the Mellons set up the Union Trust of Pittsburgh and shortly thereafter the Union Savings Bank, also in Pittsburgh, which made the family the principal financiers of the largest and most rapidly developing industrial center in the world. However, Andrew Mellon made his greatest monument the National Gallery of Art in Washington, D.C., where he served as the nation's Secretary of the Treasury from 1921 to 1931. Like his descendants, he was extremely shy and reclusive; moreover, he spoke in a gravelly whisper that many found difficult to follow.

The Mellons had large, often controlling interests in some of the most important businesses in America, among them the Pittsburgh Reduction Company, which went on to become the Aluminum Company of America (Alcoa); Union Steel and Sharon Steel, which they unloaded at a huge profit to J.P. Morgan; Pittsburgh Glass; and numerous railroads. They also invested in oil wells, including the Texas Spindletop, the most spectacular gusher ever found. It led to the formation of Gulf Oil and its endless subsidiaries. Also in the Mellon portfolio was the gigantic Koppers Company, spawned by a German engineer's invention that used waste gases from coke-making for myriad by-products. They bought several power and light companies in their infancy, as well as a grab bag of everything else from insurance companies to Nabisco. Unlike Rockefeller and other robber barons, Andrew Mellon became one of America's three billionaires without providing writers with a spate of colorful or entertaining anecdotes. He had no ingenious or maverick idea that launched his career, no get-rich-quick scheme anyone could emulate, no deadly enemy he pursued in a death struggle for great riches, no partner who inspired him to great heights. Mellon simply read balance sheets, judged character in the burgeoning heartland of America's heavy industry, and chose to participate in its growth.

After a long and distinguished career presiding over the Treasury, Mellon was appointed Ambassador to the Court of St. James, a role much prized by American Anglophile plutocrats. And there could scarcely have been a more perfect choice than this half-English millionaire public servant. His icy reserve, discretion, and aristocratic mien impressed even the grandest members of Britain's establishment, to whom he was a peer in every way.

Andrew Mellon, however, did *look* quite extraordinary, embodying as he did the physical archetype of the refined and elegant billionaire—tall, distinguished, beautifully dressed and groomed, with impeccable manners. He remained a bachelor until the age of 45, when, in 1900, he married Nora McMullen, the 21-year-old daughter of a wealthy Hertfordshire brewer, and took her to share his life in Pittsburgh. Unfortunately, Nora could not abide the sooty, industrial gloom of the Pennsylvania city and bolted back home nine years later, leaving Mellon with their children, Ailsa and Paul.

Mellon was practically unknown outside Pittsburgh until 1921, when he became Secretary of the Treasury under President Warren Harding (this after underwriting the $1.5 million deficit of the Republican Party). To qualify for the job, he had to resign from the boards of 51 corporations, but as if to compensate for the displacement, he reputedly made it his first order of business to put restrictive tariffs on many products competing with those in which he held an interest. Mellon also standardized the nation's paper currency, making every bank note the same size and color, a practice that saved the Treasury millions but forced Americans—even more so foreign tourists—to take care not to pass out $100 tips by mistake. More important, Mellon effected a consolidation of the national debt, reducing it from $26 billion in 1921 to about $16 billion in 1930. He once amazed government colleagues concerned about scrapping a war plant when he mentioned that he had taken a $12 million loss on a similar installation!

President Warren Harding with his cabinet in c. 1924. Andrew Mellon, as Secretary of the Treasury, sits second from the right in the front row. The Pittsburgh banker helped finance Henry Clay Frick and Andrew Carnegie, among many other large-scale entrepreneurs of the Gilded Age. Bold but quiet, unlike his flamboyant counterparts in New York, Mellon went on to become U.S. Secretary of the Treasury and the chief benefactor of the National Gallery in Washington, D.C.

101

MILLIONAIRES' HOUSES

The tycoons of the Gilded Age took seriously the old saying that a man's home is his castle. They were as rich as Croesus and wanted to live as such in both town and country. This was nothing new. In the seventeenth century, La Fontaine wrote that *"tout bourgeois veut vivre comme les grands seigneurs."* In Europe, where aristocratic fortunes were waning and grand families often had houses to spare, it was relatively easy to buy or rent a great pile and call in fashionable architects or decorators to do it up. In the United States, where no inventory of aristocratic housing existed, people had to build their castles from scratch. They copied any style that appealed to their fancy and bothered not at all about the anachronism of erecting vast, medieval châteaux in the middle of New York City, Chicago, or San Francisco.

Just as European monarchs used Versailles as a model for their palaces in the eighteenth century, so the newly rich of the nineteenth century generally turned to France for their inspiration. It should not surprise, therefore, that most society architects studied at the celebrated École des Beaux-Arts in Paris. France's eighteenth-century aristocracy had put up splendid *hôtels particuliers* behind high walls and forbidding carved doors on the Rue de Grenelle and Rue de Varenne, as well as throughout the Marais, but they lost most of these—along with their heads—during the French Revolution in 1789-94. As the French bourgeoisie grew and a new generation of rich South and North Americans decided to find their pleasure in what Napoleon III and Baron Haussmann had turned into the world's most luxurious city, new sandstone and granite palaces were built in a style evocative of Louis XV and Louis XVI. They rose in great numbers throughout the 16th arrondissement, as well as in the Avenue du Bois, Place des États-Unis, Avenue d'Iéna, and beautifully shaded boulevards facing the Bois de Boulogne. Their façades bristled with Corinthian columns or pilasters, sculpted putti spread graceful wings on lintels and decorative friezes, and the *étage noble* (even if no nobles were sitting on the delicate canapés) consisted of large and airy reception rooms with French windows that opened, by means of gilded hardware copied after eighteenth-century models, either on to a large formal garden or the chestnut trees planted along the street below. The grandest of these may have been the Palais de Marbre Rose, a pink-marble palace

OPPOSITE: The Palais de Marbre Rose, the folly built by the Marquis Boni de Castellane on Paris's exclusive Avenue du Bois, proved to be a bit too much even for the Gould fortune. Here, in what is a version of the Petit Trianon at Versailles, the Marquis hoped to create a place where the glory of monarchist France could be revived. To fill the palace, he was soon bidding against American tycoons for Rembrandts and furniture from the Royal inventories.

ABOVE: Baron Georges-Eugène Haussmann, who as Préfet de la Seine (1853-70) under Napoleon III rebuilt Paris in the form we know today, with its star-burst network of grand boulevards, verdant parks, and famed infrastructure of sewers, train stations, and promenades.

LEFT: Edmond-Georges Grandjean (1844-1909), *The Boulevard des Italiens*. This view shows one of Haussmann's most famous boulevards shortly after it was built, complete with long perspective, tree-lined sidewalks, and festive ranks of cafés, theaters, and *flâneurs*.

RIGHT: The elaborate courtyard of the Palais de Marbre Rose gives an idea of the lavishness of the faux 18th-century interior devised by Boni de Castellane, using money from his marriage to the American heiress, Anna Gould. However, the extravagance, in addition to a weakness for pretty mistresses, compelled the Gould family to blow the whistle. When Boni received the news that his rich wife had bolted, he put on a full-dress uniform, complete with sword and medals, lay down in the palace, and waited to die. After the dread reaper failed to appear, the Marquis de Castellane changed and went to the Jockey Club for lunch.
BELOW: The attempts of the nouveaux riches to enhance their life-style by reviving the taste of the ancien régime is nowhere better demonstrated than in the "Salon des Tapisseries de Leprince" in the house/museum built by Édouard André and Nélie Jacquemart on the Boulevard Haussmann in Paris.
OPPOSITE: The Moorish salon in the New York City home of John D. Rockefeller and his family is a splendid example of the eclecticism beloved by the Gilded Age rich, as reflected here in Babylonian columns, inlaid woods, Victorian clutter, and Oriental carpets.
PAGES 106-107: New York magnificoes such as James H. Burden outdid even the French in aping Versailles's grandeur, here seen in the music room of the Burden mansion near Fifth Avenue, an opulent mélange of marble, gilt bronze, and stucco.

built by the Marquis Boni de Castellane with money from his grandfather-in-law, Jay Gould. Here, even the kitchens were clad in precious marble.

The most elegant arrangement of all was to have a house situated between courtyard and garden, a luxury generally reserved for those who bought an old *hôtel particulier*. The parvenu wanted his palace located directly on the street, not hidden behind walls, so that all who passed could be impressed with the style in which he lived and entertained. What might be referred to as the "PPP" ("Parvenu Paris Palace") assumed extreme importance in the Gilded Age, since this was the type of opulent dwelling desired by many of the new tycoons, particularly in New York, London, San Francisco, and even Buenos Aires, where gauchos as well as Italian and German immigrants had grown rich farming the pampas.

On a more public scale, eighteenth- and nineteenth-century urban planners looked to France when imposing order on their cities. Benjamin Henry Latrobe's plan for Washington, D.C., is the most obvious early example, and later ones include Buenos Aires, with its tree-lined boulevards, and Bucharest, which was known as a little Paris, although its elegant avenues and mansions were but a façade for slums teeming with gypsies, bandits, and unemployed Greeks and Turks.

It was not only France that inspired architects. Indeed, the latter half of the nineteenth century turned into the age of eclecticism, thanks largely to Eugène-Émmanuel Viollet-le-Duc. Indeed, when a renowned Moscow architect asked Arseny Morozov in what style he wanted to build his new mansion, the merchant prince replied: "In all styles. I can afford them all." This odd vision was better expressed in a *Punch* cartoon of 1891, where an elegant, mustachioed businessman tells his architect that he wants something "nice, baronial, Queen Anne and Elisabethan, and all that; kind of quaint, Nuremburgy, you know—regular old English with French windows opening to the lawn and Venetian blinds, and sort of Swiss balconies and a loggia."

Revivals posed a dilemma to serious architects. The American Thomas R. Hastings expressed what must have been the frustration of many a fashionable architect forever required to design a French Renaissance château, a Florentine palazzo, a lacy Venetian palace, a Romanesque or Gothic enclosed cloister, or the Alhambra: "Copying destroys progress in art and all spontaneity. Our Renaissance must not be merely archaeological, the literal following of certain periods of the style. To build a

French Louis XII or Francis I or Louis XIV house, or to make an Italian *cinquecento* design, is indisputably not modern architecture." The equally distinguished and disillusioned Richard Morris Hunt rationalized that "the first thing you've got to remember is that it's your client's money you're spending. If they want you to build a house upside down, standing on its chimney, it's up to you to do it and still get the best possible result." The reverse of the coin, of course, was that new-rich clients had staggering amounts to spend, flinched at nothing that would impress their peers, and, with few exceptions, never discussed the bills, on which the architect earned a standard 5 percent.

THE GREAT HOUSE

Regardless of the style, there were several appurtenances without which the grand house of the Gilded Age could not do. The ballroom, for instance, was the largest, most elaborate, and least used of the great reception rooms, the little furniture it contained generally kept under sheets, except on those few occasions when the family received friends for an evening of dancing. Stuccowork, large crystal chandeliers, marqueterie floors, an abundance of gilded columns and mirrors, and often an overhanging balcony for the musicians (who were normally hidden behind a temporary or permanent screen) set the tone for the most ambitious social occasions. With few exceptions, white and gold were the order of the day.

The music room, often doubling as a picture gallery, was typically skylighted for better presentation of the double- and triple-hung paintings that lined the walls. While ballrooms tended to be square or rectangular, the music-room-cum-gallery was nearly always long and less festive in decoration. When not in use for an evening's entertainment, settees or benches were frequently placed in the center of the room for contemplating the art works. The walls were kept fairly free of furniture so that gilded chairs could be placed at comfortable distances from each other to accommodate the ladies attired in billowing gowns from the houses of Worth and Poiret. Red, green, or beige velvet or damask, rather than architectural embellishment, covered the walls in order not to distract attention from the paintings. The musicale was a standard event of the social seasons of the great cities and as important to an artist's career as the concert hall itself. Leading hostesses prided themselves on presenting such immortal musicians as Ignace Paderewski, Eugène Ysaye, and Anton Rubinstein, or even celebrated divas like Dame Nellie Melba and Mary Garden. Feodor Chaliapin sang in the big private houses of Paris and New York, Frédéric Chopin played in the Paris music room of James and Betty de Rothschild, and an engagement to perform in the salon of a respected social figure could often launch the career of an unknown musi-

cian or composer. It was only after the concert that refreshments were served, with drinks in the suite of reception rooms and a large, elaborate buffet in the dining hall.

The dining room was designed for extremely formal occasions and generally had to be long enough to accommodate up to a hundred guests at one table, broad enough to allow an extremely elaborate display of silver or porcelain, as well as a footman behind every chair, and high enough to lend an air of sacramental grandeur to interminable and elaborate dinners. While drawing rooms tended to be French, music rooms Italianate, and ballrooms a glorification of Classical architecture, all styles were acceptable for the dining room. It could be fashioned after a medieval refectory, a Tudor hall, a desanctified Spanish cathedral, Versailles's Hall of Mirrors, or a warm Elizabethan gallery, its walls covered in linenfold panels.

While reception rooms were created for the flaunting of wealth, a tycoon made his fortune in the library, generally the most subdued of the house's chambers. This was a place for English paneling, Regency furniture, period bookshelves, comfortable overstuffed furniture, and aristocratic portraits brought to life by embers glowing in the depths of a great marble fireplace. It was here, after business hours, that the Goulds, Harrimans, Fricks, and Vanderbilts cut their deals with J.P. Morgan and George F. Baker. Another masculine enclave was the billiard room, where men gathered on weekends or after dinner. As for salons, which today would be called drawing or living rooms, they were generally decorated in the French manner and filled with what the society decorator Elsie de Wolfe called "FFF"—the "Fine French Furniture" of the Louis XV and Louis XVI periods. Thanks to Haussmann's radical redesign of Paris,

Although by no means the most tasteful, nor the most extravagant, house in New York City, Andrew Carnegie's mansion on Fifth Avenue and 91st Street (now the Cooper-Hewitt Museum) is the only palatial residence of its kind for which a complete photographic record exists. It bears out the life-style aspirations of the super-rich and shows the spaces in which they expected to reign and receive.

OPPOSITE ABOVE LEFT: The hall is consistent with the electic Georgian-Tuscan theme of the exterior (CENTER). The figure of Mercury could be an allusion to Carnegie's beginnings in a telegraph office.

OPPOSITE ABOVE RIGHT: The drawing room in the French taste was entirely appropriate for Mrs. Carnegie's tea parties.

OPPOSITE BELOW LEFT: The picture gallery was well illuminated by a leaded-glass skylight, as well as by chandeliers and overhanging electric tubes. However, such advantages would appear to have served little purpose, given that Carnegie's evident taste in art ran to the kind of hodgepodge seen on the walls here.

OPPOSITE BELOW RIGHT: The library, with English paneling and ceiling, was meant to be a place for serious talk and the birth of great ideas, as suggested by the motto above the fireplace: "Let there be light."

ABOVE: The glassed-in conservatory, with its forest of exotic plants well protected from New York's harsh winter, was a perfect place to spend Sunday afternoon listening to the rumble of the organ concert underway in the nearby hall.

The interior of Senator William Clark's Fifth Avenue mansion was decorated with magnificent paneling imported from a château in the Loire Valley. The quality of the Louis XVI furniture is entirely equal to the splendor of the setting.

lots of splendid eighteenth-century paneling had come on the market, and dealers packed it up to send across the ocean as a background to the often royal furniture, porcelain, rugs, and tapestries they sold in large quantities. When supplies of carved-wood paneling and furniture ran low, nineteenth-century craftsmen made reproductions that fetched, in certain cases, higher prices than the originals. If not decorating *en style,* the wealthy of the Gilded Age frequently opted for a quasi-Orientalist clutter that included rug-covered pillows, brass coffeepots, fringed and tasseled curtains, fringed and beaded poufs, and reams of lace. Bear rugs, stuffed tigers, and hollowed elephants' feet indicated travel, as did cabinets displaying French and German porcelain, while heavy mahogany lintels, moldings, and fireplaces signified solid prosperity. Until the advent of electricity, oil lamps cast a golden light that was often transmuted into pink through pleated and colored silk lampshades. Great rooms were more brilliantly lit by huge crystal or bronze chandeliers reflected in large and small mirrors inserted into the rich woodwork.

Architects sought drama in the monumental entrance hall, for it was here that the tycoon first imposed his wealth and position on his guests. Other rooms could deviate from the chosen style of the house, but the entrance hall was an integral part of the architectural statement, closely married to the great dwelling's exterior design. Grand staircases ran up several stories, while sculptured reliefs, stained-glass windows, tapestries, and marble walls as well as floors set off large ferns and palms potted in great Chinese vases. Here the servants lined up in monogrammed livery to greet and see off the guests, often while standing with illuminat-

ed silver candelabra in hand. The third floor of a great mansion was devoted to family bedrooms, the one chosen by the lady of the house generally decorated in the Ritz style: imitation Louis XV white paneling, rosy pink curtains, pale Aubusson carpets, lace pillows, and painted furniture. A sunken tub in the large marble bathroom was *de rigueur* as was a *lit de repos* to recover from a hot bath.

The top floor of the house was the locus of the tiny servants' cubicles, neatly lined up like pins, all the same size, and with just enough space to get in and out of bed. One row was for the women servants, another for the men, and any night-time escapades caused immediate dismissal. A single small bathroom served the needs of the entire staff, an occasional luxury being a washbasin in each cell. The hotel-sized kitchens were in the basement, and food was carried up the stairs on heavy silver platters or occasionally sent up on a dumbwaiter.

Although household staff varied considerably, a millionaire's mansion needed at a minimum four chamber and parlor maids, a laundress to wash, and a linen woman to iron, a maid whose entire job consisted of packing and unpacking the suitcases of family members and guests, and a group of strong girls, usually Irish, to do the scrubbing. This staff was overseen by the butler, generally an Englishman who needed executive abilities and a great deal of tact, and a housekeeper, who preferably was his spouse. The butler also oversaw a minimum of four footmen, whose job was to serve, and two muscular male servants for the heavy chores. There was a chef, ideally French, and at least two *commis* (assistants), while in truly luxurious households there might even be a *patissier,* who cooked the daily bread, tea cakes, and confections served at large dinners, including great spun-sugar fantasies. Before the automobile, transport was provided by a coachman and four grooms, and later by a night and day chauffeur for the car. For the children, there were nursery maids, an English nanny, possibly a German *fräulein*, and tutors, as well as a separate cook since no chef would sully his pots with porridge, baby food, or shepherd's pie. Skeleton staffs were kept in the many residences and filled in by the permanent household staff, and for large entertainments outsiders would be brought in to serve. Wages were, of course, extremely low. In the United States, a maid earned around $12 a month at the turn of the century, and in Europe the cost of a round-trip servant's room on the Orient Express was the equivalent of a butler's annual salary.

AMERICAN ARCHITECTS IN THE GILDED AGE

Henry Hobson Richardson (1838-86) transformed American architecture in the Gilded Age, bringing order and system to its freewheeling eclecticism. In terms of the millionaire's lifestyle, Richardson played a pivotal role as the mentor of McKim, Mead & White, the most sought-after firm of architects during the Gilded Age, for private residences as well as for public commissions. Charles Follen McKim (1847-1909) and Stanford White (1853-1906) both apprenticed with Richardson when he was drafting Trinity Church, while William Rutherford Mead (1846-1928) traveled to Italy to study the monuments of the Renaissance. Florence, Rome, and Venice were the primary inspiration for the classicism these distinguished architects propagated at the end of the century.

It was Stanford White, a tireless social lion and a celebrant at countless grand occasions in New York, who convinced his rich friends to allow McKim, Mead & White to create a setting comensurate with their financial status. In the early years the architects had designed mansions in the Shingle Style for Cyrus Hall McCormick at Richfield Springs, New York, and for Robert Goelet and Isaac Bell, Jr., in Newport, Rhode Island, the summer social center of any self-respecting tycoon. Stanford White's first ambitious resort project was the casino on Newport's Bellevue Avenue, which he completed in 1881 for his friend James Gordon Bennett, Jr. This swashbuckling, romantic, and often inebriated publisher of New York's *Herald* had fun and caused trouble on both sides of the Atlantic as well as in his enormous oceangoing yachts. In Newport, he had dared a British army officer to ride a polo pony into the resort's staid and stuffy Reading Room, and was astonished to find his club membership revoked the next day. In retaliation, he ordered up a new club and, thanks to White's beautiful clubhouse, trellised gazebo, and wicker-like screens that framed generous piazzas, the Newport Casino soon became the place to go,

ABOVE: Henry Hobson Richardson, a graduate of Paris's École des Beaux-Arts, was one of the foremost architects of the Gilded Age. The power of his neo-Romanesque masterpiece, Boston's Trinity Church (1872), created a romantic revival that would dominate American architecture for the next quarter-century.

BOTTOM LEFT: During the Gilded Age, Richardson's disciples, McKim, Mead & White were America's busiest architects, who could count among their major commissions such historic undertakings as Chicago's Columbian Exposition of 1893, New York's original Madison Square Garden, and numerous private palaces, all rich in Classical or even exotic ornament. The most social member of the firm was Stanford White, who in 1906 was shot dead in Madison Square Garden by the wealthy Harry Thaw, insanely jealous of a onetime relationship between the architect and the young Mrs. Thaw. White created several Newport "cottages" once he had established his reputation with the splendid Newport Casino, built for James Gordon Bennett, Jr., following the latter's expulsion from the Newport Reading Room (ABOVE LEFT) for having dared a willing British officer to mount the stairs on a polo pony.

RIGHT: On Fifth Avenue between 51st and 52nd Streets, William Henry Vanderbilt's Triple Mansion (1879) stands just south of Alva Vanderbilt's "Petit Château de Blois," together dominating America's most fashionable thoroughfare. Alas, the Triple Mansion was little more than an overblown brownstone, extravagantly if randomly embellished with Classical elements.
BELOW: A sectional drawing gives an idea of the seraglio-like character of the enormous pile that was the Triple Mansion.
OPPOSITE: This mezzotint from a limited edition comissioned and published by William Henry Vanderbilt himself shows a corner of the northeast drawing room in the Triple Mansion. It bears superb witness to the owner's parvenu love of ostentation. The stenciled, silk-covered walls had glass butterflies applied to them. Together with masses of Victorian clutter, other rooms boasted bamboo revetments, reflecting the contemporary notion of a Japanese boudoir. Among the house's decorations was a great malachite vase by Pierre Thomire, a gift from Russia's Emperor Nicholas I to Prince Demidoff, and a reproduction in bronze of the 15th-century Gates of Paradise created by Lorenzo Ghiberti for the Baptistry of Florence's Duomo.
FAR RIGHT: The exquisitely tasteful house that Charles McKim, of McKim, Mead & White, built in Hyde Park, New York, for Frederick William Vanderbilt. It commands a sweeping view of the mighty Hudson River.

while the Reading Room emptied out. On its lawns took place many a national tennis tournament, and great actors played in its theater.

VANDERBILT HOUSES

The most spectacular—and to many the gaudi-est—mansions in Newport, however, were Alva Vanderbilt's Marble House and Cornelius Vanderbilt's The Breakers. The Vanderbilts, and later William Randolph Hearst, were America's most ambitious and extravagant home builders. The old Commodore had lived rather modestly, first in a brick dwelling on Staten Island, then in a four-story Greek Revival town house (in which he died) on Washington Place. But he was really interested in making money, while his heirs busied themselves with being accepted in what passed for New York society and then with outbidding the Astors and each other to lead it. For this, they required great palaces, the first of which was put up by William Henry Vanderbilt, the Commodore's son, at 640 Fifth Avenue along the entire block between 51st and 52nd streets. Started in 1879, the gigantic complex took only eighteen months to build, thanks to the 700 men who worked day and night throughout

the entire period. In addition, sixty sculptors and other artists were brought from Europe to decorate the façade and interior, at a cost of over \$2 million. This represented less than 1 percent of his estate when Vanderbilt died a mere four years later, and it could be considered a reasonable investment, since the twin-winged palace also housed two of his married daughters and their families. Known as the Triple Mansion, this huge brownstone enclave, with its elaborate but irrational mass of decorative detailing, was an architectural disaster, a place notable primarily for the luxury and vulgarity of its design. As a contemporary critic wrote: "One longs to find out if there is not one single room where there might be found some repose." Indeed, it is a perfect example of the early parvenu's palace.

As the Vanderbilt family became more socially aware, the quality of their houses improved, espe-

112

BELOW: Richard Morris Hunt, Alva Vanderbilt's favorite architect, received the commission to build the Vanderbilt family mausoleum at Woodlawn Cemetery outside New York City (RIGHT). Wealthy Americans clearly wanted to take their final rest in the same opulence they had enjoyed in life.

FAR RIGHT: Hunt also built for Alva and William K. Vanderbilt the "Petit Château de Blois" on Fifth Avenue at 52nd Street, a mansion inspired by French Late Gothic or Renaissance châteaux in the Loire Valley. It was the first sophisticated work of Beaux-Arts architecture to be realized on a domestic scale in New York City.

cially so once they turned to talented architects. For William Henry's son, Frederick William, McKim designed a splendid Renaissance-style palace in Hyde Park, New York; completed in 1899, it overlooks the Hudson River from a grand elliptical portico of Palladian columns. Frederick and Louise Vanderbilt liked to spend Christmas and occasional weekends in this beautiful house when not at their other residences in Newport, Bar Harbor, Palm Beach, New York State's Adirondacks, the West Coast, or Manhattan.

McKim called in his other partners for a three-story, 110-room mansion at Madison, New Jersey, modeled after Sir Christopher Wren's addition to Hampton Court and built between 1890 and 1900. "Florham," as the house was known, linked the names of Florence Adèle Vanderbilt, the daughter of William Henry, and her husband, Hamilton McKown Twombly. Stanford White designed Woodlea, at Scarborough, New York, for Margaret Vanderbilt Shepard, William Henry's second child. A 74-room Italian Renaissance mansion, also overlooking the Hudson, the house boasted a modification of a Greek amphitheater that seated 1,500 people. Finally, at Centerport, Long Island, McKim created Eagle's Nest for William Kissam Vanderbilt, Jr. Under construction from 1908 to 1939, this was an extraordinary Hispano-Moorish-Portuguese folly whose interior decoration followed the combined Louis XV-Elizabethan-Tudor-Renaissance obsession.

RICHARD MORRIS HUNT'S CREATIONS AND INFLUENCE

Over a doorway at Eagle's Nest is the near-life-sized limestone statue of the architect Richard Morris Hunt (1827-95), in the guise of a stonemason,

which once adorned the façade of the grand château he built in 1878-82 for William Kissam and Alva Vanderbilt at 660 Fifth Avenue. McKim used to say that whenever he walked past this Loire castle in Manhattan, he would sleep peacefully just knowing it existed. This was as much a tribute to New York's plutocracy as to one of the Gilded Age's great architects, who—despite the many splendors put up by McKim, Mead & White for the Commodore's descendants—was the Vanderbilt family architect par excellence. In William K. and Alva's "Petit Château de Blois," an American architect managed for the first time to plan a house not only in the manner of Renaissance France but also in keeping with the life-style of an American millionaire. There seems to be no record of why Alva Vanderbilt sought out Hunt; perhaps she felt that, as the first American to study at the École des Beaux-Arts, he could fulfill her dream of building a verifiably European castle. "I don't care what style it is," she told him "as long as it's medieval." Thus began a collaboration between architect and patron without precedent in the New World. "She's a wonder," said Hunt. "It is as much as one man's brain can do to keep up with the Vanderbilt work."

Alva decided to upstage the rest of high society and so gave Hunt $2 million to build a castle in which she could receive like a queen. The architect dug out the sketches he had once made of the Loire châteaux and used as his inspiration not only Blois

but also the house of the 15th-century banker Jacques Coeur in Bourges. Prior to the Vanderbilt château, millionaires' houses had been little more than expanded brownstones like the Triple Mansion, and the idea of a period castle revolutionized the plutocrats' sense of possibility for their residences. The exterior, carved in Indiana limestone by European artists, was topped by a blue slate roof with copper cresting. Fleur-de-lis reliefs graced the central tower, and the walls of the entrance hall, fashioned of French marble imported from Caen, displayed delicate filigree accurate in every detail to the style of the era evoked. In this great space, warmed by a magnificent French Renaissance fireplace and lit by Gothic stained-glass windows, two footmen in maroon livery always stood ready to greet the family and guests.

The Vanderbilts decided to die like kings, and William Henry, after seeing his son's château, asked Hunt to design the family mausoleum on the highest hill of Staten Island, where the old Commodore had launched his empire. The first design, which could have been a setting for one of Alva's balls, horrified William Henry. "You entirely misunderstand me, Mr. Hunt," he said. "We are plain, quiet, unostentatious people, and we don't want to be buried in anything as showy as that would be." Notwithstanding, the final product, based on the Romanesque Chapel of St. Gilles at Arles, was America's most elaborate house of the dead.

The Vanderbilts' Fifth Avenue château inspired a number of less lugubrious commissions, all for palaces in Newport. First came Ogden Goelet's neo-Gothic Ochre Court (1888-92), followed by August Belmont's Belcourt Castle (1891-94), which was modeled upon Louis XIII's hunting lodge at

FAR LEFT: The entrance hall in the "Petit Château de Blois," with its grand sweep and rich, sculptural décor, continues the French Renaissance style of the exterior. It must have been particularly impressive when Vanderbilt footmen in maroon livery stood on every step bearing silver candelabras. ABOVE: The house at 1 West 57th Street, built by George Browne Post for Alice and Cornelius Vanderbilt II at a cost of $3 million. In 1892, the huge French Renaissance palace, which would soon face the Plaza Hotel on the north, was expanded to include 137 rooms, making it the largest private town house ever erected in the United States. It took up 200 feet along Fifth Avenue (the present site of Bergdorf-Goodman), and the distinguished team of artists who decorated the vast interior included Louis Comfort Tiffany, John La Farge, and Augustus Saint-Gaudens.

The Vanderbilts commissioned the grandest of the grand "cottages" in Newport.
FAR RIGHT: The entrance to Alva Vanderbilt's Marble House, in the full glory of its Beaux-Arts classicism.
BELOW: Every inch of the surface in the Marble House ballroom is animated with exuberant rococo relief work and mirrors. The latter once reflected not only the brown and gold décor but also the low romantic light from candles in the massive putti-bedecked chandeliers based on those at Château de Maisons-Laffitte outside Paris. Between the study and the sitting room on the mezzanine of this palatial house are bas-relief portraits of Jules Hardouin-Mansart, Louis XIV's architect and the creator of Maisons-Laffitte, and the Vanderbilts' favorite architect, Richard Morris Hunt. The images bore testimony to the esteem in which Alva held both of her aesthetic mentors.
OPPOSITE ABOVE: "The Breakers," commissioned from Richard Morris Hunt by Cornelius Vanderbilt II, is even larger than Marble House, but it falls short of the latter's elegance, despite the obvious attempt by one branch of the family to outshine the other.
OPPOSITE BELOW: The dining hall in "The Breakers." Today, the mansion, unlike Marble House, resembles more a grand hotel than a princely palace, perhaps because Hunt found a better-informed patron in Alva Vanderbilt than in her sister-in-law.

Versailles and whose entire ground floor was devoted to the owner's celebrated horses and carriages. Finally, there were the most famous Vanderbilt residences of all: Marble House (1888-92) and The Breakers (1892-95).

Marble House, the symbol of Alva's role as co-queen, with Caroline Astor, of New York society, was modeled in part on the White House in Washington, D.C., but with details from Marie Antoinette's Petit Trianon at Versailles. The architect and his patrons spared nothing in either the construction or the decoration of this *fin-de-siècle* masterpiece, erected behind a high fence so that members of the summer colony would have no idea of its magnificence until the house had been completed. So much marble was used—yellow Siena and black-veined Brescia from Italy, pink-veined Numidian from western Algeria, and, for the façade, white stone from Westchester County, New York—that a private wharf and warehouse were needed to

BELOW: The façade of George Vanderbilt's Biltmore, completed in 1895, on the edge of a vast, virgin forest outside Asheville, North Carolina. Biltmore sprung from the brain of the first true intellectual to appear among the Vanderbilts. Touring Europe with his architect, Richard Morris Hunt, the maecenas bought so many antique treasures that the house had to be tremendously expanded to contain them all. With its 255 rooms, many of them royally magnificent, Biltmore surpasses in size and opulence the Loire châteaux that inspired it. To build the place, Vanderbilt had first to establish an entire new village, complete with railroad station, sawmill, and a factory that turned out the 32,000 bricks laid every day that Biltmore was under construction.

OPPOSITE: The library at Biltmore is a soaring hall with a ceiling frescoed by Giovanni Antonio Pellegrini and imported from the Palazzo Pisani in Venice. The handsome walls are lined with George Vanderbilt's collection of some 20,000 books devoted mostly to art, gardening, and architecture.

unload and preserve the material. Of the $11 million spent on the palace, only $2 million went for construction, the balance going toward interior decoration. The ballroom, a perfect example of the Napoleon III interpretation of the Louis XV style, was—and still is—arguably the most opulent space ever created in the United States.

The Breakers, Newport's grandest "cottage" as well as the apogee of Richard Morris Hunt's work in that seaside town, was designed for Cornelius Vanderbilt II to replace an earlier mansion destroyed by fire in 1892. Construction of the new—and completely fireproof—stone house took a mere two years, with at times over 200 builders and carvers at work on the site. For his inspiration, Hunt turned to the Italian Renaissance, specifically to the great waterfront palaces of Genoa. Like its sixteenth-century prototypes, the three-story Breakers (which also included two basement levels and an attic) abounded in terraces, arcades, and loggias, all of which signified its primary purpose as a summer residence. The mansion boasted over seventy rooms (albeit half of them for staff), and, like Marble House, it exhibited a wide variety of stone, marble, and gold. Carved panels of Caen stone inlaid with colored marble adorned the great hall, pale gray-green Cippolino marble revetted the sides of the billiard room, and gold wall panels shimmered under the silver and gold coffered ceiling of the grand salon. Twelve red alabaster columns topped by gilt-bronze Corinthian capitals lined the state dining room, the palazzo's most extravagantly decorated space, whose double-height walls rose to meet life-sized figures in the arches and a ceiling painting entitled *Aurora at Dawn*.

While working on these Baroque- and Renaissance-revival seaside excursions, Hunt did not forget the Middle Ages. In the first half of the 1890s he built one Loire château for Elbridge T. Gerry on the southeast corner of Fifth Avenue at 61st Street and another for Alva's competition, Mrs. Astor and her son John Jacob, on Fifth Avenue at 65th Street—making a short cab ride up or down Fifth Avenue a much easier way to experience the Loire Valley than crossing the Atlantic on a heaving liner. Appropriately, Hunt's last great building—like his first—was a Gothic château, this one for George Washington Vanderbilt outside Asheville, North Carolina. With its 255 rooms, Biltmore is the largest private dwelling ever constructed in the United States. Henry James would characterize the place as "a thing of the high Rothschild manner." Its name, subsequently adopted by countless American hotels, was derived from Bildt, the Dutch village where the family originated, and "more," an Old English word for rolling upland countryside. George Vanderbilt started out in 1888 with an estate of 2,000 acres and plans for a château along the lines of Alva's New York castle. He then got swept away by the ambitious Hunt while they traveled throughout Europe in 1889 to buy treasures for the house. Having acquired far more than needed, they decided to enlarge the plans rather than return the objects. Hunt enlisted Frederick Law Olmsted to do the landscaping, and soon the acreage multiplied sixtyfold. In fact, the project required so much building material that Vanderbilt organized his own wood-carving, tile, and brick workshops on the estate. The rich exterior of the house, finished in 1895, appropriated elements of several Loire châteaux, including the freestanding exterior staircase at Blois, in an extremely successful mix, one that becomes quite breathtaking when approached through the beautifully landscaped grounds. In George Vanderbilt both Hunt and Olmsted found a merchant prince along the lines of Cosimo de' Medici, and under his enlightened patronage they created their finest and last masterpiece.

RIGHT: The block-long, genuinely palatial mansion, on Fifth Avenue between 70th and 71st Streets in New York City, that Carrère & Hastings designed for Henry Clay Frick. The coke baron sought a distinguished home not only for himself and his family but also for the fabulous collection of European art and furniture still housed there and now open to the public as the Frick Collection.

BELOW: For Whitehall, his Palm Beach palace, Henry Morrison Flagler imported Fifth Avenue to tropical Florida at a cost of $4 million. Here, he managed to combine styles from almost all the Bourbon reigns—Louis XIV, XV, and XVI—throughout the reception rooms. Velvet, silk, and satin from Europe's finest shops were used to embellish sixteen great suites. Whitehall launched the fashion of wintering in a private palace rather than a hotel suite, which radically altered the life-styles of millionaires seeking respite from New York's bleaker months.

ECLECTICISM AND CLASSICISM MOVE SOUTH

Among the other great society architects were John Merven Carrère and Thomas Hastings, who trained at the École des Beaux-Arts and in the drafting room of McKim, Mead & White. Their most lasting commissions were the Henry Clay Frick mansion on Fifth Avenue and 70th Street, the New York Public Library, and the office buildings of the Senate and House of Representatives in Washington, D.C. These two distinguished partners received their first major commission from Standard Oil's Henry Morrison Flagler, who attended New York's West Presbyterian Church, where Hastings's father was pastor. Flagler decided to give the young partners a crack at designing his Ponce de León Hotel in St. Augustine, Florida, launched in 1888. The architects felt that the swampy northern Florida landscape would be an inappropriate place to build the mansard-roofed palace hotels of the spa city of Saratoga Springs, New York, and decided to look to sunny Spain for their inspiration. Henry James described the resulting creation as "breaking out, on every pretext, into circular arches and embroidered screens, into courts and cloisters, arcades and fountains, fantastic projections and lordly towers, and is in all sorts of ways, and in the highest sense of the word, the most amusing of hotels." Across the way, at about the same time, Carrère & Hastings built a second hotel in the Spanish style, the Alcazar.

Further south, in Palm Beach, Flagler commissioned one of the largest hotels in the world, the Royal Poinciana, in 1893. The yellow and white wood and shingle palace was so long that exhausted clients had to ride from one end to the other in a rickshaw-like vehicle pedaled from behind by a black driver. A year later, he built the Palm Beach Inn (later known as the Breakers Hotel) directly on the ocean. Both hotels were designed by Theodore Blake, a draftsman at Carrère & Hastings, and in 1901 the principals returned to erect the 55-room, all-marble Whitehall, Flagler's Southern answer to the Newport palace, which he presented as a gift to his third wife, Mary Lily Kenan. It must have inspired many tycoons to think of building their own houses for greater privacy and more personal ostentation, but they desisted from doing so until the war years and the appearance on the scene of Addison Mizner, who—with Stanford White and Richard Morris Hunt—completed the triumvirate of America's major society architects.

"Citizen Kane"

William Randolph Hearst was the last of the Gilded Age palace builders, going through 54 houses and apartments in his lifetime. He filled them with mountains of both trash and treasure from all periods, countries, and styles, bought mostly in Europe. The money had been made by his father, George, who amassed millions from the Comstock Lode as well as from other mines, forests, and California real estate. Newspaper publishing did not generate the Hearst fortune, as commonly believed, and William Randolph nearly depleted what he inherited with his house building and art collecting. The most important of the residences were an entire apartment building in New York, the Clarendon; St. Donat's, a 135-room medieval castle in Wales; Wynton, an enormous hunting and fishing lodge for sixty guests in California's McCloud River; and—most famous of all—San Simeon in California's San Luis Obispo and Monterey counties. This was the Mission-style masterpiece of Julia

Morgan, one of the first women architects, and probably the finest on the West Coast. Morgan and Hearst started working together in 1919, and their great project included three guest houses, the main castle (La Casa Grande), a $1 million swimming pool of white marble embellished with antique-green mosaics, formal gardens, and a private zoo. The main entrance high on a hill overlooking the Pacific incorporated elements taken from several Gothic cathedrals, and the 36 bells in its two Spanish Renaissance towers pealed forth greetings to important (or attractive) visitors. The ceiling of the great assembly hall originally adorned the Palazzo Montenegro in Brescia, while the Flemish tapestries on the walls of San Simeon had been woven after cartoons by Giulio Romano and Rubens. The renowned refectory, a high Gothic hall of state with two rows of choir stalls and colorful flying standards, glowed with light reflected from magnificent old silver. The bed Hearst slept in had been Cardinal Richelieu's. The fantastic, mishmash castle seldom sheltered fewer than a hundred visitors, many of whom stayed for a weekend of tennis, swimming, and after-dinner movies starring their friends.

European Palaces

Palace building in Europe was more a phenomenon of the seventeenth and eighteenth centuries than the nineteenth, with the exception of Paris, where large parts of the city were razed and reconstructed by Baron Haussmann on the orders of

BELOW: William Randolph Hearst, popularly known as the model for the character Citizen Kane immortalized by Orson Welles, almost went bankrupt on several occasions as a consequence of his passion for building and furnishing lavish residences, some fifty of them before he died.

BELOW LEFT: The most astonishing of Hearst's many mansions was San Simeon, overlooking the Pacific Ocean in California's San Luis Obispo and Monterey counties. The statue-encircled swimming pool—evidently inspired by Hadrian's villa outside Rome—became the center of jolly weekends when beautiful film stars arrived in Hearst's private railway car from Hollywood.

ABOVE: The Refectory and the Assembly Room at San Simeon are filled with the hodgepodge of European art that Hearst bought in bulk and kept in warehouses until he found a place for it in one of his numerous houses. He acquired entire Gothic rooms, ceilings, carved choir stalls, sarcophagi, columns, tapestries, and anything else that suited his considerable fancy.

OPPOSITE: The Earl of Spencer's house in St. James's Place, leased by Barney Barnato, a cockney music-hall performer who found his way to South Africa and to the top of the heap among the monopolists in control of South African diamonds and gold. Although snubbed by London society and denied the peerage granted to most of the other South African mining millionaires, Barnato probably had more fun than all the rest of them combined, entertaining his raffish circle in the resplendent world of a Regency mansion.

FAR RIGHT AND BELOW: In 1903, Luton Hoo, the exquisite country seat designed by Robert Adam for Lord Bute, with gardens by Capability Brown, became the property of Julius Wernher, a key player in the "cartelization" of South African diamond and gold mines. Soon thereafter, the partnership of Charles Mewès and Arthur Davis, the designers responsible for the hotels of César Ritz, restyled Luton Hoo in the Louis XVI manner. As an Edwardian country house, it may be the finest ever realized.

Napoleon III. The palace hotel was a far more popular expression of the rich man's desire to live like a king, and the great resort hotels of Nice, Cannes, Monte Carlo, Carlsbad, Marienbad, Biarritz, Baden-Baden, Bad Homburg, St. Moritz, Lausanne, Lucerne, and Deauville became enormously comfortable and expensive second homes for the surgent bourgeoisie. These would eventually be joined there by the more adventurous members of established aristocracy in a perpetual round of dinners, balls, and entertainments. The movement of the rich from resort hotels to private houses that took place in the United States was far slower and less important in Europe, and the aristocracy, which made up society, mostly visited each other's country homes and castles.

The very rich, however, bought or leased the town houses of the old aristocracy and often had them expanded and totally redecorated in Belle Époque style. In London, the unpopular South African J.B. Robinson (known as "The Buccaneer") leased the palace of the Earl of Dudley in Park Lane, built in 1826, and filled its eighty-foot picture gallery with his own Rembrandts, Gainsboroughs, Italian Old Masters, and Dutch paintings. Sir Julius Wernher bought the Marquess of Bath's house next to the Ritz on Piccadilly, which he redecorated so opulently that a visitor, Beatrice Webb, wrote that "wealth, wealth, wealth was screamed aloud wherever one turned. There might just as well have been a Goddess of Gold erected for overt worship." (When hotel keeper César Ritz asked him whether he might sell his house, Wernher asked Ritz whether he might sell his hotel, since he was thinking of expanding.) That most showy of all South

African magnates, the cockney Barney Barnato, rented the Earl of Spencer's superb Regency palace in St. James's Place, where he entertained vaudeville stars, jockeys, racing trainers, boxers, and chorus girls. The banker Sir Ernest Cassel bought the enormous house of Lord Tweedmouth, on Park Lane and Upper Brook Street, and embellished it with 800 tons of Sarravezza marble from Michelangelo's quarry in Tuscany. The place was sarcastically referred to as the "Giant's Lavatory," and Cassel filled it with his splendid French furniture, Bouchers, and Fragonards. Finally, the Duke of Hamilton's house, built by William Kent, was bought by a Welsh iron caster, Ivor Bertie, who added a winter garden and a white and gold ballroom of extraordinary grandeur.

It was much the same in the country. William Waldorf Astor embellished Cliveden—purchased from the Duke of Westminster for $6 million—with the Fountain of Love, the largest private gusher in the world, and he spent $10 million simply on the expansion of tiny Hever castle, reputedly the birthplace of Anne Boleyn. Here, Astor created artificial lakes, bridges, and a formal Renaissance garden, at the same time that he also built a large group of houses connected to the castle, for guests and servants, all in the Tudor style. The Julius Wernhers first rented, then bought, Luton Hoo, the beautiful house that Robert Adam had designed in Bedfordshire for Lord Bute, with gardens by Capability Brown. Adam considered it his masterpiece "both in point of elegance and contrivance," but a fire in 1843 caused considerable damage. A rich Liverpudlian land speculator, John Shaw Leigh, acquired the house the same year, then restored and redecorated it in the eclectic Victorian style, complete with a Persian-carpeted conservatory full of exotic plants and birds singing from silver and gold cages. Wernher decided to gut most of the interior when he bought Luton Hoo in 1903, and commissioned Mewès and Davis, the favorite designers of Ritz and Albert Ballin's Hamburg-Amerika Line, to redo the place mostly in the Louis XVI style and at enormous cost. An outstanding example of Edwardian taste in a country house, and perhaps the finest work of its date and style in England, Luton Hoo gained Davis important commissions to rehabilitate such other country piles as Leeds Castle, Combe Court, and Polesden Lacey for their new owners.

BELOW: Joseph Paxton, a famous landscape gardener and designer of the Crystal Palace for London's Great Exhibition of 1851, created several Rothschild houses: Mentmore and Aston Clinton in England, the Château de Ferrières in France, and the Château de Prégny near Geneva. The Family appreciated Paxton's skill at laying out splendid formal gardens as much as they did the spectacular main halls he illuminated with great iron and glass ceilings.

RIGHT: The main courtyard and entrance at Mentmore Towers, built in 1859 by Paxton for Baron Mayer Amschel Rothschild. Mentmore is Paxton's only surviving work in Britain and a perfect example of the Jacobite revival. The architect took the basic plan from the Reform Club designed by Sir Charles Barry, co-architect with Charles Pugin of the neo-Gothic Houses of Parliament.

FAR RIGHT: Paxton's Château de Prégny commissioned by Adolphe de Rothschild of the Family's Neapolitan branch.

ROTHSCHILD HOUSES

Charles Mewès and Arthur Davis may have been the closest thing in Europe to American society architects, and they even designed the occasional tycoon palace: Jules Porgès's château at Rochefort-en-Yvelines, inspired by the Palais de la Légion d'Honneur, Albert Ballin's imposing palace in Hamburg, and William K. Vanderbilt's new home in Paris. The large amount of energy they spent on remodeling and redecorating old houses, designing hotels, and ritzing up ocean liners are a clear demonstration that private palace building was not a great activity of Europe's Gilded Age rich. Every rule, however, has its exceptions, and here, as in so many other contexts, the Rothschilds were exceptional. The Family thrived on being unique, and their circuit consisted of the monarchs, prime ministers, and heads of state who frequented them for loans. Other people's houses were of little interest to the Rothschilds, and with their incredible fortunes they created some of Europe's most impressive nineteenth-century palaces suitable for entertaining their royal and imperial guests in the style to which they were accustomed.

Such was the scale of Rothschild houses, collections, and entertaining that everybody—including Queen Victoria, Kaiser Wilhelm, and Napoleon III—asked to be invited. Although the Family could have afforded to buy a great many large palaces, they felt obliged to build their own, generally out of the architectural context of the country in which they lived. Their favorite architect was Joseph Paxton, designer of London's Crystal Palace for the international exposition of 1851. This enormous iron-and-glass, greenhouse-like structure was the prototype for important new covered shopping gal-

leries as well as the departure platforms for the many railway stations then being built in Europe. Paxton's early career as a landscape gardener also fit the Rothschild ambition to create extravagant formal gardens replete with hothouses, statuary, and baroque fountains.

Paxton's first Rothschild commission was for Mentmore Towers, the country house of Baron Mayer Amschel Rothschild in Buckinghamshire's Vale of Aylesbury. This area had become a hunting preserve of sorts for the English branch of the Family who took to the hounds with their usual degree of extravagance and enthusiasm. Mentmore's great clerestory hall, hung with priceless tapestries, was illuminated during the day by a large glass skylight and at night by enormous glass lanterns from the Doges' barge in Venice. Its luxury was such that Lady Eastlake wrote: "I do not believe that the Medici were ever so lodged in the height of their glory." There was every modern convenience, and Mayer even encased his washbasins in valuable eighteenth-century commodes that he had sawed in two. As a result of Mentmore's glory, Sir Anthony Rothschild, Mayer's

LEFT: Built of Caen stone, the entrance hall at Mentmore was paved with Sicilian and Rouge Royal marble, the better to display Mayer Amschel Rothschild's famed collection of antique sculpture. Marble stairs lead to a grand hall whose main feature is the monumental black-and-white marble fireplace designed by Rubens for his house at Antwerp.

BELOW: Like all Rothschilds, Mayer Amschel could not resist 18th-century France, which is elegantly reflected in the ground-floor dining room at Mentmore, with its white and gold boiseries appropriated from the Hôtel de Villars in Paris. So chock-a-block was the great house with Italian and French 18th-century furnishings that even the bathroom sinks rested in chopped-up Louis XVI commodes. It also contained furniture from the Doge's palace and barge in Venice, as well as many Old Master paintings and other priceless works of Renaissance and Baroque art.

BELOW: Buckinghamshire was once almost cluttered with Rothschild follies, but the most extraordinary of these creations may be Waddesdon Manor in the Vale of Aylesbury, a French château famous not only for its fabulous collections but also for its hothouses, remarkable cuisine, and weekends aglitter with politicians, financiers, and British royals. Building French castles in the traditional English countryside required the sort of *chutzpah* that only the Rothschilds could carry off.
ABOVE: Despite the extraordinary qualities of Mentmore, Paxton's greatest achievement was undoubtedly Baron James de Rothschild's Château de Ferrières, seen here in a period engraving.
OPPOSITE ABOVE: Philippe Jullian has claimed that Ferrières possessed the splendor of Veronese combined with the comfort of a grand hotel. The centerpiece of the lavish entrance hall was a bronze Hercules holding a globe topped by the Rothschild arms.
OPPOSITE BELOW: The opulent "Cordova Leather Salon" at Ferrières provided an agreeable place to recover from an extravagant dinner prepared by Carême, a legendary chef who left the service of the Czar of Russia for the more generous patronage of Baron James.

elder brother, asked Paxton to enlarge nearby Aston Clinton House, purchased in 1851, while Adolphe de Rothschild, the son of Neapolitan Carl Mayer, commissioned him to do up his Château de Prégny, near Geneva. This large Victorian palace, decorated in *le goût Rothschild*, was filled with works of art and precious furniture. Exotic birds sang in a plush aviary, and the hothouses of Baroness Julie were renowned the world over.

Paxton's Rothschildian masterpiece, however, was Baron James's Château de Ferrières in the Brie district east of Paris. The Baron had acquired the 7,880-acre estate in 1829 from the Duc d'Otrante, heir of the turncoat revolutionary Fouché, and the blunt, business-like new owner instructed Paxton: "Make me a Mentmore, only twice the size." No one could accuse the Rothschilds of not being competitive. Fouché's château was knocked down, and in its place rose the foremost example of the Second Empire style, an immense Italianate villa complete with columns, pilasters, busts of Roman emperors, and imposing colonnaded turrets. The house had five private apartments for the family and eighteen suites for guests, the lot of them served by a hundred-member staff, the latter dressed in the Rothschild blue livery. Phillippe Jullian describes Ferrières as "having the magnificence of a Veronese adapted to a grand hotel." Baroness Betty entrusted the décor to the fashionable artist Eugène Lami,

who mixed sixteenth-century Italy with seventeenth-century France. The centerpiece was the great hall, rising two floors by means of a grand staircase, whose coffered ceiling evoked the Doges' Palace (which Lami and the Baroness had visited to obtain decorating ideas). Germany's Kaiser Wilhelm, green with envy, said that even kings could not afford such luxury.

Royal visits to Rothschilds were by no means limited to Ferrières, although they were usually less spectacular. One of the favorite country retreats most favored by the Prince of Wales was Baron Ferdinand's Waddesdon Manor in Buckinghamshire (on whose staircase His Royal Highness broke a leg); indeed, he spoke of its beauty and comforts with such relish that Queen Victoria asked to be invited. Ferdinand had bought his 3,200-acre estate from the Duke of Marlborough in 1874 and picked as his architect G.-H. Destailleur, whose father and grandfather had been architects to the Duc d'Orléans. He asked Destailleur to erect something resembling the Valois's sixteenth-century châteaux in the Touraine, a rather more specific request than that of Alva Vanderbilt, who wanted anything medieval for her Fifth Avenue mansion. Baron Ferdinand and his sister Alice took charge of the decoration, buying splendid eighteenth-century fireplaces and paneling from the Paris houses of the Maréchal de Richelieu, the Duc de Lauzun, and the notoriously rich Fermier-Général Beaujon, who had also owned the Hôtel de l'Élysée. Ferdinand, a ferocious art collector, also inherited major art works from two members of the French branch, and in consequence could display in his beautiful rooms the most complete and perfect of all the Family collections.

There were many other extravagant Rothschild country houses in Great Britain and on the Continent. In France alone seven entered the Family through marriage, and Beatrix Ephrussi, Baron Alphonse's daughter, commissioned one of the grandest estates in the South of France, overlook-

BELOW: Baroness Hélène van Zuylen (née Rothschild) married a Dutch aristocrat whose ambition was to re-create his family's past by building the immense Kasteel de Haar near Utrecht to replace the one destroyed in the 17th century during the Battle of Orange.

RIGHT: President of the Automobile Club in its early years, Baron van Zuylen enjoyed organizing rallies for sporting friends, here seen lined up at the turn of the century near the moat around the castle he built in the Netherlands with Rothschild money. This colossal structure, which dwarfs even Newport's largest houses, is a splendid example of the 19th-century vogue for eclectic historicism. But while the detailing on the façade corresponds quite accurately to genuinely ancient manor houses in the neighborhood, the highly imaginative interior offers a kind of supreme luxury unknown to premodern times.

OPPOSITE: The breathtaking entrance hall at Kasteel de Haar, with its filigreed marble, stained-glass windows, and tapestries, is nothing less than a cathedral adapted to private use. The castle, while open to the public most of the year, is entirely occupied by the present Baron van Zuylen and his family in September, when guests are still received in the high style long characteristic of the Rothschilds.

ing the Mediterranean at Cap Ferrat. Built like Ferrières in the Franco-Italian style, this harbor for Russian grand dukes, American millionaires, English peers, and Italian princes boasted a famous spread of English, Spanish, Japanese, and Mediterranean gardens. To create them, Mme. Ephrussi had leveled entire hills for the sake of better views and proper climactic effects. The Viennese Rothschilds, the richest family in Austria-Hungary, were master builders as well, an extraordinary achievement considering that when Salomon Mayer arrived in Austria to establish the family fortune, he as a Jew was not allowed to own or rent property, which forced him to take over most of the city's finest hotel, Zum Römischer Kaiser. Baron Albert's palace on the Prinz Eugenstrasse, with its gold ballroom and silver dining room, was referred to as "the Albert Memorial" by his English cousins. Outside Vienna, Baron Albert also maintained large and luxurious shooting estates at Schilensdorf and Schloss Enzesfeld. It was at the latter that another Prince of Wales pined away in exile while his American fiancée, Wallis Warfield Simpson, got her divorce. Rothschild money also built the largest and most extraordinary private house in the Netherlands, the Kasteel de Haar in the flatlands near Utrecht. This was the result of a union between a Dutch nobleman living in Paris, Baron van Zuylen van Nyvelt, and Hélène Betty, the granddaughter of Baron James, whom he married largely in order to have the enormous funds necessary to replace the family castle that had been razed during the Battle of Orange. The van Zuylens hired the Netherlands' most distinguished architect, P.J.H. Cuypers, who had designed Amsterdam's new train station as

well as its Rijksmuseum, and instructed him to build a medieval Dutch castle, complete with moat and towers, on the Rothschildian scale. That meant formal French gardens, a private golf course, large stables for carriage horses, and fifty bedrooms decorated in styles from Tudor to Ritz. On the elaborate beams of the Gothic salon the Rothschilds left their mark, the Star of David alternating with the van Zuylen crest and its motto: *Non Titubans*.

Rothschildian splendor was not limited to the countryside. In Paris, they had a large house on the Rue du Faubourg St. Honoré, today the residence of the United States Ambassador, and another opposite the Élysée Palace on the Avenue de Marigny, which is where the French government presently houses its most important visitors. The Rothschilds also lived in the former residence of the Princesse Mathilde on the Rue de Courcelles, and they built important town houses in Haussmann's new residential sections on the Avenue du Bois and Avenue de Friedland. In London, Lionel de Rothschild erected an enormous house at 147 and 148 Piccadilly, next to the Duke of Wellington's Apsley House, which was inherited by his son Nathaniel, the first Lord Rothschild, in 1879. It was here that Disraeli obtained the funds needed to buy the Suez Canal from Khedive Ishmael of Egypt. Nathaniel's neighbors then included *mischpoche* galore, who occupied new palaces at 107, 142, and 143 Piccadilly, as well as in St. James's and Hamilton Places. The descendants of Frankfurt's coin peddler, Mayer Amschel, had moved from the "House of the Red Shield" in the Frankfurt ghetto to the most opulent dwellings in Europe in two generations, and were certainly among the best-housed families in history.

The Villa Hügel designed and built by Alfred Krupp himself when the aristocratic neighbors of his vast steel works in Essen refused to sell him any one of their feudal estates. The main building, with its enormous glassed-in winter garden, contains 160 rooms.
FAR RIGHT: Alfred Krupp built the Villa Hügel of nonflammable iron and steel, as if it were a factory. Indeed, it was a technological wonder in the 19th-century, equipped with one of the first air-conditioning systems, needed to protect the industrialist and his family from the toxic discharges of the Krupp works.
RIGHT: Alfred Krupp von Bohlen und Halbach, flanked by his son Arnd and his "foreign manager" Berthold Beitz, in 1961 on the occasion of the 150th anniversary of the founding of the Krupp works. Behind them stand the company's entire staff of foreign representatives, whose very number corresponds to the overwhelming scale of the Villa Hügel.
BELOW: Bertha Krupp (1886-1957), heiress to Germany's mighty steel works in Essen, and her husband, the aristocratic Gustav von Bohlen und Halbach (1870-1950).

THE KRUPPS' VILLA HÜGEL

Little in Europe could be compared to the Paxton Rothschild houses except the Villa Hügel, built in 1870 in Essen by Alfred Krupp. This was the fourth residence constructed by Krupp, who tended to increase the size and costliness of the abodes as his success grew. A few years after beginning his career in a tiny, peasant-style hut, Krupp built a three-story house on his factory grounds. When the steel forges shook the place, chinaware fell from the walls and shattered. "It's only a few porcelain plates," he said to his wife Bertha. "I'll make the customers pay for them." To console her, he erected, again on the factory grounds, a more elegant home with a large glass-encased winter garden and orangery, a small, formal French garden with fountains, and lily ponds. The flowers and peacocks quickly died from the soot that poured out of the blast furnaces' tall chimneys. With Bertha complaining that the smoke would be the death of her and their young son Fritz, Krupp attempted to buy a castle nearby. However, the local nobility would have cheerfully faced a firing squad rather than sell to the rough steelmaker and the granddaughter of a pastry cook to the Archbishop of Cologne; thus, the new tycoon decided to show them all what a steel king could do with his money.

Krupp insisted on building the Villa Hügel near his ever-expanding factory grounds, but attempted to filter the air through an elaborate system of ventilators and shafts, fixing the temperature by means of one of the earliest air-conditioning systems ever installed in a large private house.

Among other daring things, he invented windows that could not be opened, and placed his own study over the stables on the theory that manure inspired creative thinking. Villa Hügel, dominating the vast Krupp factories from a hill, was several palaces rolled into one, all in the traditional neo-classical-cum-eclectic Victorian style. Serving as his own architect, Krupp placed a Renaissance façade on the main building, which had 160 rooms, some longer than a city block, and built a gallery to join this mass with an additional 60 rooms in the Little House.

The Villa Hügel's decorators had a hard task, since Krupp forbade the use of any wood. He was terrified of fire and refused even to have potentially flammable books, tapestries, or paintings in the house. Everything was made from iron forged in his factory and stone imported from France. The technical complications were such that it took three years to build the Villa Hügel, whose elaborate systems rarely worked properly. Bertha gave up and moved out with Fritz for most of the year, living in comfortable spas and resort hotels nearby. She did return for a few days on such important occasions as the Kaiser's visits, but Alfred spent most of his life alone with his 110 servants. It was the house and its owners that inspired Luchino Visconti's terrifying film of 1969 entitled *The Damned*, in which a family of German industrialists divide and then crumble under the Nazis. The Villa Hügel had also provided the setting when Krupp's descendants discussed with Kaiser Wilhelm's officer corps the weapons with which they hoped to emerge victorious in World War I, a catastrophic event that brought the Gilded Age to its end.

Safely sealed against the industrially polluted atmosphere around Essen, this immense, glassed-in chamber at the heart of the Krupp family's Villa Hügel has for over a century served as winter garden, banquet hall, ballroom, and concert hall. It has also been graced by the presence of virtually every important political, social, industrial, and financial figure to emerge in modern Germany. Not only in sheer scale but also in its Teutonic sobriety, the great nave-like interior stands in marked contrast to the fanciful Beaux-Arts confections and the *goût Rothschild* favored by the Gilded Age architects and their patrons in Paris, London, New York, and Newport. The beautiful paneling is fashioned not of flammable wood but of the same fireproof metals used by the Krupp factories to make heavy armaments.

COLLECTORS

Art collecting has long been linked to power, whether in the form of patronage or plunder. Popes, princes, and monarchs alike sought immortality by amassing masterpieces as a demonstration of their enlightened identification with the finer things in life. The Hermitage is a monument to Catherine the Great, the Uffizi to the Medici, the Zwinger in Dresden to Augustus the Strong, and the Louvre—in many ways—to both Napoleon I and Napoleon III. It was to be expected, therefore, that when the super-rich parvenu made it in a big way, he would head for the art dealer. Private galleries became the status symbol par excellence in the new mansions put up at the turn of the century, and if, as Henry Clay Frick once said, railroads were the Rembrandts of investment, a Rembrandt or two on the wall was the ultimate sign of taste, power, and prestige.

For perpetuity, there is, of course, philanthropy, in the interest of which the Rockefellers and Fords have dispersed billions of dollars, putting their names on hospitals, scholarships, public works, and endless other world-class benefits. Yet, somehow, all that is not as tangible as a repository of fine art, which can be viewed within a few hours, its treasures there for all to see, palpable and pleasing to the senses, endlessly impressive. Best of all, it can be enjoyed by the tycoon-collector during his own lifetime, for there is little pleasure in knowing that hard-earned money will perhaps be squandered by self-seeking trustees. Blessedly, art can be left where it always hung and knock as many socks off future generations as it did off one's own.

Until World War I, the relationship between artists or their work and collectors was largely dominated by such semipublic institutions as academies and salons, whose exhibitions—usually annual—did much to establish taste and thus the price or even acceptability of art.

OPPOSITE: In this painting by the British artist George Bernard (1828-1917) or his circle, two elegant, well-chaperoned young ladies attend the annual exhibition at London's Royal Academy.

BELOW: The art gallery in the Fifth Avenue house of the William B. Astors, double- and quadruple-hung mainly with "official" art—paintings by such academically correct masters as Ziem, Bouguereau, and Millet. The pompous, overbearing Second Empire décor—with its stuccoed ceiling and Louis XIV fireplace—provided the parvenu glitz needed for the space in which the Mrs. Astor gave her annual ball, attended by New York's "Four Hundred." This was the exclusionary number of socially prominent guests who could be received there with comfort.

ABOVE: Many of the pictures owned by the Astors and their peers in high society were bought from dealers in New York and Paris, or, far less often, at auctions such as the well-attended one at the Galerie Georges-Petit in Paris, here depicted by the French artist Gustave François (1883-1968).

RIGHT: Under the influence of sophisticated dealers such as Knoedler and Duveen, America's great industrialists and bankers gradually became serious collectors of Old Master art. One of Joe Duveen's favorite clients was the Kuhn, Loeb partner and railroad financier Otto Kahn, seen here relaxing with his wife in the paneled library of their regal Fifth Avenue mansion. Over the fireplace hangs a Rembrandt portrait while a painting by the Flemish master Patinir rests on an easel in the background. A German-born Junker of immense culture and sophistication, Kahn was a leading patron of the Metropolitan Opera, a theatrical producer who brought Max Reinhardt to the United States, and an international traveler as well as bon vivant with an appetite for blond operatic sopranos. With Duveen's costly aid, Kahn filled the salon of his New York house with masterpieces.

BELOW: Joseph Duveen, later Lord Duveen of Millbank, adopted aggressive though subtle techniques to ween parvenu collectors from their addiction to stodgy academic art and introduce them to the giddy satisfactions of collecting of Old Masterworks. He succeeded handsomely with Otto Kahn, Henry Clay Frick, Isabella Stewart Gardner, and Paul Mellon, among others.

A GREAT OPPORTUNITY

The Gilded Age provided an unparalleled opportunity for collecting. As the great families of Europe tasted the bitter fruits of revolt and reform, they began to have trouble making ends meet and thus sold off many of their possessions. Smaller landholdings could not yield enough to keep their owners in the style to which they had become accustomed. Only the rare feudal lord had marketable skills, and there were not enough dollar heiresses to go around. Even if there had been, many impecunious nobles felt it beneath their dignity to marry below their station. Few wanted to sell their estates, given that castle-hopping was more or less a year-round occupation. So, the next best thing was to take a few pictures off the wall, get rid of some furniture, empty the vitrines of precious enamels and bronzes, remove the priceless illuminated manuscript from the library shelf, and slip the master drawings out of the folders where they had rested unwatched and ignored for decades, even centuries. Thanks to the Bolsheviks, extraordinary opportunities presented themselves. In 1930 the bankrupt Soviet government unloaded for hard currency the masterpieces of Raphael, Rembrandt, and others collected by Catherine the Great for her Hermitage; and before that such Russian grandees as Prince Felix Yusupov, murderer of Rasputin, had debarked in Paris with some of the Empire's greatest treasures. Once Germany was unified by Bismarck, a number of Teutonic princes—in effect, small potentates—lost their taxing power and sold out as well. In post-unification Italy, grand and newly impoverished aristocrats unloaded Renaissance and Baroque treasures from their palazzi and private chapels. Life-styles, gambling debts, and womanizing forced dozens of English peers to sell ancestral portraits, masterpieces bought on the Grand Tour, and royal French furniture purchased by their great-grandfathers after Versailles and the Tuileries had been sacked during the Revolution of 1789-94.

There were no export controls, and national artistic patrimony had yet to become a notion; consequently, most of this extraordinary loot crossed the Atlantic to be unloaded in the Port of New York. Notwithstanding American wealth, a great deal was siphoned off by the Rothschilds in Paris, London, and Vienna, as well as by Sir Richard Wallace, Alfred Beit, and a few other British parvenus. For many, collecting was a lifetime occupation.

Collecting styles are as different as the styles collected. Some millionaires placed themselves in the hands of dealers or "experts." In the United States, the very rich made the fortunes of Lord Duveen and Bernard Berenson, who were singly and jointly responsible for placing many masterpieces in the collections of Collis P. Huntington, Isabella Stewart Gardner, Henry Clay Frick, Andrew Mellon, Jules Bache, and J.P. Morgan. Such dealers as Knoedler, Wildenstein, and Duveen maintained elaborate offices with red- and

LEFT: One of the exhibition rooms in the large art gallery maintained by Duveen Brothers in London's New Bond Street. It was in this kind of prestigious environment that Joe Duveen made loyal clients of such major collectors as Sir Edward Cecil Guinness, J.P. Morgan, Benjamin Altman, and Samuel H. Kress.

BELOW: In his passion to acquire and sell Old Masters, Joe Duveen bought up whole collections of major European art, sometimes holding them for decades as inventory stashed away in the crowded storerooms of his posh New York gallery. Eventually, he sold everything as his clients' taste caught up with his own.

brown-velvet inner sanctums in London, Paris, and New York, and transferred their treasures from one to the other depending on the location and whims of their clients. Those who did not maintain branches in New York, such as Agnew's and Colnaghi's, placed their pictures with competition who did. In fact, it is the dealers as much as the collectors who convey the elegant frenzy of this golden age of collecting.

THE DUVEENS

Although there were many important art dealers in Paris, London, and New York at the end of the nineteenth century, nobody seems to have so captivated the public's curiosity as the short, unattractive, aggressive, and often obnoxious Joseph Duveen (1869-1939). This is largely owing to the witty biography by S.N. Behrman, originally published in *The New Yorker*, against which other dealers' biographies—mostly written by family members and destined as gifts for clients—pale in comparison.

Joseph Joel Duveen was the first truly important family dealer, beginning in 1879 when he founded the legendary London and New York firm known as Duveen Brothers. Prior to this, Joseph Joel had been based in Hull, where he sold Oriental porcelain, delftware, and other objets d'art in his father-in-law's jewelry shops throughout Britain. He realized that the big money was to be made not in the provinces but in London, where newly rich businessmen from the United States, Great Britain,

and various parts of the Empire were spending vast fortunes decorating their recently purchased or built town palaces with fine old French furniture, tapestries, rare porcelain, and fashionable paintings by either contemporary artists or Old Masters. Meanwhile, in 1876, Joseph Joel's brother Henry was sent off to New York and Boston to establish a beachhead in the New World, where money was flowing like water.

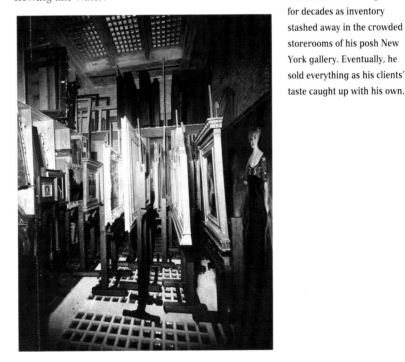

RIGHT: It was in this modest house on Fifth Avenue at 31st Street that Henry Duveen first established the New York outpost of Duveen Brothers, the family firm of English art dealers that had begun in Hull before moving to London. As the window display suggests, Duveen Brothers dealt mainly in rare porcelain, as well as other decorative arts, before upscaling to Old Master art.

ABOVE: Sir Edward Cecil Guinness, Bart., helped launch Joe Duveen into Old Master art when the young dealer proved clever enough to recognize his new client the first time he ventured into the London gallery of Duveen Brothers, until then known mainly for purveying objets d'art rather than great paintings.

RIGHT: Joe Duveen, nattily dressed in blue blazer and white flannels, waits on the deck of a transatlantic liner to collar a prospective client. He was not above bribing deck stewards to place him next to potential collectors, or of paying Fifth Avenue butlers to keep him informed about competitors' attempts to cultivate his favorite clients.

In many ways the Duveens were like the Rothschilds. Quick, cunning, courageous, and hardworking, they understood above all the strength of the *mischpoche*, and this is where they proved lethal rivals to other American dealers. The traditional pattern for the New York trade at the time was to travel to Europe during the slack months of May to October (when their clients were abroad) and to stock up for the next season. With no way of foreseeing the many bubbles and busts that characterized the American financial scene, they were often left holding a warehouse of temporarily unsalable goods when some of their important clients filed for bankruptcy. All Henry Duveen had to do was cable his needs to Joseph Joel, and the goods would be on the next boat. Thus, while many American dealers went broke, the Duveens prospered. And, in the end, it was the American connection that carried them, for in general, then as now, the Europeans sold and the Americans bought.

LORD DUVEEN OF MILLBANK

In retrospect, grand as Joseph Joel and Henry became, their appearance on the entertaining and endlessly fascinating stage of the art-dealing drama seems but preparation for the entrance of Joseph Joel's son, Joseph (known to many as Joe), later Lord Duveen of Millbank and arguably the most flamboyant, outrageous, and important dealer of the first quarter of this century, when the great American museum and private collections were formed. Prior to the arrival of Joe, Duveen Brothers had sold some decorative French and English pictures by Largillière, Watteau, Hubert Robert, and Thomas Lawrence but nothing truly major, and it was great

paintings rather than fine French furniture and porcelain that made Duveen a legendary firm. The credit for this goes to Joe, who first set out for the United States in 1886 at the age of seventeen.

After sizing up the American scene, young Joe returned to London and was present at the shop when an Irish gentleman and his wife came in and asked to see some screens. Joseph Joel had made several up from embossed Cordoba leather and old tapestries, and the couple started buying them at a rapid clip. Joseph Joel, desperate to discover who these clients were, sent his son out to speak to their coachman. Joe slipped a piece of paper to his father with the name E.C. Guinness. "You may think it strange, Mr. Duveen, that I am buying so many screens," said the wife, to which the art dealer responded: "Not at all, Lady Guinness. You have many fine homes, and you are quite right to supply them with screens." The Guinnesses, flattered at being recognized, bought lots more. Joseph Joel was delighted, Joe frustrated that he had nothing more important to offer them. Sir Edward Cecil Guinness, later Lord Iveagh, was then one of the most important picture collectors in Britain, as well as the main client of Agnew's, the venerable picture dealers on Old Bond Street, and Duveen was still picture poor.

THE KING OF OLD MASTERS

The Guinness visit proved to be a turning point for Duveen. Joe was well aware of the potential hornet's nest that could be stirred up by selling Old Master pictures—questions as to condition, attribution, second versions, even authenticity. A few major mistakes could destroy the reputation of a dealer, and connoisseurship of 500 years of Western painting was a thornier problem than K'ang Hsi vases or Riesener furniture. Consequently, young Joseph headed for Berlin to befriend and seek the advice of Dr. Wilhelm von Bode, director of the Kaiser Friedrich Museum and one of the greatest experts of his day. He also approached other connoisseurs throughout the world to help him plot his course. Joe was too smart to rush in, but in 1901 he created a splash by paying the biggest price ever reached at auction, £14,050 (approximately $70,250) for John Hoppner's portrait of Lady Louisa Manners, in its day a sum many times what the picture

would be worth now. With this, he also established a pattern of overpaying, which dazzled vendors and brought him a large share of the great works of art on sale at any time. It was in 1906, however, that two major events occurred that were drastically to change Duveen Brothers and the history of art dealing. In that year Joe purchased the famous Oskar Hainauer collection for $2.5 million and as a result met Bernard Berenson, who became his main adviser in an odd partnership that lasted until the great dealer's death in 1939.

Buying the right pictures on Berenson's advice was crucial, and selling them constituted as great an art. There were few dealers as deadly as Joe Duveen when it came to matching picture to collector. He chose his clients as carefully as his paintings, which generally needed to be bright, colorful, and life-enhancing. Women's portraits sold better than men's, and Crucifixions were avoided at all costs. (Tycoons did not want to be depressed.)

BELOW: The renowned art historian Bernard Berenson was the *éminence grise* behind the flamboyant power and success of Joe Duveen as a dealer in Old Master art. Although aesthetically and ethically uncomfortable, the relationship between the scholar and the dealer endured for decades, mainly because it allowed Berenson to live in the luxury to which he soon grew addicted. Here, late in life, "B.B." is seen at his beloved Villa I Tatti in Fiesole, surrounded by books and a priceless *Madonna and Child* by Domenico Veneziano.
LEFT: A disciple of George Santayana and one of Harvard's most brilliant students, young Bernard Berenson was chosen by Isabella Stewart Gardner, the slightly eccentric Boston dowager, to help her assemble a collection of Old Master paintings. Her portrait reproduced here, a work by John Singer Sargent, caused a scandal in Boston, which thought a respectable lady should not pose in decolleté and bare arms.

BELOW: The magnificent gallery, on New York's Fifth Avenue 56th Street, that Carrère and Hastings designed for Duveen at the height of his career as a dealer in Old Master art.
FAR RIGHT: The mansion that William T. Sears built for Isabella Stewart Gardner on Boston's Fenway Court could scarcely have been more anachronistic in the Puritan world of "Bean City," where the chill atmosphere was never entirely a matter of climate. For the flower-filled courtyard of the North Cloister, Tiffany discovered his model in a Venetian palazzo. The enclosure became a perfect invitation to visit the Renaissance salons upstairs.
ABOVE: In Mrs. Gardner's Red Salon hangs what is probably the finest Titian in the United States—*The Rape of Europa*, acquired for the collector by Bernard Berenson. Flanking the door on the other side is Velázquez's portrait of Philip I of Spain. The gilded Venetian furniture completes the ensemble in all its sensuous delight.

Duveen also created the illusion that he could sell only to those ready to buy "a Duveen," a tactic that made mid-level millionaires feel as if buying one of his pictures were an indication of finally having made it. Joe was brilliant at setting one collector against another, dispensing his favors as if they were the gift of the gods, and his ways of meeting prospects were legendary. He bribed stewards on the great liners to give him a deck chair next to a prospective client, and had every butler in New York and London on his payroll in order to be informed fully of his clients' movements and visitors. S.N. Behrman describes Joe and Bertram Boggis, his assistant, preparing for a meeting with a tycoon to sell a particular picture. "Now, you're Morgan, and I'm Duveen," began the cockney-accented Boggis as he summoned all the arguments why he did not want the picture while Duveen polished his sales pitch.

In the wake of the Hainauer coup in 1906 came the purchase of the Rodolphe Kann collection in Paris for 23 million francs (approximately $4.6 million). Virtually a self-contained museum, the Kann collection, aside from magnificent tapestries, French furniture, Oriental ceramics, and unique works of art, was chock-a-block with Dutch, Flemish, and Italian pictures, including eleven Rembrandts, all major masterpieces and now among the glories of the Metropolitan Museum and the National Gallery in Washington, thanks to their purchase by Altman, Mellon, and Kress. Following up on this bold move, Duveen purchased the collection of Maurice Kann (Rodolphe's brother) for

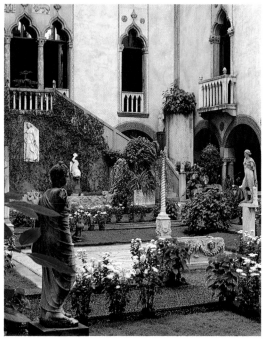

nearly an equivalent amount, doing so at a time when Berenson's Italian finds were crossing the Atlantic in great numbers.

Amazingly, Joe sometimes kept pictures for decades, which suggests the degree to which his taste outpaced that of his rich clients, many of whom preferred the prettier, more academic paintings of Bouguereau or Ziem to the darkly romantic, soulful Rembrandt. The miracle was financing the enormous stock. When Joseph Joel died, he left the business to his widow and his brother Henry, as

BELOW: Collis P. Huntington, the California railroad king, was one of Joe Duveen's important clients who eagerly collected English paintings as well as the decorative arts of royal France. These treasures, including a vast collection of books and manuscripts, are now housed in the Huntington Library in Pasadena, California.

well as to Joe, who decided to buy the other two out. Consequently, by 1908, as sole proprietor of the firm, Joe found himself $17 million in debt, and this impressive sum rose to $25 million toward the end of his life, a colossal figure considering that J.P. Morgan's gross estate was $75 million. As another tycoon quipped at the great banker's funeral: "And to think, he wasn't even that rich." By milllionaire standards maybe, but for an art dealer it was a lot

of money, and Duveen survived thanks to his many banker-clients who financed his worldwide operation. At its height, this included an enormous mansion on Fifth Avenue and 56th Street modeled after Jacques-Ange Gabriel's Marine Ministry in Paris, a shop on London's New Bond Street, and a large gallery on the Place Vendôme in Paris. Joe was first knighted in 1919 and then, in 1933, elevated to the peerage, as Lord Duveen of Millbank, in recognition of his generous gifts of paintings and entire wings to the British Museum, the National Portrait Gallery, the Tate, and London's National Gallery. In all, he gave away $10 million in his lifetime, munificence matched only by that of his major clients. His real legacy, however, was paid for by others, and it would be fair to say that about 75 percent of the Italian masterpieces in American museums are there thanks to Duveen and, of course, to Berenson, his trusted mentor. After Joe's death, Lincoln Kirstein wrote that in a quarter of a century historians would be examining the Duveen stock books as they did the Medici inventories. He was right, even though the stock books are now under lock and key at the Metropolitan Museum. And by the 1950s, the books were about all that remained.

In his greed and ambition, Joe Duveen made one fatal mistake: He forgot the concept of the *mischpoche*. The Duveen family were scattered in other galleries and businesses, and Joe's only child, Dorothy, married a London surgeon and busied herself supporting socialist causes while living in Britain tax-free, thanks to an arrangement Joe had reached with the government after leaving the

ABOVE LEFT: The Savonnerie carpet in this room at the Huntington Library once graced the Grande Galerie in the Louvre. The chairs covered in Gobelins tapestry were made for Madame de Pompadour. FAR LEFT: *The Blue Boy*, a portrait of Jonathan Buttall, by Thomas Gainsborough now hangs in the Huntington Library. Purportedly, Joe Duveen bought the painting for Collis P. Huntington after the collector admired its reproduction in the "Gainsborough Suite" on the *Aquitania*. But when Duveen obtained the original, from the Duke of Westminster, and had it cleaned, Huntington was at first disappointed to find the color blue rather than green as in the imitation.

Duveen bequest to the National Gallery. Paris closed, then London, and faithful Boggis moved the library, stock books, and what little inventory was left after his employer's death to a smaller building on 79th Street, shortly to become the extremely successful Acquavella Galleries, leaders in the sale of Impressionist and Post-Impressionist pictures. Joe's hated main competitors—Wildenstein, Knoedler's, Colnaghi's, Agnew's—are still in business, actively buying and selling in London, Paris, and New York, but the greatest dealer of all time is but a memory. Dorothy died in London in 1987, after returning from her winter home in Jamaica's Montego Bay, a tropical paradise where she embellished her living and dining rooms with plastic flowers.

AGNEW'S

Just as Sir Edward Cecil Guinness's first visit to Duveen Brothers was so significant, it worked the same magic for Agnew's, the Old Bond Street picture dealers who counted the Irish magnate as their most important customer. That fateful dealer-client relationship developed in 1887, some sixty years after the firm had opened its doors.

Sir Edward one day dropped by, unheralded and unannounced, and asked to see Agnew's finest pictures. He had just been rebuffed at a nearby gallery, where a staff member told him that the partners were out to lunch. The more polished Agnew salesman slowly started to bring out fine pictures, strictly against policy, while praying that

BELOW: Thomas Agnew, as portrayed by John Prescott Knight (1803-81). In partnership with the Italian Vittorini Zanetti, Agnew opened his first art gallery in Manchester in the early 19th century.

RIGHT: Here, in Agnew's newly built galleries at 39 (later 43) Old Bond Street, William Agnew, who became known as "the prince of dealers," shows a set of prints to a top-hatted client. Agnew's, like Colnaghi's, sold optical instruments, picture frames, scientific instruments, and even firecrackers and lottery tickets before getting into prints and pictures.

RIGHT BELOW: In the Gilded Age, Bond Street was, as now, the center of London's art trade, where many a masterpiece changed hands, often for shipment to the New World.

his employers would soon come back from their lunch and not fire him on the spot for disobeying orders. When they did return, however, Guinness introduced himself and bought an important Boucher and a Cuyp. Two weeks later he returned and purchased three works by Reynolds and one by Romney. During the next year he bought 78 pictures, 27 in the month of July alone. In all, Guinness acquired 240 pictures and drawings from Agnew's, including 34 by Reynolds, 16 by Romney, and major pictures by Vermeer, Hals, Rembrandt, Greuze, Canaletto, Guardi, Van Dyck, and Claude, among others. Much of Lord Iveagh's collection is today the glory of Kenwood House in Hampstead, while additional pictures remain in the hands of his descendants.

While Joe Duveen would have liked to consider himself a monopolist in masterpieces, he did have some heavy competition, especially from Knoedler's in New York, who not only pursued his super-wealthy pet clients with equal zeal, but also followed Duveen Brothers in their geographical movements around New York City as the art world inevitably migrated uptown. Millions of Americans might stand in lines to collect unemployment insurance and crash-ruined stockbrokers sell apples on street corners, but the newly rich went on furiously competing with one other, driven by rival dealers to pay astronomic prices for Old Master pictures.

MELLON AND FRICK AS COLLECTORS

Andrew Mellon and Henry Clay Frick had a close business and personal relationship. When Frick became a millionaire in 1879 at the age of thirty, he asked Mellon to join him on a trip to Europe to celebrate his inauguration into the pantheon of American success, as well as Mellon's installation as

head of the family bank. The two somewhat reclusive tycoons thus set out with a pair of friends on a trip to Venice via Ireland, London, and Paris. In London both were deeply impressed by the Wallace Collection, and decided that this would form the model for their future collecting. Upon his return, Frick spoke to a friend of how much Americans enjoyed traveling through Europe to see famous pictures, adding: "I am going to try to bring some of them here where all Americans may have the opportunity of seeing them without crossing the ocean."

In 1881 Frick bought his first picture, *In the Louvre* by Luis Jiménez, and for a decade—until the sale of his interests to J.P. Morgan and their amalgamation into United States Steel—he steadily bought a hodgepodge of fashionable Salon pictures to decorate his house in Pittsburgh. As the midwinter gloom settled over the heartland of American industry, the Fricks would sit in their heavy, mahogany-paneled reception rooms and bask in the comfort of these rather lugubrious, yellowing *fin-de-siècle* pastiches. For a few years after the great steel merger, Frick was kept busy with Morgan's giant conglomerate, while Carnegie paid little attention to United States Steel and gave himself

over entirely to philanthropy, setting up libraries around the United States, Ireland, and Great Britain, as well as building his concert hall and universities. After the merger, Frick devoted a third of his time to art, a third to his investments, and a third to philanthropy.

FAR LEFT: An interior at Kenwood House in Hampstead, where Lord Iveagh, Agnew's most important client, would house his fabulous collection.
BELOW: America's two greatest collectors of Old Master art were surely Henry Clay Frick (*far left*) and his friendly banker Andrew Mellon (*seated*), seen here in a rare photograph taken during their tour of Europe together with two friends, the latter brought along for the conversation the taciturn tycoons seemed incapable of. A visit to the Wallace Collection in London inspired Frick and Mellon to build similar institutions at home for the edification of their fellow citizens in the still young United States.
LEFT: By the time Mellon and Frick reached Venice, their party had expanded somewhat, in number if not in madcap gaiety. Even in the world's most voluptuous city, they appear to have remained serious and purposeful.

The palace built on New York's Fifth Avenue at 70th Street by Henry Clay Frick is the grandest of all the Gilded Age mansions now open to the public. Even as the Frick Collection, it retains the aura of a private treasure house. (See also page 120).

RIGHT: Installed in the Du Barry Room is the most important decorative ensemble ever executed by Jean Honoré Fragonard (1732-1806), who painted the wall panels on commission from Madame du Barry for her new dining pavilion at the Château de Louveciennes. By the time the cycle was finished, Louis XV's mistress no longer wanted the pictures, probably because their sparkling Rococo hedonism seemed old-fashioned relative to the rising taste for Neoclassical sobriety, or yet because the lover in the story looked embarrassingly like the King. As a result, Fragonard installed his multipart masterpiece in the home of relatives in Provence, where he took refuge during the French Revolution. J.P. Morgan bought the paintings but left them rolled up, after which his estate sold the entire series to Frick for the intimate room they now glorify, the setting properly enhanced by period furniture and porcelain as well as by a view over Central Park across the street.
BELOW: Frick's paneled Living Hall, filled with superb Renaissance bronzes and El Greco's *Saint Jerome* flanked by Hans Holbein the Younger's portraits of Sir Thomas More and Thomas Cromwell.
OPPOSITE: The Frick Collection's *Wisdom and Strength* by Paolo Veronese allegorizes two essential attributes of the tycoon, at the same time that it epitomizes the rich color and sensuality of Venetian painting at the end of the Renaissance.

In 1905 Frick decided to move to New York City, keeping his large house and a small office in Pittsburgh, and lodged himself comfortably in the George W. Vanderbilt mansion on Fifth Avenue, which he rented for a large sum. Here he hung his ever-growing collection of now mostly démodé pictures, although by 1899 he clearly had a larger purpose in mind—and a close involvement with major dealers who helped him achieve it. In that year he enriched his collection with a Rembrandt and a Nattier, in 1901 with Monet, Turner, Ruisdael, and Vermeer, and in 1902 with Hobbema, Cuyp, and Reynolds. The year Frick moved to New York saw the arrival of a Raeburn, an El Greco, a Van Dyck, and Titian's magnificent portrait of Pietro Arentino (for which he paid $475,000), among other masterpieces. Frick's fortune was about $50 million at the time of the U.S. Steel deal, and the purchase in 1913 of three Gainsboroughs, three Rembrandts, two Guardis, a Van Dyck, and an El Greco must have made a definite dent even in such a large fortune. From Knoedler's alone, Frick bought a total of 229 paintings for $7,350,950 between 1895 and 1916, and that represented slightly more than half of the pictures presently exhibited in the Frick Collection. Considering that this sum does not include the collection's priceless furniture, sculpture, bronzes, and enamels, nor the cost of the splendid, specially commissioned Carrère & Hastings building on Fifth Avenue between 70th and 71st streets, Frick's munificence was truly extraordinary. At his death in 1919 the collection was appraised at $30 million, and he left an endowment of $15 million for its upkeep.

ANDREW MELLON'S BOUNTY

Asked by his old friend John Bowman why he collected art, Andrew Mellon replied: "Every man wants to connect his life with something he thinks eternal. If you turn that over in your mind you will find the answer to your question." Clearly, Mellon had the same preoccupation as his old pal Frick, but he went about it in quite a different way. While Frick bought steadily, gradually refining his taste

BELOW: Andrew Mellon with his son Paul, a passionate collector in his own right and still a chief benefactor of the National Gallery in Washington, D.C., whose president the younger Mellon became in 1963.

RIGHT: One of the signal gifts made to the National Gallery by Andrew Mellon was Vermeer's *The Girl in the Red Hat* (c. 1665). The great banker had long displayed the painting on the piano in his lavish, though rented, apartment on Massachusetts Avenue in Washington, D.C. Mellon's biographer noted that "British and Dutch painters were the ones among whom he found himself most at home—the beautiful English ladies and proud gentlemen of the late eighteenth century and the very human faces of the Dutch masters."

and knowledge, Mellon mostly acquired his collection in great blocks. The ultimate repository of his holdings was the National Gallery of Art, on the Mall in Washington, D.C., whose building Mellon commissioned from John Russell Pope at a cost of $15 million. To the institution he gave an endowment of $5 million and almost 400 major Old Master paintings and 23 important pieces of sculpture. His children, Ailsa and Paul, continued to support the gallery, enriching it with a remarkable collection of Impressionist and modern pictures.

At the opening of the museum in 1937, Mellon's collection was appraised quite modestly at $50 million. The press coverage pointed out that it included "three Raphaels, three Vermeers, eight Rembrandts, four Botticellis, two Masaccios, a Cimabue, a Fra Angelico, a Perugino, and three Titians," before going on to list a glorious roster of practically every

other major artist up to the early nineteenth century. Noticeably missing was a work by Leonardo da Vinci, a master particularly well represented in London's National Gallery, which was Mellon's inspiration for his own monument. The lacuna was corrected nearly forty years later when the gallery purchased, from the Liechtenstein family, Leonardo's portrait of Ginevra de' Benci. Andrew Mellon did not name his museum after himself, and such discretion carried over even into the building's surface material. Convinced that the nation's gallery should be clad in marble, he took pains to choose a special pink stone that did not look like marble in order to avoid gaudiness and ostentation. Yet, when the architects discovered substantial differences in the material's color, the task of matching the enormous blocks emptied several Tennessee quarries at astronomical expense.

Providentially, about the same time that Mellon began buying for his national gallery, the Soviets were on the brink of selling *their* national treasures, and Knoedler's stepped forward to act as middlemen. Throughout the 1920s, the bankrupt Soviet regime (which had not yet even been recognized by most civilized nations) was desperately in need of hard currency, and started dumping oil and the decorative objects they had confiscated from Czarist Russia's landed aristocracy and Imperial family. At boutiques in the Metropol Hotel in Moscow and the Astoria in Leningrad, Fabergé treasures were sold by weight and snapped up by the likes of Marjorie Merriweather Post, who, with her husband Joseph Davies (from 1936 to 1938 the American envoy to the Soviet government), was living in royal style on her great sailing sloop, the *Sea Cloud*, berthed in Leningrad's harbor. In addition, the Soviets sent trains full of what they considered decadent bourgeois rubbish to be auctioned in Berlin. Calouste Gulbenkian, the Armenian collector and petroleum magnate, who handled Russian oil sales abroad, took to offering the Soviets substantial sums for the silver and Old Master pictures in their collections.

On behalf of the Soviets, a German dealer, F. Zatzenstein (who later changed his name to Matthiesen and also ran a gallery in London), contacted Colnaghi's in London, asking them to explore with their American associates the possibility of finding a wealthy collector who would outbid Gulbenkian and who had the means to buy major masterpieces in large quantities for a substantial amount of money. Colnaghi's went to Knoedler's, and the latter went to their most important client, Andrew Mellon, who together with the National Gallery made a very simple deal. The 75-year-old Secretary of the Treasury empowered Knoedler's to purchase for him paintings from the Hermitage for a 25 percent commission. If Mellon decided not to keep certain pictures, Knoedler's would sell them and give him 25 percent of the profit.

Everybody was happy about this major transaction—except Joe Duveen. To be left out of the largest art deal of all time was galling to the salesman extraordinaire, particularly since Duveen had been in Russia to look at the pictures and declined to buy them in view of what he considered the Soviets' excessive greed. This was highly unusual for Duveen, who prided himself in overpaying for the best, and following the Mellon transaction he

Raphael's *Alba Madonna* (c. 1510) was the most important painting bought by Andrew Mellon from the Soviet government during its desperate 1930s campaign to raise hard currency by selling nationalized treasures from the former Czarist collections. The price paid for the *Alba Madonna* made it popularly known as "the million-dollar picture." In all, Mellon acquired 21 masterpieces from the Hermitage, remitting a total of $6,654,000, an astronomical sum at the time. The haul included Botticelli's *Adoration of the Magi*, Raphael's *Saint George and the Dragon*, Titian's *Venus with a Mirror*, four van Dycks, five Rembrandts, and a host of paintings by Rubens, van Eyck, and Frans Hals. And what the legendary purchase failed to provide—paintings by Giorgione and Leonardo da Vinci—would come from other donors, such as Samuel H. Kress, who gave the National Gallery Giorgione's *Adoration of the Magi* in 1939 (see page 147). Then, in 1967, Ailsa Mellon Bruce, Andrew Mellon's daughter and the sister of Paul, purchased for the National Gallery the mysterious portrait of Ginevra da Benci from the Liechtenstein family, in yet another transfer of cultural wealth from European royalty to the New World.

RIGHT: Davis E. Finley, the first director of the National Gallery of Art, and Senator Tom Connelly of Texas listen as the architect John Russell Pope explains his plans for the great museum. Finley had been Andrew Mellon's attorney, while Connelly was the Senator responsible for the legislation allowing the construction of the National Gallery. The building, undoubtedly Pope's masterpiece, emerged from the perfect match of a gifted Beaux-Arts architect with a generous, enlightened patron. Pope also designed Washington's National Archives, Jefferson Memorial, and Scottish Rite Temple, the latter inspired by the Mausoleum at Halicarnassus. In New York, Pope transformed the Frick mansion into the Frick Collection, a public institution. BELOW: The National Gallery's central rotunda, which John Russell Pope based on nothing less than the Pantheon in Rome, articulates the museum's ambitious purpose, doing so in marble and on a grandiose scale. From this rotunda extend the long, lateral wings, a balanced sequence of galleries renowned for their noble proportions and splendid lighting. Neither Pope nor Mellon would live to see the completion of their great project.

did buy the odd masterpiece from the Hermitage. After the Russian deal, Duveen decided to go full speed ahead with the biggest customer in the art market. "Mellon has arrived," he said to a fellow dealer. "Now, he's ready for *me*."

In 1934 Mellon, now retired from the Treasury, was sued by the government for $3,089,000 in back taxes, largely because he had donated more than $3 million of the Hermitage pictures to his own charitable trust, which the government claimed was a tax dodge. They called in Duveen—by then Lord Duveen—as an expert witness, given that he now enjoyed the status of America's pre-eminent dealer. Duveen testified that Mellon's collection was "the finest in the universe," but he also claimed that as early as 1928 he had discussed with Mellon the project of a national gallery. The charges were dropped, but if Mellon had ever harbored doubts about his great project—which is highly unlikely—the die was now cast. Duveen rented an apartment below Mellon's in his building near Dupont Circle in Washington, spent a fortune decorating it in the red velvets and plush that best set off Old Master art, hired a caretaker and guards, filled the flat with all the pictures he felt should go to the nation via Mellon, and went back to New York. The distinguished tycoon, never one to spoil himself, gradually got to prefer Duveen's opulent flat to his own, wandered down in his dressing gown and slippers, and even entertained his guests there. Gradually, he came to love the masterpieces Duveen had casually left him and decided in 1936 to acquire the con-

tents of the apartment lock, stock, and barrel for $21 million, three times what he had paid for the Hermitage loot. Most of the 42 pictures did end up in the National Gallery, as well as most of the Dreyfus collection of Renaissance sculpture, which Duveen had bought in 1930 and sold to Mellon in 1937, the year the collector died. Perhaps Mellon

BELOW: Samuel H. Kress, whose massive fortune derived from a coast-to-coast chain of five-and-dime stores, originally housed his astonishing collection of Italian paintings in the penthouse apartment he occupied on New York's Fifth Avenue. The 1,300 canvases and panels in the collection included major works by Giotto, Duccio, Sassetta, Fra Angelico, Bellini, and Titian among others. Many experts considered the hoard to be the most important private collection of its kind. By contributing it to the National Gallery in Washington, D.C., Kress became the institution's principal donor after Mellon himself, the credit for which was claimed by both Duveen and Davis Finley.

ABOVE: The most important work in the Kress donation may be *The Adoration of the Shepherds* (c. 1505-10), attributed at various times to Giorgione, Titian, and Bellini. Duveen attempted to coerce Berenson into certifying that it was by Giorgione rather than his far more prolific student Titian. This precipitated a final break in the difficult but long and fruitful collaboration between the great dealer and his revered advisor. Kress used to display the painting in the window of his Fifth Avenue store during the Christmas season in order to attract customers. It was as beloved a holiday symbol as the tall tree at nearby Rockefeller Center.

bought en bloc because he felt death approaching and wanted to fill the cavernous gallery, or perhaps the dealer's salesmanship was too strong to resist. At any rate, such was the contribution made by Duveen to Washington's great museum that he came to consider it practically his own. Once Mellon was gone, he pursued the five-and-dime-store magnate, Samuel H. Kress, to perfect his enormous collection and replace Mellon as the leading contributor to the gallery. With this Kress found a new purpose in his old age, and the masterpieces he bestowed upon the museum—including Titian's *Adoration of the Shepherds*, which he enjoyed displaying in the window of his Fifth Avenue shop—beautifully rounded out the collection Mellon had so impulsively collected.

John Pierpont Morgan was the most important art collector of his time, no mean feat considering the competition both in the United States and abroad. Moreover, he began collecting only at the age of 53. Then, as Aline Saarinen wrote: "He meant to gather for America an undreamed-of collection of art so great and complete that a trip to Europe would be superfluous."
BELOW: With his encyclopedic range of interests, Morgan recruited a bevy of excellent advisors, the most influential of whom was his curator, Belle da Costa Green, here portrayed in a drawing by the fashionable French artist Paul Helleu.
FAR RIGHT: At one time, Morgan kept most of his art treasures in his London mansion.

ABOVE RIGHT: The original Morgan Library on Madison Avenue and 36th Street, a fine Beaux-Arts structure designed by McKim, Mead & White and conceived as an annex to the Morgan's own house. For a prototype of this Renaissance palace of 1902, the architects looked to the Villa Giulia in Rome.
OPPOSITE: Among the great paintings collected by J.P. Morgan was Raphael's *Madonna and Child Enthroned, with Saints*, now in the Metropolitan Museum of Art.

J.P. MORGAN AS COLLECTOR

When the famed banker J.P. Morgan died in 1913, more than half of his estate consisted of rare books, paintings, and works of art. Morgan's collecting, like that of Mellon and Frick, started only later in life, following the death of his father, Junius. Already 53 years old, he had received an impressive classical education both in Europe and the United States, and held wide interests that would be reflected in his collecting. Such was the scale of his purchases and the intermingling of his and the bank's funds that on occasion there were temporary cash shortages at the great institution. As his wife put it, Morgan would "buy anything from a pyramid to the tooth of Mary Magdalene," the latter being housed in a magnificent reliquary at the Metropolitan Museum of Art, whose board chairman he became in 1904. On one trip to Paris in 1906, he spent $750,000 on objets d'art, and he financed almost single-handedly the excavations carried out by the Metropolitan in Egypt, where he kept a large and comfortable dahabiah for cruising on the Nile.

Morgan was guided by an extremely bright young curator, Belle da Costa Greene, who continued to work at the Morgan Library for nearly a quarter-century after the founder's death. She came to be feared as well as respected by the long line of dealers at the door on 36th Street and, even more so, at the collector's London house at Prince's Gate, overlooking Hyde Park, where most of the collection was kept. The objects on display were so magnificent, and their renown so universal, that King Edward VII requested an invitation to visit.

In 1909, the possibility of death duties in Britain compelled Morgan to ship his hoard to New York, where the public would see it for the first time. He hoped to create in Manhattan "a greater museum than anyone at that time dreamed it was possible to realize, and a library that would go down in history as comparing favorably to the Vatican, the Laurentian Library in Florence, and the most sumptuous assemblage of rare books in Paris, London, and Vienna." As president of the Metropolitan Museum and its guiding force, Morgan went far toward achieving the first part of his dream. He wanted the

RIGHT: In its early days, the Metropolitan Museum of Art in New York City became a virtual fiefdom of J.P. Morgan. Trustee in 1888 and chairman of the board in 1904, the great financier chose the museum's directors, packed its board, and controlled the staff. Shortly before his death in 1913, he arranged for almost the whole of his vast collection to be exhibited there.

BELOW: Despite his failure to have a wing added to the Met as a home for his collection, Morgan bequeathed to the institution many a treasure, including this 13th-century silver and cabochon reliquary head of Saint Yrieix from Limoges.

entire collection to be permanently installed at the Metropolitan, but, in one of the greatest blunders in its history, the city refused to allocated funds for a special wing needed to house it. Largely as a consequence, Morgan left the disposition of one of the finest, and certainly the most interesting, collections of all time to his son, John Pierpont Morgan II (called Jack). Eventually, however, the Metropolitan received over 4,000 pieces from the Morgan estate, a legacy that is the backbone of the museum's renowned medieval department.

The Wadsworth Atheneum in Hartford, Connecticut, where Pierpont was born, also received Morgan treasures, while others were sold to benefit growing art collections both in the United States and abroad. Frick bought the Renaissance bronzes as well as the Fragonard panels made for Madame du Barry, and Ghirlandaio's portrait of Giovanna Tornabuoni, Morgan's favorite painting, became the favorite painting of Baron Thyssen in Lugano. Still further Morgan pictures, following their acquisition by such collectors as John G. Johnson, Benjamin Altman, Robert Lehman, and Andrew Mellon, would subsequently enter the Thyssen collection, the Metropolitan, the National Gallery in Washington, and the Philadelphia Museum of Art.

Morgan's dream of a great library would nevertheless be realized, and this alone seems to be a sufficient monument to the greatest financier of modern times. Had the collection survived intact, however, it could have proudly stood comparison with the agglomerations of the Renaissance princes whom J.P. Morgan justly considered his peers.

One of the most admired works in the Morgan Library, a museum famous for its illuminated manuscripts, is the 9th-century *Lindau Gospel*, a Swiss codex named for a monastery in Germany. The repoussé gold cover studded with precious stones suggests the veneration in which this Gospel was held. After Morgan bought it in 1899, for £10,000, the *Lindau Gospel* became the first building block of a legendary collection that includes illustrated scientific and medical books, bestiaries, first editions, splendid individual leaves of medieval illumination, master drawings, and holograph music scores. Thanks to his classical education at the University of Göttingen, Morgan had the intellectual capacity to savor his collection in all its richness. Indeed, he spent even longer hours studying the books and manuscripts than he did assembling them.

LE STYLE ROTHSCHILD

While American tycoons, as a rule, went after a mélange of Italian Renaissance works of art for their walls, English country-house style for their dining rooms, and eighteenth-century French taste for their salons and the bedrooms of their wives, an important group of European parvenus immersed themselves almost entirely in the bucolic, ultra-refined, and civilized world of eighteenth-century France. For these collectors, furniture and objets d'art of the *dix-huitième siècle* were safe, fashionable, and elegant, and collecting as well as decorating with them an appropriate manner to display wealth. They made a tasteful ensemble, but also an impressive one: shiny, curvilinear, gilded, orna-

mented, and beautiful. Royal support of the Sèvres and Vincennes porcelain manufacturers, the Gobelins tapestry workshops, and literally an army of *ébénistes, bronziers, ciseleurs*, and *orfèvriers*, all brought together by the *marchands-merciers*, made possible the most brilliant expression ever achieved in the decorative arts. Under the ancien régime, a flood of orders came to Paris from Catherine the Great by way of Voltaire, from Frederick the Great for Schloss Charlottenburg and Sans Souci, and from a large, rich French aristocracy. The breakup of France's royal and noble collections came with the Revolution of 1789-94, and the first big buyers were English grandees who got Bourbon furniture for a song from the bloodthirsty mob that had rea-

son to hate every Rococo curve. The next largest clients, beginning in the mid-nineteenth century, were the Rothschilds.

The Family have always been extremely secretive about their collecting, although a few Rothschilds commissioned illustrated catalogues for private circulation. The second generation—particularly Baron James in Paris—were already substantial accumulators, but due to many intermarriages, treasures did not always follow a straight line of succession. Notwithstanding, if put together even today, the Family holdings of masterpieces of French eighteenth-century decorative arts would dwarf that of any of the world's great museums. *Le goût Rothschild*, which characterized all their houses, was what French kings would have loved far more than Versailles, since it combined the most splendid of their coveted treasures with the ulti-

mate in modern comfort. Instead of cold and windy reception rooms, priceless Savonneries lay on heavy red carpets, thick damask curtains absorbed the chill, and comfortable upholstered sofas and armchairs offered an alternative to stiff-backed *sièges à la reine*. Rothschild houses were filled with cabinets full of Sèvres pink or green elephant vases, Limoges enamels, jewel-studded *tabatières* (snuffboxes) and presentation boxes, among other delights that had cost Marie Antoinette her head.

The best place in which the public can bask in Rothschildian splendor is Waddesdon Manor in Buckinghamshire, which passed to the National Trust, courtesy the recently deceased Dorothy de Rothschild. In Paris, however, there are many museums in the style of nearly equivalent quality that preserve the collections and lifestyles of such splendid collectors as Count Moïse Nissim de

Waddesdon Manor in Buckinghamshire houses treasures from several Rothschild collections, thanks in part to the Family's penchant for intermarriage. Baron Ferdinand, the builder of Waddesdon and a great collector, was the son of Baron Anselm of Paris, who had married a daughter of Nathan Rothschild, the title-spurning founder of the English Rothschilds. The childless Ferdinand left the estate to his sister Alice, a spinster who in turn bequeathed it to her grand nephew Jimmy (ABOVE), the son of Baron Edmond, another renowned collector, this one the Paris-based son of Nathan Rothschild who had married the only daughter of Baron James, the founder of the French branch of the Family.
OPPOSITE: The Red Drawing Room at Waddesdon Manor is a perfect example of what became known as *le goût Rothschild*. This means sumptuously upholstered Gilded Age interiors containing, as here, a Royal Savonnerie carpet, Louis XV *sièges à la reine* covered in Gobelins tapestry, a Riesener commode from Versailles, Sèvres vases on a Louis XV carved-marble fireplace, and portraits by Thomas Gainsborough on brocaded walls.
LEFT: Among the emulators of Rothschild taste was Moïse Nissim de Camondo, whose small salon in Paris is now part of a museum open, like Waddesdon, to the public.

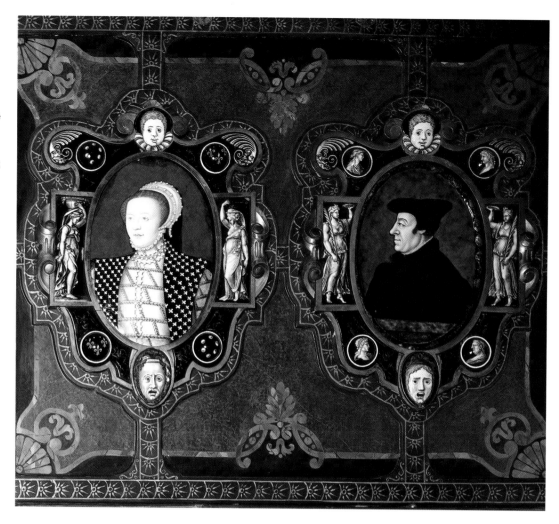

OPPOSITE: Ingres's portrait of Betty de Rothschild, the beautiful niece and wife of Baron James, the founder of the French Rothschilds, remains in the collection of her direct descendant, Baron Guy. A great patroness of the arts, Baroness Betty invited Chopin to play in her salon, befriended Heine, and became an intimate of both Queen Amélie, the consort of the Orléanist monarch Louis-Philippe, and Empress Eugénie, wife of the parvenu Emperor Napoleon III. She also helped form the family collections, which would begin with Goya, Rembrandt, and Vermeer.
RIGHT: These splendid Limoges enamels are part of the collection assembled by Baron Édouard de Rothschild, the father of the present Baron Guy.
BELOW: Another passion of the Rothschilds was 18th-century French furniture, especially items of royal provenance. During the German Occupation of France (1940-44), Field Marshall Goering launched a campaign to round up as much Rothschild loot as possible, storing it in a German castle against the day when he could furnish Karinhall and his other residences.

Camondo, Jules Marmottan, Henri Cernuschi, Adolphe d'Ennery, Édouard André and Nélie Jacquemart, and Ernest Cognacq (and his wife, Louise Jay), owner of La Samaritaine, who actually made his treasures one of the attractions of that large and popular department store.

Many new collectors of eighteenth-century French furniture and decorative arts covered their walls with contemporaneous paintings by Boucher, Fragonard, Greuze, Lancret, Chardin, and others that were mostly obtained from the venerable firm founded by Nathan Wildenstein in Paris in the 1870s. The scholarly Wildenstein was, in fact, largely responsible for rehabilitating eighteenth-century French painting, which, since the Revolution, had come to be considered superficial, frivolous, and lacking in strength or conviction, and the firm has never ceased to be linked in collectors' minds to the period. Notwithstanding, Nathan also sold masterpieces of Dutch, Flemish, and Italian paintings in Paris and later in New York, where he opened a gallery in 1902. This was run by his talented son, Georges, who inherited the mantle of his father as one of the greatest experts on French painting and, until his death in 1963, ruled over large and elaborate selling palaces built in the eighteenth-century style on the Rue de la Boëtie in Paris, East 64th Street in New York, and New Bond Street in London, as well as in Buenos Aires and Johannesburg. Part of the Wildenstein tradition is holding on to treasures for decades, and nobody really knows what lies hidden in the family's secret bomb-proof shelters somewhere in the mountains of the American West. As a result, the Wildensteins are not only far richer today than most of their clients; they are the leading art dealership still in family hands.

COLLECTORS OF THE NEW

Frick, Morgan, Mellon, Kress, Altman, Widener, and company all looked back in time. They used their vast wealth to emulate the princes of the past and to buy immortality. In the main aloof, reserved, and impeccably turned out, theirs was a world somewhat at odds with the times in which they lived. While string quartets played in their private picture galleries, Diaghilev and Stravinsky were shocking Paris with *Le Sacre du Printemps*, and Picasso was reinventing pictorial art with *Les Demoiselles d'Avignon*. Impressionism passed them by, as did Post-Impressionism, Fauvism, and Cubism. Duveen steered his charges clear of "modern painting," and the nearest most of them got to the art of their times was Manet and Corot, the latter not so far from the Barbizon School to be unsafe to hang. And yet, there were a few exceptions to the rule among the parvenus, a small and open-minded group of men and women who were willing to look beyond the established galleries into the more vibrant—and often ruder—world of the artist's studio, particularly in Paris, the center of the avant-garde.

The main defender of the Impressionists was Paul Durand-Ruel, the son of Jean Durand-Ruel, a Paris purveyor of stationery and artist's supplies who had fallen into art dealing as a sideline, exchanging his stock against the paintings of struggling artists. He eventually divided the two flourishing activities and opened a shop on the Rue de la Paix, with colors and canvas on the first floor and a popular exhibition space on the second. The pillars of the gallery were Théodore Rousseau, Dupré, Diaz, and Millet, all Barbizon masters who were still not overly appreciated in the 1850s.

Paul assumed control of the gallery when his father died in 1865, traveled extensively abroad selling pictures, and soon realized enough success to be a major force in the Paris art market, bidding

Paul Durand-Ruel, the courageous Parisian art dealer who courted bankruptcy in order to support the Impressionists, not only in Paris but in London and New York as well. Finally, his American clients saved him from ruin, just as his sales to them would eventually become the glory of such major American museums as the Metropolitan and Chicago's Art Institute.

up at auction the prices of the artists he supported. "To keep prices up," he explained, "you must never be in a hurry to sell and be ready to bid at sales for works by your artists." After the start of the Franco-Prussian War, he moved most of his stock to London and hung it at a gallery on 159 New Bond Street. In January 1871, Daubigny introduced him to the struggling, largely unknown Monet, who was painting his renowned series devoted to the Thames and the Houses of Parliament, after which Durand-Ruel purchased several of his pictures as well as those of Pissarro, who was also in London at the time. Between 1870 and 1875, he organized ten London exhibitions of the work of Manet, Monet, Sisley, Pissarro, and Degas, along with such older favorites as Diaz, Isabey, Ziem, and Cabanel. In 1873, on a visit to Manet's studio, he bought 23 pictures for 35,000 francs and returned a few days later for another lot, including a masterpiece, *La Musique aux Tuileries*. Everyone thought him mad, and to meet his obligations Durand-Ruel was forced to sell at a loss the by then far more popular paintings of Corot, Delacroix, and Millet.

Durand-Ruel persevered, living from hand to mouth as he went on organizing unsuccessful Impressionist shows in London, Boston, Rotterdam, and Berlin. Then, in March 1886, while already over 1 million francs in debt, he accepted an invitation from the American Art Association and crossed the Atlantic with some 300 Impressionist canvases for exhibition in New York. Americans would prove far more receptive to the new than Europeans, and Durand-Ruel decided to open a permanent gallery in New York, which became his salvation. He satisfied his creditors, and in 1888, after returning to France a rich man, he could finally create a serious market for the immortal artists he had courageously supported, despite all odds. "If I had died at sixty," he once said, "I should have been insolvent; my estate would have been a mountain of debts and unappreciated and unsaleable art-masterpieces." Instead, he was the savior of the Impressionists, and his galleries and warehouse—not to mention his clients' salons—were filled with finally admired, eminently marketable masterpieces.

THE UNITED STATES DISCOVERS IMPRESSIONISM

It was at Durand-Ruel's avant-garde gallery that Mary Cassatt (1844-1926) first encountered the art of Manet, Courbet, and Degas. The talented young painter had left Philadelphia in 1868 to pursue a career as an artist in Europe. Her father was horrified at the idea of his refined daughter engaging in *la vie de bohème*, but, well-chaperoned, she traveled throughout Europe for six years, studying the Old Masters and developing her skills before settling in Paris in 1874. The great Degas took Cassatt under his wing in 1877, and, with him as her

LEFT: Claude Monet (1840-1926), *On the Seine at Bennecourt*, 1868 (Art Institute of Chicago). This landmark painting in the history of Impressionism, with its magical sense of both flatness and depth, was one of the many works by Monet that the Potter Palmers bought for their castellated house on Chicago's Lake Shore Drive.

FAR LEFT: Mary Cassatt, *The Cup of Tea*, 1879 (Metropolitan Museum of Art, New York City). Chaperoned by her mother or sister, the highborn, thoroughly genteel Mary Cassatt abandoned Philadelphia for Paris and the avant-garde world of the Impressionists. While sharing in their aesthetic experiments as well as in their revolutionary exhibitions, Cassatt also urged her wealthy, conservative family and friends back home to invest in Impressionist art, at a time when Europeans would generally tolerate nothing more challenging than Barbizon.

BELOW: The heavily rusticated neo-Romanesque castle built by the Potter Palmers on Chicago's Lake Shore Drive. However retardataire her taste in architecture, Berthe Potter Palmer was daringly avant-garde in her art collecting. After a visit with Monet, she bought so many of his canvases that the pictures ended up making a frieze around the ballroom in the great picturesque fortress seen here.

lodestar, she became a significant figure in the Impressionist movement, with close artistic and professional ties to Monet, Renoir, Berthe Morisot, Pissarro, and Sisley. She shared their intellectual ferment in the cafés and ateliers of Montmartre; equally important, she bought their paintings for herself and her brother Alexander. Moreover, she introduced her rich American friends, in particular Mrs. Potter Palmer and the Henry O. Havemeyers, to Durand-Ruel in Paris and New York. Finally, it was the Havemeyers' purchase of forty Impressionist paintings at the New York gallery (incidentally situated in a building the sugar king owned) that saved the dealer and in effect launched Impressionism.

Berthe Potter Palmer came most glitteringly into her own during her reign over the 1893 World's Columbian Exposition, which brought to Chicago all the excitement of the universal expositions that had earlier mesmerized large crowds in London and Paris. One of the largest pavilions was the Fine Arts Palace, which had an important exhibition entitled "Foreign Masterpieces Owned by Americans." Among the lenders were Cornelius Vanderbilt, Alfred Corning Clark, Jay Gould, John G. Johnson, and William H. Crocker. As might be expected, their contributions included a number of Barbizon pictures. But for the first time in such an official setting there were paintings by Manet, Pissarro, Sisley, and Degas, lent, for the most part, by Alexander Cassatt, the Havemeyers, and the Palmers, who had bought the works largely under the guidance of the first American Impressionist, Mary Cassatt.

Chicago was, in every way, a Francophile city. Its great retailing emporiums featured Paris fashions; its manufacturers exhibited their equipment in France's international expositions; and its newly rich citizens were better received in Paris than in New York, where their way was blocked by Caro-

RIGHT: It was in this elaborately Rococo salon—in a Moscow palace once owned by the princely Troubetskoy family—that the Muscovite merchant prince Sergei Shchukin hung many of the 37 Matisses he would own by the time the Bolshevik Revolution put a stop to private enterprise in Russia. FAR RIGHT: Pierre-Auguste Renoir (1841-1919), *Nude*, 1876 (Pushkin Museum, Moscow). Ivan Morozov, a wealthy Muscovite textile industrialist, collected the paintings of Impressionists like Renoir as well as the works of the Post-Impressionists, especially Bonnard. He also acquired several of Matisse's Moroccan pictures, but then balked at the radicalism of Picasso.

line Astor and Ward McAllister. In Paris they became major clients of the art galleries, beginning with Berthe Potter Palmer, who, in 1891, visited Monet in his studio and bought her first of many paintings by this master. Eventually there were enough of them to make a frieze around her ballroom. She visited Whistler in Rome, and purchased major paintings from Renoir in his Paris studio, including two undisputed masterpieces, *Luncheon of the Boating Party* and *Two Little Circus Girls*, for all of $1,750. Monet's *Argenteuil-sur-Seine* cost her $1,500, and she acquired three Pissarros for $650. Most of these works ended up at the Chicago Art Institute, of which she was a munificent benefactor. Other Chicago millionaires, such as Martin A. Ryerson, followed in her tracks, buying many Impressionist paintings that would also enrich Chicago's finest museum. Again at the urging of Mary Cassatt, H.O. Havemeyer delved heavily into Spanish painting, purchasing highly important El Grecos and Goyas that, along with the Havemeyer Impressionists, are among the most salient splendors of the Metropolitan Museum of Art.

It is fair to say that Americans were far ahead of Europeans in patronizing the Impressionists and their followers. The wives of nineteenth-century tycoons got the same excitement out of visiting the ateliers of Renoir, Degas, and Pissarro as today's newly rich do from touring the lofts of New York's East Village. In later years, it was the adventurous Americans Gertrude and Leo Stein who first caught on to Matisse and Picasso, and it was the bearded and scholarly dealer, Ambroise Vollard, who helped

launch the avant-garde masters of twentieth-century art just as Durand-Ruel had served the Impressionists. As a result Vollard, as well as Gertrude Stein, played crucial roles in one of the great collecting adventures of the twentieth century, undertaken by a few parvenu Russian merchant princes.

THE MERCHANT PRINCES

Long hidden away in the reserves of the Hermitage in St. Petersburg and the Pushkin Museum in Moscow was one of the most amazing collections ever amassed of Impressionist, Post-Impressionist, and early twentieth-century avant-garde painting. It comprised hundreds of masterpieces by such revolutionary modernists as Matisse, Picasso, and Braque, all executed prior to the Russian Revolution of 1917, but soon thereafter deemed antithetical to the revolutionary spirit as redefined by the paranoid Soviet Union. One paradox was that these very paintings had been the inspiration of the artists of the Revolution itself—Russian Expressionists, Suprematists, and Constructivists such as Kandinsky, Malevich, Tatlin, Popova, Rosanova, and Rodchenko—-whose art later also came to be buried under the long Stalinist dictatorship. Equally paradoxical was the fact that the bulk of these extraordinary works had been collected by two solid, bourgeois businessmen—Ivan Morozov (1871-1921) and Sergei Ivanovich Shchukin (1854-1937)—whose appetite for the most advanced art in Paris surged years ahead of that of their contemporaries in Europe.

Ivan Morozov was the major collector of Pierre Bonnard's work in Russia, and he even commissioned the artist to do an important series of decorative panels for his Moscow house, enhancing the thirteen Bonnards already there. A great admirer of Maurice Denis, Ivan commissioned the Nabis master to create a suite of thirteen decorative panels for his music room, and Denis came to Moscow in 1909 to supervise their installation. They complemented several of the artist's major paintings that Morozov had already purchased on trips to Paris. During one visit to the French capital in 1907, he bought three important Tahitian Gauguins from Vollard, Monet's *Landscape with Grainstacks,* and Renoir's *Under the Arbor at the Moulin de la Galette,* as well as three major Cézannes, later joined by ten other splendid paintings of this key modernist. Ivan also acquired a Henri-Edmond Cross landscape and several Van Goghs, including his *Café at Arles* and *Night Café.* There was hardly a picture that would not be the pride of a serious museum, and the scale of Ivan's collecting of modern art was equivalent in every way to Andrew Mellon's purchases of Old Masters

a few decades later. Morozov bought several Moroccan landscapes and the occasional still life by Matisse, but found Picasso's work difficult to understand.

It was Sergei Ivanovich Shchukin who introduced Morozov to Matisse and Picasso in 1908. By this time the most important collector of these two pivotal twentieth-century masters, Shchukin was Matisse's most devoted patron and the only person ever to own more Picassos than the artist himself. Even today, no collector of modern art has matched either the quantity or the quality of the modernist works amassed by this merchant prince before 1914. The Shchukins, like the Morozovs, had made their fortune in textiles, and Sergei Ivanovich too was part of an immense clan. He had five brothers and five sisters, and all the boys were brought up to be part of the family business. Sergei Ivanovich often visited Paris, attended to the family business, and, at his brother's extravagant house on the Avenue Wagram, met leading figures of the art world, such as Rodin, Degas, and the Durand-Ruels. He also saw Lenin, who kept up with intellectual Russian exiles in the Shchukin Paris salon. It was on one of these visits that Sergei began to collect, rather conservatively buying the works of Zuloaga, Burne-Jones, Whistler, and Courbet.

Soon Shchukin was drawn into the more adventurous world of Gauguin and Cézanne, which led to the Durand-Ruel gallery, where he made his initial purchase of a "modern" picture, Claude Monet's *Lilacs at Argenteuil,* the first work of the Impressionist master to arrive in Russia. He would acquire, in a short period, thirteen works by Monet, including two versions of the *Cathedral at Rouen,* sixteen Gauguins, five works by Degas, sixteen of Derain's finest pictures (many of them from his

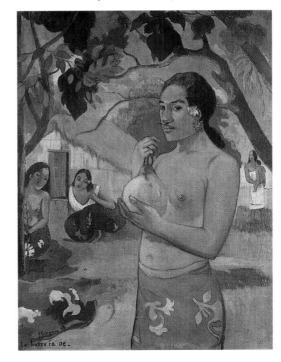

LEFT: Gertrude Stein in the courtyard pavilion at 27 Rue de Fleurus in Paris, where she received almost everyone in the world—writers, artists, composers, intellectuals, industrialists, bankers, collectors—interested in the modern and the experimental. With her brother Leo, Stein collected Matisse and Picasso at such an early date that the two artists might very well not have survived without the Americans' support. It was in the Rue de Fleurus that Sergei Shchukin saw Matisse's *Joy of Life* (now in the Barnes Collection, Philadelphia) and an oil sketch of *Music,* which together inspired him to commission two large murals entitled simply *Danse* and *Musique,* which Matisse would deliver in 1910 (see page 160). BELOW: Paul Gauguin (1848-1903), *Rave te hiti ramu,* 1898 (Hermitage, St. Petersburg). This was one of the three Gauguins that the daring Russian collector Ivan Morozov bought from Vollard during a visit to Paris in 1907.

BELOW: Henri Matisse (1869-1954), *La Desserte rouge*, 1908 (Hermitage, St. Petersburg). This extraordinarily rich variation on the Fauve aesthetic of wildly heightened color and liberated drawing held great appeal for the Russian collector Sergei Shchukin, who as a manufacturer and importer of textiles shared Matisse's love of all-over pattern and design. Nothing could be more expressive of the artist's lifelong theme, taken from a poem by Charles Baudelaire: *luxe, calme et volupté*.

RIGHT: Henri Matisse, *La Danse II*, 1909-10 (Hermitage, St. Petersburg). Emboldened by Matisse's most advanced art, Sergei Shchukin commissioned this "mural" painting, together with *Musique*, for the grand staircase of his 18th-century mansion in Moscow. In *La Danse II*, Matisse vastly enlarged and simplified the arabesque pattern of *La Desserte rouge*, at the same time that he also humanized the abstract result by translating pattern into figuration.

Fauve period), nine Marquets, four Van Goghs, and eight Cézannes. Shchukin seldom followed any advice, going through a dealer's entire stock and picking those works that struck his extraordinary eye. "If a picture gives you a psychological shock," he was fond of saying, "buy it. It's a good one." This was an amazing aesthetic for a bourgeois Muscovite merchant who started collecting only late in life. With such an open mind, it is not surprising that he was highly receptive to the work of both Matisse and Picasso, and it was his patronage of these artists that made history.

Shchukin first encountered Matisse's painting at what became the scandalous *Fauve* ("Wild Beast") Salon d'Automne of 1905. He reacted by making a studio visit to the "King of the Fauves"—so-called for the "wild" intensity and freshness of his colors and drawing—the visit arranged by Ambroise Vollard. He bought the first of his 37 Matisses, which were eventually hung together in a special salon of the Troubetskoy Palace in Moscow, an immense eighteenth-century mansion that Sergei's father had acquired from the cash-starved descendants of one of Russia's most aristocratic and snobbish families. They would have been horrified by the avant-garde pictures filling their walls as well as the textile depot built in the courtyard. The Shchukins changed practically nothing, leaving the eighteenth-century frescoes on the high ceilings, the damasks on the walls, the silk curtains on the elegant French windows, and the Oriental carpets on the parquet floors. In the Troubetskoys' elaborate rooms, chock-a-block with daring works from the School of Paris, the Shchukin family gave elaborate dinners and private concerts, with an amazing mixture of diplomats, aristocrats, artists, critics, intellectuals, and politicians. Rachmaninoff played, Chaliapin sang, quartets and occasionally a symphony orchestra performed works by Bach, Beethoven, and Mozart.

Shchukin's most daring plunge came with Picasso. While in Paris, it was inevitable that he would visit Leo and Gertrude Stein and be sought out by Daniel-Henry Kahnweiler, the avant-garde dealer for Picasso and other Cubists, who was making the same sacrifice for his artists as the Durand-Ruels had for the Impressionists a few decades earlier. Arranged by Vollard, the first meeting of the elegantly dressed, conservative merchant prince with the sandaled American expatriates in the Rue de Fleurus must have been quite strange. Yet, the Steins' salon was, in a curious, modest way, the Paris equivalent of the Troubetskoy Palace, for the siblings had drawn together in one place much the same mixture of painters, poets, collectors, intellectuals, politicians, and celebrities. Their far smaller walls were also double-hung with masterpieces by Cézanne, Braque, and Picasso, among others, which must have made the merchant prince feel oddly at home. The Vollard-Kahnweiler-Stein axis carried Shchukin on to the cutting edge of the Paris art scene; in fact, it was at the Steins that he saw Matisse's *Joy of Life* as well as an oil sketch of *Music* and conceived the idea of commissioning the two large now-historic murals entitled *Musique* and *Danse* for his Moscow palace.

Until 1914, Shchukin was Picasso's most loyal client, especially so once the artist fell into disfavor with his small circle of supporters, appalled as they were in 1907 by *Les Demoiselles d'Avignon*. The Russian Maecenas had an opportunity to buy the picture, but, like many of the faithful, he believed Picasso had now gone too far. Otherwise, what may be *the* watershed picture of the twentieth century would have ended up in Moscow, hidden away from the public for nearly half a century. Still, during the next seven years Shchukin became Picasso's chief patron, and even Kahnweiler admitted that almost no one else, other than Gertrude Stein, was buying his work. The Picasso collection hung in a small and, appropriately, undecorated room of the Troubetskoy palace, which became a pilgrimage site for every

venturesome Russian artist as soon as Shchukin began opening the house to the public on Sundays.

After the 1917 Revolution, Shchukin sent his wife and daughter out of Russia and stayed behind, largely to protect the collection. Arrested by the Bolsheviks, he was told that his fortune exceeded 30 million gold rubles, to which he replied, rather elegantly: "I didn't know I was so rich." A group of anarchists broke into Ivan Morozov's house and slept, drank, and gambled amidst the Gauguins and Cézannes. The experience so unnerved the great collector that very shortly he went into a severe physical and psychological decline. A.V. Lunacharsky, the charismatic new Minister of Culture, informed both merchant princes that their holdings were state property and would be administered by the People's Commissariat for Enlightenment. Making the best of it, Shchukin moved into the caretaker's lodge, while both he and his daughter served as guides to the collection until they left for Paris in 1918. Morozov followed soon thereafter, living off a small bank account he had maintained in Berlin to pay for pictures. The Troubetskoy Palace became the First Museum of Modern Western Painting and Morozov's palace the Second, and thousands of forward-looking art lovers poured through the doors to see the great pictures they had heard so much about. In exile Shchukin kept up with the artists whose work he had left behind—Matisse, Picasso, and Renoir, among others—while Morozov sank into an ever-growing isolation until his death in 1921. In 1928 the two collections were brought together in one location, Morozov's former home. Although for many years kept in the dark by Stalinist disapproval, today they are proudly exhibited in the Hermitage in St. Petersburg and in Moscow's Pushkin Museum.

FAR LEFT: Pablo Picasso (1881-1973), *Acrobat with a Ball*, 1904-05 (Pushkin Museum, Moscow).
ABOVE: Pablo Picasso, *Portrait of Ambroise Vollard*, 1910 (Pushkin Museum, Moscow). When Picasso moved in a mere five years from his deeply poetic, soulful works of the Rose Period, such as the painting at the far left, to the largely monochromatic, fractured syntax of Analytic Cubism, he left the 19th century behind and created the lingua franca of 20th-century art. Thanks to Vollard and his fellow dealer Kahnweiler, Sergei Shchukin joined Gertrude Stein and a handful of others in following Picasso through his momentous invention of high-modernist art.

TRAVEL

In a period of less than forty years, between 1850 and 1890, travel attained a pinnacle of comfort and luxury that has never been equaled. Most of Europe's grand hotels were built, serving guests who arrived by the recently constructed rail lines. Not only did these crisscross the United States as well as Europe, they would soon stretch beyond Russia to the far reaches of Siberia, linking the West to Asia by train. In Europe, engineers tunneled through the Alps. They also spanned great rivers and gorges with concrete and steel bridges, the effect of which was to couple Edinburgh to far-off Palermo and everything in between. This, in turn, vastly enlarged the exchange of goods and people. Long-distance travel along the rails fostered the sleeping car and luxury train, thanks to George Pullman and Georges Nagelmackers. Meanwhile, the steam engine, and later the turbine, allowed shipbuilders to expand the size and increase the speed of steel-hulled ships, giving birth to the modern ocean liner.

Easy and comfortable travel spawned the development of new resorts and spas as well as the opulent casinos of Baden-Baden and the South of France. For the super-rich this golden age of travel meant private railway cars, seaworthy steam yachts, large suites (including private dining rooms and servant quarters) on ocean liners, long stays in palatial hotels, and active participation in international society. The descendants of tycoons, with little to do but spend their inherited fortunes, could now contemplate getting away from the cold winter by taking a trip up the Nile, shooting big game in Africa, visiting maharajas in India, or simply being social in Palm Beach, gambling in Monte Carlo, walking on Nice's Promenade des Anglais, or visiting volcanoes and Greek temples in Sicily. For the more athletic there were the new mountain resorts where skiing was about to become a popular sport. Today's "jet set" could very well find a true ancestor in the *fin de siècle*'s "steamer set," whose members regulated their lives around "sea-

OPPOSITE: The title of this assembly of images from an 1897 issue of *The Illustrated London News* tells the whole story: "Triumph of Steam and Electricity." Contrasting the old and the new, together with portraits of the latter's inventors, the artist made clear how steam and electricity would power more capacious and faster transport as well as better illuminated streets, houses, and hotels.
ABOVE: Thanks to advanced technology, the Gilded Age could enjoy the new phenomenon called "resorts," such as Monte Carlo, places now reachable within hours or days rather than the weeks required before the advent of steam and electricity.
LEFT: Once the new mobility made Monte Carlo possible, the Gilded Age could amuse itself there by gambling away fortunes in high, melodramatic style, as staged here in a painting by Christian Ludwig Bokelman (1844-94).

BELOW: Luxury on the rails was invented in the United States, where the sheer vastness of the land motivated Americans to discover rapid, efficient, and comfortable ways to link their nation together.

FREE
OF EXTRA CHARGE

THE NEWEST & BEST
PALACE RECLINING CHAIR CARS
ARE RUN IN ALL THROUGH TRAINS
VIA

CHICAGO & ALTON R.R.
FREE OF EXTRA CHARGE

FROM CHICAGO TO
ST. LOUIS AND
KANSAS CITY.

FRANK BOWMAN, Traveling Passenger Agent,
668 Broadway, ALBANY, N. Y.

ABOVE RIGHT: In Europe, luxury travel provided a crucial inducement to take in the world's fairs that began with London's Great Exhibition of 1851.

FAR RIGHT: To recover from its increasingly good life, the Gilded Age could travel by luxury train to such newly developed, fashionable spas as Carlsbad, here photographed in the 1870s.

sons" during which old and new money came together in various playgrounds according to the time of the year. Needless to say, everybody would have been far less peripatetic if luxury travel had not evolved.

The pioneer of modern railway travel was George Mortiner Pullman. Born in Brockton, New York, in 1831, Pullman parlayed one luxurious private sleeping car into a vast enterprise that finally allowed Americans to cross their great continental expanse in relative ease. For the super-rich, he produced personal railway cars that were either attached to trains on their regular runs or coupled in tandem with other private cars on to a special engine. It was such a multicar train that J.P. Morgan chartered for a group of Episcopal clergymen traveling from New York to San Francisco. One car possessed a domed Tiffany skylight under which the gentlemen received their morning shaves in leather barber chairs; another constituted an elegant dining room; still others provided saloons for chatting and a rolling-stock chapel. Goulds, Vanderbilts, Goelets, and Stanfords all had their own multi-carriage trains that transported them, their families, and guests across the country. The pennywise Morgan either chartered a train from Pullman or borrowed one from his railroad clients. Pullman's main competitor in this highly lucrative industry was the Vanderbilt-controlled Wagner Palace Car Company, with which Pullman merged in 1899.

Private railroad cars, known as "varnish" because of their lustrous wood paneling, escalated in price from $50,000 at the end of the Civil War to $500,000 between the two World Wars. A standard car contained a bathroom with a bronze tub (whose curled-in edge kept the water from sloshing on to the floor), a small kitchen, mahogany-lined saloon,

a dining table for up to eight people, and several bedrooms with comfortable beds. Generally, a single car was attached to the end of the train in order to prevent the hoi polloi from coming through, and many had a small "observation platform" on which the owners sat to behold the passing landscape in the fresh air. Before hopeful future American presidents rushed around in chartered planes to appear on television, they addressed their constituents on railroad sidings from these observation platforms, which have become part of the nation's political folklore. Cars had their own servants dressed in family livery, and on the rich man's train, life followed the rituals of New York, Palm Beach, or Newport. Ladies and gentlemen dressed for dinner, their meal generally prepared by a French chef and

LEFT: George Mortimer Pullman created the luxury railway car, which he then developed into one of the first great business combines, run from his own industrial city outside Chicago. Bit by bit, Pullman constructed and operated an intercontinental—eventually international—fleet of such rolling stock.

FAR LEFT: Pullman became the leading supplier of private railroad cars to the nouveaux riches, as well as to heads of state. The latter included Mexico's Porfirio Diáz, who could thus travel throughout his largely arid, hot country cushioned in all the comfort of Second Empire Paris.

BELOW: A poster promoting the pleasures of dining à la Pullman while traveling across the endless expanses of Midwestern America.

served by an English butler. These servants, independent from the house staff, worked only on the rails. Tycoon trains were equipped with their own gold or silver monogrammed plate, and all contained a safe for the jewelry ladies wore in the evening. Decoration was at the owner's whim and could vary from the wicker furniture chosen by Flagler, a symbol of his involvement with Florida resorts, to the velvet and plush of Second Empire Paris. In 1898, Pullman fashioned one of his most elaborate trains for Mexico's dictator, Porfirio Díaz; it comprised frescoed ceilings, silk-covered Louis XV chairs, and passementerie dripping from every curtain and sofa.

A rich owner's needs were always accounted for. Pullman, who liked harness racing, had a car for his horses, carriages, grooms, and coachmen, while the dyspeptic Jay Gould took along his own cow, whose milk had the butterfat content soothing to his digestion. The Budweisers arranged for ice-cold beer to flow from a spigot in their guest rooms, and famous musicians traveled with grand pianos and accompanists. Many of the private cars and trains belonged to the great railroaders, who were allowed to travel along the tracks of their competitors free of charge. Otherwise, there was a steep tariff, which, added on to the fee for hitching one's wagon to an existing train, staff salaries, and the maintenance of one's varnish in good state, made the cost of traveling by private car or train absolutely staggering. Mrs. Edward T. Stotesbury, the New York and Palm Beach socialite, once told a reporter that "the only thing that's economical about our car is the solid-gold plumbing. It saves polishing, you know." Varnish was a very personal affair, and cars seldom changed hands. Rich owners usually preferred to destroy their cars rather than sell them and pass their glory to some unknown arriviste. This explains why so few have survived. What still exists, however, are private railroad sidings such as the ones guests of the Waldorf-Astoria used to park their varnish when staying at the hotel. For the opening of this palace in 1932, so many of the rich came that cars had to be parked in Grand Central Station.

RIGHT: The multilingual staff recruited and trained by Georges Nagelmackers for the Compagnie Internationale des Wagons-Lits, which coddled European rail travelers just as Pullman did Americans. Indeed, Nagelmackers felt no compunction about pirating Pullman's ideas, which he then surpassed so that his passengers could sleep between cool linens in elegantly marquetried compartments while the staff took care of customs formalities.

BELOW: Nagelmackers realized his greatest creation when he launched the legendary Orient Express, which would link Paris with Istanbul through the Balkans. It was not for everyone, since the price of a round-trip ticket could have rented a superb town house in London's West End for an entire year.

EUROPEAN TRAINS

The private railroad car was never as popular in Europe, except with royalty. Distances were shorter and the rich somewhat poorer; moreover, the quality of existing trains ran so high that even the moneyed felt no need to possess their own varnish. Also, luxury travel was the purview of the extremely rich, unlike in the United States, where literally everybody was on the go. A trip on one of the grand European expresses could be as brilliant a social event as dinner at Maxim's on Friday night. Here, one did not have to worry about mixing with the middle class. The quality of these trains was largely owing to Georges Nagelmackers and his Compagnie Internationale des Wagons-Lits, whose trademark was the highly polished, deep-blue paint on cars embellished with silver arms and staffed by polylingual conductors attired in impeccable brown livery and the Wagons-Lits kepi, or stiff cap.

Nagelmackers's greatest creation was the Orient Express, whose astonishing luxury set the still unsurpassed standard for super-rich rail travel. With the Orient Express the age of luxury land travel had been launched with a bang, and in no time CIWL cars were rolling all across Europe, even to the Russian steppes. As they went, their interior design kept up with the times as well as with the ever-growing love of creature comforts on the part of rich passengers. Nowhere was this more evident than in the famous "Blue Train" from Paris to the newly fashionable South of France, an Art Deco masterpiece with a car for dancing the turkey-trot. The Cairo-Luxor Express, renamed the "Star of Egypt" once the service included Aswan, was cooled to 77°F, even with an outside temperature of around 100°F, thanks to air blown across 300 pounds of ice. One could go from London to Paris on the Golden Arrow, while resting on large plush armchairs and served tea or lunch from the small kitchen in every car. The Channel had to be crossed by ferry; however, since the train was identical on the other side and the luggage checked through, many passengers thought their luxury car had also come across by boat. (In fact, the Golden Arrow made the London-Dover run, the Flèche d'Or Calais-Paris.) The St. Petersburg-Paris-Nice-Lisbon Express brought grand dukes to the casinos and merchant princes to the bankers and art dealers of Paris; on the way back, it bore mimosa and carnations to decorate ballrooms during the Russian Imperial capital's winter season. On this express, it became the custom to dress in white tie for dinner and to dance until the early hours of the morning.

To super-rich Americans, this meant that Europe could be reached quickly, in the luxury they required and on a fairly reliable schedule. Likewise, wealthy Europeans could come over and invest their money in the new world where gold seemed to pop out of sidewalk grates. Meanwhile, the new technology ennabled poor Europeans to escape from their mis-

The most legendary train was, of course, the Trans-Siberian from Moscow to Vladivostok, with a spur through Mongolia on to the warm waters of China's Port Arthur. For this enterprise, Nagelmackers mounted a fantastic exhibition of Louis XVI-style cars, complete with a piano so that passengers could sing their way across the barren, blizzard-swept steppes. In the end, however, he never risked such elegant rolling stock on Siberia's rickety, slave-built road. Still, there was both a Russian and a CIWL service right through the wilderness, a journey which, at the time, took almost two weeks to complete, with passengers traversing frozen Lake Baikal on dog-pulled sleds. Far less arduous and venturesome than all this was a transatlantic crossing on one of the great new ocean liners.

THE OCEAN LINER

The development of the propeller, in place of the paddle wheel, and the riveted-steel hull toward the end of the nineteenth century brought a quantum increase in the size and speed of transatlantic liners.

erable lot by means of cheap tickets for steerage class, which had finally become at least sanitary and bearable, with three square meals a day. The class differences aboard ship proved as striking as those on shore. The room in which the *Olympic*'s first-class passengers rested from their steam bath was larger than the kitchens serving close to 1,000 steerage passengers. On their deck the rich also found posted signs asking them not to create chaos by tossing food to the poor, who swarmed on lower decks nursing their children, singing, or dancing.

FAR LEFT: Thanks to the high standards maintained by the CIWL, no demand arose on the Continent or in Britain for the private railway car, except among reigning families. This was true as well in Czarist Russia, where Nagelmackers placed his cars on the Trans-Siberian Railroad and sent them rolling across the steppes.
LEFT: Passengers and baggage being loaded on a liner docked at Liverpool. The new behemoths of the sea changed life drastically in Britain's passenger ports, employing armies of engineers, stewards, sailors, and porters.
BELOW: Sent off by a throng of well-wishers, the White Star Line's *Olympic* departs on her maiden voyage from Southampton to New York in 1912. But even with state-of-the-art technology, luxury travel on the high seas still presented certain risks during the Gilded Age. Not only did the *Titanic*, the almost identical sister ship of the *Olympic*, sink on her maiden voyage in 1912, with the loss of some 1,500 lives, but the *Olympic* too went down, in Greek waters, during World War I.

BELOW: The Cunard Line's *Aquitainia* leaving New York midday on a voyage to Southampton.

RIGHT: Among the endless delights of transatlantic crossings on luxury liners was relaxing in a deck chair under a full moon, always with the possibility of new romance. Painting by Calvin Rae Smith.

FAR RIGHT: Evenings aboard luxury liners could be very formal, as this man in full fig and monocle demonstrates for the Compagnie Générale Transatlantique. Many thought it particularly chic to travel with the French Line.

OPPOSITE: The main salon of the *Erin*, the yacht owned by Sir Thomas Lipton, Britain's immensely rich shopkeeper and tea-maker who was also the most celebrated yachtsman of his time. Sir Thomas took special pleasure in racing his *Shamrock* against Edward VII's *Britannia* at Cowes. During regattas, he shared the comforts of the *Erin* with many guests, entertaining them at candlelit suppers, to which the royal and the rich eagerly accepted invitations. The yacht's decoration seems to have been intended to give passengers the illusion of having remained on terra firma. Presumably, the hideous porcelain was either bolted down or stowed away once the ship left port.

For the privileged who crossed the Atlantic, the first order of business was to study the printed passenger list slipped under the door, since this offered the key to a week or more of frenetic cocktail and dinner parties organized either in one's own small private dining room, in larger private suites off the main dining saloon, or even in the saloon itself. On first and last nights the dress code allowed suits for the gentlemen and gowns for the ladies; otherwise, full evening dresses was de rigueur, the grandest Cartier jewels and Poiret dresses being reserved for the captain's dinner, the next to last night out. Days passed in a delightful schedule of walks on deck (requiring tweeds and a cap for the gentleman), a little exercise in the gymnasium or pool, shuffleboard, and amateur entertainment, which might include watching members of the crew slug it out. All this was punctuated by nonstop drinking and eating—breakfast in bed, bouillon on deck at 11 A.M. ("elevenses"), cocktails, lunch, tea to chamber music, cocktails again, an especially elaborate dinner, and a midnight buffet after dancing. Gambling was prevalent, from big-stakes poker to the ship's pool, an activity more or less concentrated in the wood-paneled gentleman's lounge. Finally, romance was a full-time occupation among the younger generation.

Along with the development of ocean liners came the building of private yachts, without doubt the ultimate status symbol for a tycoon. In the mid-nineteenth century private yachts often surpassed public passenger ships in both size and comfort. When launched in 1843, Queen Victoria's 225-foot paddle steamer, *Victoria and Albert,* was the ultimate in luxury, and in 1855, after only twenty royal outings, the vessel was retired in favor of an even larger ship. The *Victoria and Albert II,* a propeller-

driven yacht with a crew of 240, was a comfortable floating palace in which all details of court protocol obtained. Queen Victoria may have been the world's grandest monarch, with the wealth of the Empire behind her, but Commodore Vanderbilt's *North Star* was 45 feet longer than the *Victoria and Albert* and no less grand. Built in 1853 when his fortune had grown to $11 million (a sum that would increase twentyfold before the Commodore died), the yacht boasted a large Louis XV-style saloon with rosewood chairs and cushions, another reception saloon with a sofa that sat twenty guests, and a marble and granite banquet hall crowned by a ceiling decorated with heroes of the New World. All the staterooms could have come from a Vanderbilt mansion, and there were enough of them to accommodate ten of his children, seven of his sons-in-

and a granddaughter, as well as the family physician and a chaplain, both accompanied by their wives on the ship's maiden voyage. The large ship paddled its way across the Atlantic in eleven days, to be greeted by cheering crowds in Southampton. In an article describing the vessel and its crossing, a reporter suggested that it was "time that *parvenu* should be looked on as a word of honour." After a stop in Copenhagen, the *North Star* berthed at Kronstadt in Imperial Russia, where she so impressed Grand Duke Constantine, High Admiral of the Russian Navy, that he convinced his brother, Czar Alexander I, to order a steam yacht for the Imperial family modeled after the Commodore's. Vanderbilt also inspired his fellow tycoons to take to the waves. In 1870, the members of the New York Yacht Club owned four steam yachts; twenty years later the number had risen to 71.

Among the most famous American yacht owners were James Gordon Bennett, Jr., proprietor of the *New York Herald*, J.P. Morgan and his partner Anthony J. Drexel; and various descendants of the

FAR RIGHT: Three generations of English monarchs aboard the royal yacht *Britannia*: Edward VII with his son and grandson, the future George V and Edward VIII (later Duke of Windsor).

RIGHT: Young Queen Victoria and Prince Albert aboard the royal yacht, on their way to France in the company of King Louis-Philippe.

Croesus-rich Commodore. Bennett's first transatlantic yacht was the 227-foot *Namouna*, staffed by fifty officers and crew and designed like an English country house, with cabins paneled in oak, maple, cherry, and other precious woods. It cost $150,000 a year to run, an enormous amount considering that the ship itself cost $200,000 to build and decorate. (*Herald* employees referred to the yacht as the *Pneumonia*.) His next yacht, *Lysistrata*, was designed by Britain's pre-eminent architect, George Watson, and constructed in Scotland in 1900 for the then stupendous sum of $600,000. With enormous reception rooms, dozens of cabins, and a hundred-member crew, the 314-foot vessel represented luxury on a scale virtually beyond any other ship known at the time, and it largely proved Bennett's undoing. The publisher devoted far less time to the newspa-

per his father had founded than to yachting, and when he died in 1918, at age 77, Bennett had squandered a fortune of some $40 million.

Drexel's slightly longer *Margarita*, also designed by Watson, had a double hull, ten watertight compartments, and a 5,000-horsepower engine, equivalent to that used on the *Britannia*. Fully lit by electricity, *Margarita* boasted an interior décor that seemed designed to convince her owner that he had remained on land in an electric, antique-filled mansion. His partner, J.P. Morgan, possessed three splendid yachts, all called *Corsair*, and kept recalcitrant businessmen prisoner on the high seas until they conceded to his terms. It was Morgan who went down in yachting history for telling Henry Clay Pierce, the oilman, that he had no right to a yacht if he had to ask how much it cost to run.

Gilded Age America considered a large and expensive motor yacht an essential of life. During warm weather, multimillionaires sailed to work from their estates on Long Island, tying up at a New York Yacht Club slip strategically located near Wall Street.

LEFT: George Gould, son of the notorious robber baron, found his yacht extremely useful for commuting between New York and Paris, where his daughter had become first the Marquise de Castallane and then the Duchesse de Talleyrand-Périgord.

FAR LEFT: The American financier J.P. Morgan with Sir Thomas Lipton on his right at Cowes in c. 1903. Morgan owned a succession of big yachts dubbed *Corsair*, and when queried about how much it would cost to keep such a vessel, he answered gruffly that if you had to ask the question you could not afford one.

BELOW: The Francophile James Gordon Bennett, Jr., took few lessons from Morgan or his even own father, the founder of New York's *Herald Tribune*, preferring instead to squander an immense fortune on yachts, women, and parties.

European tycoons, as well as feudal grandees, owned large oceangoing yachts. The Duke of Westminster offered Coco Chanel a sublime emerald necklace aboard his *Cutty Sark*, a converted destroyer, only to have her toss it into the sea, boasting that her favors could not be bought for a few stones. The Duke and Duchess of Bedford sailed to the North Pole in 1901 on their 244-foot yacht *Sapphire*, and after Baron Edmond de Rothschild sailed to Palestine on his own luxury liner, a reluctant pioneer told him that he would prefer to remain on the Promised Yacht rather than return to the hard life in the Promised Land. Among England's newly rich, Sir Thomas Lipton received the luxurious yacht prize for his 287-foot, 1,242-ton *Erin*. Among both American millionaires and English peers, the *Erin* was the preferred ship from which to observe the sailing action at Cowes, an event that often included Lipton's *Shamrock* racing against Edward VII's *Britannia*. Seventy people could lunch on deck, and each night a more limited number of guests dined in full evening dress in a brass and polished-wood saloon gently lit by blue-shaded oil lamps. Other big yacht owners who frequented Cowes were Sir Edward Cecil Guinness, the stout brewer, Richard Hennessy of cognac fame, and John Gretton, the monarch of Bass ale, who were collectively referred to by snobby Brits as "the Beerage." Regardless of ownership, by the beginning of this century the oceangoing luxury yacht had pretty much been standardized. It hovered between 200 and 300 feet long, weighed 1,500-2,000 tons, and had a clipper bow and narrow stern, a single, tall yellow funnel, and two vestigial masts that, at best, flew storm sails and more often served for bunting. When it came to décor, an oceangoing style had not yet evolved, and the designer's purpose seemed to be to make owners and guests feel as if they had never left home, be this Fifth Avenue, Newport, the English countryside, or the Avenue du Bois. For the very rich, a yacht was a floating palace that transported them in the comfort on which they had become hooked, as well as the ultimate status symbol.

The Grand Hotel

The increase in transatlantic travel, the rise of the middle class in the United States and Europe, and facilitated transport along the rails—all fostered the development of the grand hotel as an institution of luxurious living. The large hotel was, in fact, an American invention, the first example being New York's City Hotel of 1794-96, built with 73 rooms on five floors at a time when the European traveler had to put up with roadside inns and small city hostelries. But the first truly *grand* American hotels were built in resorts, particularly at New York State's Saratoga Springs, New Jersey's Cape May and Atlantic City, and, slightly later, in Florida at St. Augustine and Palm Beach. Living in these hotels

was, for America's early super-rich, the equivalent of *schloss*-hopping for Europe's aristocracy.

The first large European hotels originated in England as part and parcel of the luxurious new railroad stations. First came P.C. Hardwick's Great Western Hotel (1852-54) at London's Paddington Station, built in the French Renaissance style with a royal waiting room for Queen Victoria; then the Grosvenor (1860-61) next to Victoria Station; and finally the Charing Cross on the Strand (1863-64). These were essentially travelers' hotels; tycoons had to wait until 1864 and the arrival of the Italian-Gothic-French-Renaissance Langham, which permitted them to live in their accustomed manner. Complete with two paneled libraries and an Ambassadors' Audience Room, this palace came into being for the purpose of accommodating the large number of visitors drawn to the 1864 International Exhibition from all over the world. For the crowds expected to attend the universal expositions in Paris, Napoleon III encouraged financiers to erect luxury hotels along the French capital's finest avenues. The first was the Grand Hôtel du Louvre on the Rue de Rivoli, built for the 1855 exposition, and the second the extravagant Grand Hôtel for the 1862 fair. With its enormous gilded ballrooms, rich-

The railroad station and the hotel—utterly interdependent institutions—provided the Gilded Age with two of its most representative symbols and two of its signal opportunities for monumental public architecture. The very names adopted for the hotels—Royal, Rex, Regina, Grand, Excelsior, or simply Palace—suggest the kind of bourgeois aspiration they embodied. But whatever their name or location, the hotels almost invariably articulated the international language of Beaux-Arts taste.
ABOVE FAR RIGHT: The Hôtel du Louvre in Paris built for the Universal Exposition of 1855.
RIGHT: The palatial Grosvenor Hotel in London.
BELOW: The Grand Hôtel stands today, as it did when built in the 1860s, across the street from Paris's ornate Opéra, whose architect, Charles Garnier, designed many of the public rooms in the hotel.
OPPOSITE: The extravagant ballroom in the Hôtel Continental, today Intercontinental, on Paris's Rue de Castiglione.

ly frescoed dining room, and domed *salon de thé*, all placed within an enormous triangle of 700 bedrooms, the Grand Hôtel would compete quite effectively with the opulent gaudiness of Charles Garnier's Opéra, then under construction across the street.

With money burning holes in their pockets, the newly rich wanted to see the world and in comfort; thus, the grand hotels of London and Paris would soon be imitated in Berlin, Frankfurt, Vienna, Moscow, and St. Petersburg. Meanwhile, their success spawned countless commercial palaces in Europe's new resorts. The purpose of all this was to permit the affluent voyager to live like a king, which meant that the palace hotel, as its name would indicate, had indeed to be modeled after royal residences. Palatial elements included classical façades, grand staircases covered in custom-designed Aubusson carpets, interconnecting public rooms (*enfilades*) derived from rooms of state, lavish marble-faced and frescoed dining rooms, private theaters, gilded ballrooms replete with stucco angels and Classical statuary, masses of plush upholstery, flowered carpets, and crystal chandeliers. Liveried footmen completed the monarchical ambience, and the standard hotel appellations—Regina, Royal, Imperial, Majestic, Excelsior, Hermitage—were a code for what the owners intended and the guests expected.

At palace hotels such as the Grand in Paris (FAR RIGHT), the Majestic on Paris's Avenue Kléber (BELOW), and the London Ritz (BOTTOM), service provided the key ingredient that kept the rich and the influential coming back for years on end. Even when fully occupied, the grandest of the Gilded Age hotels boasted more staff than

CÉSAR RITZ

These parvenu palaces still needed a wizard to wave his wand and make them aristocratic and royal dwellings once again. The greatest such magician of all time was César Ritz, the only hotelier ever given the opportunity several times to incorporate in his own palace everything he knew his difficult clients would want. First came Rome's Grand Hotel

guests. The celebrated chef, Escoffier, made the restaurants in the Ritz hotels magnets for wealthy gourmets, serving everyone from Edward VII to Marcel Proust and such legendary divas as Nellie Melba ("Pêche Melba") and Luisa Tetrazzini ("Chicken Tettrazini").

ABOVE: César Ritz was the king of hoteliers for all times. Born in 1850 into a modest Swiss peasant family, Ritz revolutionized the hotel business by applying unprecedented standards of cuisine, service, housekeeping, refined taste, and comfort.
OPPOSITE BELOW: The original ballroom in the London Ritz on Piccadilly.
ABOVE LEFT: The salon in the grandest of the suites at the Paris Ritz overlooking the Place Vendôme.
BELOW: A cartoon sending up the snob scene in the bar at Ritz's Grand Hotel in Rome, where the Princes Pio di Savoia, Trebia, and Belmonte, together with Counts Conturbia and Potocki, perform their courtly rites while long-bearded, Hassidic Mr. Rembelinski sits glumly on the sidelines.

of 1893; then, in 1899, London's new Carlton at the bottom of the Haymarket; next, in 1906, the London Ritz on Green Park; and finally the Paris Ritz of 1898. For these, the genial hotelier chose the design firm of the Alsatian-Frenchman Charles Mewès and the Englishman Arthur Davis. The unsung heroes of Ritz's triumph, Mewès and Davis were largely responsible for the Ritz style, which became the inspiration of grand hotels everywhere on the planet. This could best be described as the world of Louis XVI lit in delicate rose and reflected in thousands of mirrors, with every possible modern comfort. A stickler for cleanliness, Ritz stripped hotel walls of their dust-collecting damask and velvet, providing instead Louis XV and XVI *boiseries*. These, like the imitation eighteenth-century chairs, were painted pale gray or beige. Practically every room had its marble bath at a time when luxury hotels provided no more than one or two such facilities per floor. The public spaces abounded in marble, gilded brass, and wrought iron, with crystal chandeliers and classical façades setting the tone for the entire establishment. Essentially, Mewès created for hotel guests much the same ambience that American society architects like Richard Morris Hunt and Stanford White were giving their super-rich clients, and millionaires felt at home the moment they stepped through Ritz's elegant portals. But they paid heavily for this luxury—a home away from home—which included the ministrations of such famous maîtres d'hôtel as the Paris Ritz's Olivier, who served Marcel Proust late at night, lit a fire for him, and carefully closed the padded doors to keep out drafts. In the buzzing baronial halls one met kings, maharajas, statesmen, millionaires, aristocrats, and their coteries in what quickly became a roving house party around Europe. Ritz offered not only sublime comfort and beauty but also an unmatched opportunity for social climbing, an essential sport for most newly rich ladies and gentlemen.

THE GRAND TOUR

The new technology of travel afforded the rich a life-style that remained mostly unchanged until World War II. When the blossoms fell in New York's Central Park and the first warm days of spring announced the coming of heavy, humid summer, the servants in many a fine town house started packing big steamer trunks for the annual exodus to Europe, whence the family would return only in early August for the Newport season. The trunks were labeled according to destination—London, Paris, Carlsbad, Venice, Biarritz—and formed self-contained units to satisfy the strict dress codes of the

places to be visited. On a bright June morning appeared the polished truck of a company that specialized in transporting heavy baggage to the long row of ocean liners waiting at the Hudson River piers. One trunk was marked to be taken to the suite of cabins; the others went into the hold. The railway and shipping magnates always arranged for their trunks to be the last loaded and, as a result, the first off. The servants accompanied the trunks, supervised the loading, and found their way to the suite and the tiny cabins in which they would travel. At home, meanwhile, the brougham or, a few years later, the family automobile with liveried chauffeur and footman arrived to ferry the privileged travelers across town. The bon-voyage party in their suite served as a prelude to the full week of partying that would follow all the way across the Atlantic.

After the liner's arrival in Southampton, liveried representatives from Claridge's, the Savoy, or the Ritz awaited their rich clients, saw the mountain of luggage through customs, and conveyed it to London in special trucks that often arrived before the guests had disembarked from the beautifully appointed boat train at Victoria Station. Once in London, rich, social, and Anglophilic Americans cashed in chits from the English blue bloods they had entertained in New York, Newport, or Palm Beach, and got themselves into the whirl of the season, which included balls, lunch and dinner parties, theater, and country weekends. There was the occasional reciprocation, which, more often than not, consisted of elaborate feasts at the Savoy or Ritz under the supervision of the noted chef, Auguste Escoffier. The tycoons did deals with their English bankers while their wives spent time with the latest titled progeny of the daughter they had married off to England's waning peers. Then there was racing, whose highlight was Royal Ascot, where the likes of William K. Vanderbilt would run his fillies against those of the Rothschilds, the Aga Khan, and Edward VII. After a few weeks of such activity, some wealthy Americans went off to their own country houses. Otto Kahn, for example, often parked his children in a great house near London, while Andrew Carnegie repaired to his Scottish castle. Meanwhile, others left for the Continent.

Paris was where ladies loaded up on clothes while, often, their husbands passed the afternoon in bed with seductive courtesans. Mornings were spent sightseeing or promenading in elegant calèches in the Bois de Boulogne, and evenings were the time to see Sarah Bernhardt or Loïe Fuller in the theater, followed by supper at Voisin. Occasionally, rich Americans would be invited to the extraordinarily elaborate parties of Paris's Second Empire society; for the most part, however, French aristos never really warmed to Americans, whose intercourse was limited by an inability to speak the language.

The balance of the summer for the international rich centered around the spas, where they pretended to recover from year-round gluttony by imbibing often foul-tasting waters. With the possible exception of Baden-Baden, where well-heeled Russians built elaborate private villas, spa life was an entirely public activity in grand hotels, kurhouses, casinos, and restaurants. Italy beckoned to the more serious, although the rich were so busy dancing on the Lido or attending parties in rented palaces along the Grand Canal that they had little time to visit monuments or museums. (Many of the ladies had been forced to visit them, in any case, while being "finished" in British-run schools.) Notwithstanding, art dealers arranged to fill the palace walls of down-and-out nobles with paintings of varying degrees of authenticity for a quick sale—while collectors were temporarily away from the rapacious clutches of Duveen, Knoedler, and Wildenstein.

WINTER TRAVELS

Cold-weather rituals were somewhat different, and more for European than American delectation. New World tycoons and their spouses were otherwise engaged making money, social climbing, or turning winter into summer in Florida. Also, hiber-

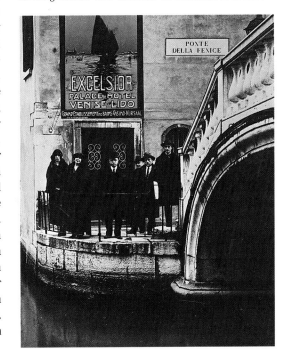

FAR LEFT: Adding to the infinite pleasures of traveling about Europe in luxury were the elegant as well as useful products from the Paris luggage-maker Louis Vuitton, whose eternally classic style is as much a cachet today as it was in the Gilded Age.
OPPOSITE: Jean Beraud (1849-1936), *The Gardens of Paris, or the Beauties of the Night,* 1905 (Musée Carnavalet, Paris). For the benefit of gentlemen with overactive libidos, Paris teemed with ladies of the night, especially in or around such nocturnal pleasure gardens as the cafés concerts.

ABOVE: The Gilded Age found splendid shooting in Scotland, Spain, and Hungary. After a shoot, it was not unusual to see bellboys carrying the fruits of a day's sport to be cooked by the hotel chef.
LEFT: Venice had much to offer both the culturally aroused and the hedonistic, the one at the Accademia or the opera and the other on the Lido, an island in the Venetian Lagoon. Here, the Queen of Romania and Princess Irene prepare to cross a bridge over the canal near Venice's historic opera house, La Fenice.

RIGHT: In St. Petersburg, racing on the frozen Neva with horse- or reindeer-drawn sleighs transformed the Russian winter into a wonderland. A favorite late-night entertainment was mounting a troika, under the cover of mink-lined blankets, and racing across the iced-over bay for supper and gypsy music until the rosy break of dawn.

FAR RIGHT: The Empress Maria-Feodorovna of Russia arrives at the Hôtel de la Turbie on the French Riviera in 1896. After Mardi Gras, which marked the end of St. Petersburg's social season, Russian grandees fled the austerities of Lent for the good life in southern Europe.

nal crossings on the stormy, iceberg-filled Atlantic were something to be avoided except when absolutely necessary. The favorite winter destinations for rich Europeans at the end of the century were St. Petersburg, Cairo, and India. St. Moritz would become truly popular only with ski lifts in the 1920s, inasmuch as hours of trekking up mountains for a few minutes of downhill racing was considered fun by only the most sporting.

A far more agreeable winter activity for many well-off Europeans was to sit covered with furs in a droshky making its way along the canals of Russia's Imperial capital. The beautiful and extravagant St. Petersburg never seemed more so than when covered with snow in February. Once the waters had frozen, Eskimos trekked down from the Arctic circle with their reindeer, set up tepees on the ice, and made a small fortune taking rich people's children for rides on the ice. This was the pinnacle of the social season, a yearly round of grand-ducal receptions, balls in ancient palaces of extraordinary luxury, and evenings at the Imperial Marjinsky Theater watching Tchaikovsky's latest ballets, followed by troika sleigh rides to the outlying islands and gypsy music until dawn.

Russian grandees were regular travelers to Paris, the South of France, London, and Berlin. At home they offered lavish hospitality to foreigners, who delighted in shopping at Fabergé, located just off the Nevsky Prospekt, then one of the world's most glamorous streets, or at the Gostinny Dvor, a two-floor Oriental bazaar stocked with soft sables and mink coats, folk jewelry from the far reaches of the Empire, colorful embroideries, and carvings in

wood and ivory. Splendid restaurants such as Cubat and Medved ("Bear") employed French chefs who lightened hearty Russian specialties, thereby rendering them even more delicious. From St. Petersburg, it was overnight in a luxury train to Moscow, where the fortunate few could visit the palaces of merchant princes and see their extraordinary art collections, watch Feodor Chaliapin re-create *Boris Godunov* at the Bolshoi Theater, or sense for a few hours that they had penetrated the Russian soul at Stanislavsky's Moscow Art Theater. The hotels of St.

Petersburg and Moscow—the Astoria, Hôtel de l'Europe, Nationale, and Metropol—were up to the best European standards, their immense halls filled in mid-winter with a profusion of tropical plants that bloomed even as frost obscured the windows.

enlarged fifty years later, it had all the amenities of a European palace hotel, including French chefs and Swiss chambermaids, with Egyptians employed only for the most menial labor. From Shepheard's famous terrace, sheltered by a striped

EGYPT

Very different from all this was mid-winter in Egypt, without doubt the most desirable of all travel experiences. Rich Europeans, as well as a few moneyed Americans, made their way by ship to Alexandria, a cosmopolitan town where Greeks, Jews, Cypriots, Italians, and Arabs traded with each other and the world in heavily accented French. Cotton, the foundation of Egypt's wealth, was mostly grown in the astonishingly fertile delta that travelers crossed in a CIWL Pullman car between Alexandria and Cairo. Here the Nile deposited literally mountains of silt carried by its downstream current all the way from the very heart of Africa.

At the turn of the century, Cairo was a prosperous and cosmopolitan city ruled over by the Khedive, the Ottoman viceroy. The aristocracy of beys and pashas at his rather formal court inhabited large Western-style palaces along the Nile in new and grandiose residential quarters such as Garden City and Zamalek. It was in Cairo, whose "season" lasted from Christmas to early spring, that visitors first attempted to solve the riddle of the Sphinx and encountered the lost world of the pharaohs. The inevitable lodging of the well-to-do was Shepheard's, an elegant stone hotel outside the old city walls on Ezbekiyah Boulevard, now known as El-Gumhuriya Street. Dating from 1841 and greatly

awning, tourists watched with unending fascination the life of the teeming city. The other grand hotel was the Gezireh Palace, built in 1869 by Ismail Pasha to receive the royals who attended the opening of the Suez Canal.

At Shepheard's or the Gezireh Palace one might find Anna Pavlova taking sun in the garden with Sergei Diaghelev, J.P. Morgan on the way to an excavation he was sponsoring for the Metropolitan Museum, Lord Carnarvon negotiating the disposition of King Tut's treasure, or wealthy French and German travelers preparing to venture up the Nile. Most went on large paddle steamers belonging to Thomas Cook, who had a virtual monopoly on organized tourism in Egypt. These large, flat-bottomed ships offered comfortable cabins, libraries

LEFT: Charles Theodore Frère (1814-88), *The Empress Eugénie Visiting the Pyramids.* Traveling up the Nile to the Valley of the Kings became a favorite winter escape for wealthy Europeans and Americans. In 1869, Napoleon III and his Empress arrived for the opening of the French-built Suez Canal. Many would follow in their fashionable wake, though hardly in the privileged Oriental style seen here.
ABOVE: Shepheard's became the favorite hotel of the rich and the powerful making a winter sojourn in Cairo. However, Napoleon III and Empress Eugénie stayed in the Gezireh Palace, turned into a small luxury hotel for the occasion.
LEFT BELOW: On the terrace at Shepheard's overlooking the Nile, East met West with mixed results.

RIGHT TOP: John S. Goodall (b. 1908), *Egypt*. Traveling up the Nile became the ultimate purpose of a winter sojourn in Egypt. The vehicle was usually one of the gleaming paddle steamers run by Thomas Cook.
BELOW: Once in Luxor, the Gilded Age traveler could enjoy being spoiled all over again in the new Winter Palace Hotel.
RIGHT: Edward, Prince of Wales (*fifth from the left*), and his party visiting the Temple at Karnak on 16 March 1862.
FAR RIGHT: While in the Valley of the Kings, many a Gilded Age traveler visited the colossi of Menhotep in the hope that they would sing, as some terrified travelers had reported hearing the statues do.

filled with British periodicals and books, European chefs, and obligatory dress for dinner. In other words, tourists were cut off from local life as much as if they lived at Shepheard's. "Real" travelers went to the banks of the Nile in Cairo and rented either a *cangia* or a *dahabiah*, the former immortalized by Gustave Flaubert, who hired one to sail up the Nile in 1849 with his friend, the photographer Maxime Du Camp.

Luxor, the mid-station on this splendid voyage of discovery, was the landing site nearest the Valley of the Kings, with its extraordinary tombs, the Temple of Amenhotep, the largest religious building ever constructed, and the Great Temple of Amun at Karnak. Farther up the Nile lay Aswan, the winter resort par excellence for moneyed Europeans, a sort of Egyptian Palm Beach. Comfortably warmed by the desert sun, the rich—elderly, retired, or merely idle—passed their days basking on the terrace of the beautiful new Cataract Hotel, walking in the green formal grandeur of Elephantine Island, or riding in the encroaching desert. From Aswan, one could explore the brown rocks and yellow sand of the Nubian desert on a donkey or on board the dahabiah pulled up the rapids by dozens of well-muscled, rope-tugging Nubians stationed on both banks of the river. Above floated Philae Island, a place so holy that one could not land on its shores without permission, and the Temple of Abu Simbel, where a single beam of light reached into the dark sanctuary every October to mark the anniversary of the birth of Ramses. When not focused on temples and tombs, travelers

shot crocodiles and watched the lazy, ambling progress of camel caravans—the latter laden with precious spices, African slaves, and caged leopards—before coasting down the rapids on their way home.

INDIA

Maharajas figured prominently in the world of Edwardian society, and the most important and urbane of them spent several months in Europe annually during the oppressive monsoon rains, which, fortunately, came at the time of the London and Paris seasons. Colossally rich in their own right and fiercely loyal to Great Britain, these princes emulated the life-style of English grandees, who accepted them as their equals. However, certain Indian princes, such as Kapurthala and Patiala, were more Francophile. The former, after building himself a large Versailles-like palace in the desert, filled it with precious French furniture, while the latter became Cartier's biggest client, his arrival at 13 Rue de la Paix the highlight of the jeweler's year.

Some of these Asian princes traveled with large retinues across the hot Indian Ocean with their holy water and polo ponies, and, like the rich Argentines, they helped make the sport of polo fashionable at Hurlingham and Windsor, later inspiring the creation of Club Le Polo in Paris's Bois de Boulogne. In the evening, dressed in gold-embroidered fabric, their chests and turbans aglitter with large diamonds, emeralds, and rubies, the maharajas lent a much-appreciated exotic touch to the dazzling balls in the great houses of London and Paris. They hardly ever visited the racially conscious United States, fearful of being ostracized or refused lodging in the grand hotels, which turned away black people. Several bought country houses in Britain, particularly in Surrey and around Newmarket, where they kept stables of horses bred to race at Ascot, Longchamp, and Baden-Baden. The princes went home in early September, accompanied by large crates of Maple's furniture and Baccarat chandeliers to decorate their opulent palaces.

When winter arrived in Europe, the warmth of India was an extremely appealing alternative to snow and frost; so, the rich and titled frequently set off on a P&O liner to trade on the hospitality they had extended to their friends among the Indian nobility. Indians of all social strata are extremely hospitable by nature, and many of the princes were interrelated by marriage. Consequently, to know one or two Indian royals was to find every palace opened up. Any self-respecting prince had several large homes in which he received hundreds of guests for the marriages of his many daughters and for elaborate house parties, which included shooting tigers or birds, sticking pigs, playing polo, and drinking endless magnums of French champagne.

The center of both Royal and Imperial India was Delhi. Old Delhi, with its Red Fort, had been the capital of the great Mughal Emperor, the enemy of the neighboring Rajput princes, and New Delhi was the capital and administrative center of the Raj, eventually run from the stupendous Viceroy's House (1923-31), designed by Sir Edwin Lutyens to express the highest aspirations of the British Empire. Traveling grandees found themselves nearly always received in the vice-regal palace with a degree of pomp that surpassed even that of the maharajas. There, uniformed and turbaned servants stood behind every chair, while the military executed tattoos in the vast Mughal-style

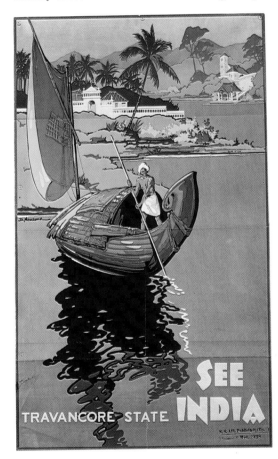

gardens. For visits around the country, the viceroy took his guests in the only white-painted train in India, a long procession of dining rooms, staff quarters, saloons, and bedrooms. From Delhi, well-connected travelers went to house parties given by such Indian Princely Families as Jaipur, Bikaner, Udaipur, Baroda, and Patiala. The maharajas of Jaipur put up as many guests as possible in the pink city palace, while accommodating others in Rambagh Palace just outside town. During Jaipur's annual polo tournaments, so many Europeans dis-

LEFT: John S. Goodall (b. 1908), *Bombay*. When European travelers reached India during the Gilded Age it was almost always aboard a P&O liner and at the teeming, malodorous port city of Bombay. For maximum comfort, the knowing avoided direct sunlight by lodging port out and starboard home—the origin of the word "posh," which still means the "best" wherever English is spoken.

BELOW: A particularly rewarding experience for travelers to India was a tour of the South, where Travancore State offered beautiful beaches washed by both the Indian Ocean and the waters of the Arabian Gulf.

RIGHT: Bombay's Great Indian Peninsula Terminus, the focal point for one of the largest and most efficient railway systems in the world, thanks to the British Raj.
BELOW: His Royal Highness Maharaja Dhuleep Singh, like most Indian potentates, maintained a private train, which he used to collect friends for boar or tiger hunts.
BELOW RIGHT: A lithograph after E. Hobday, depicting a luncheon break by British colonials in India during a day-long boar hunt (National Army Museum, London).
OPPOSITE: The Maharaja of Bikaner and three British guests pose following a successful afternoon of shooting kudu. Seldom did an invitation from this potentate go unaccepted, since he gave the most luxurious hunt parties in all of India.

embarked that special tents had to be pitched in the garden and dinner prepared every night for hundreds of guests.

The most prized invitation for good shoots came from the Maharaja of Bikaner, who built a small palace in the countryside next to a large artificial lake, which swallowed up most of the desert's scarce, badly needed water and attracted flocks of migrating birds from Europe. For entertainment, Bikaner's famous camel regiment raced their dromedaries, the only camels in the world capable of jumping hurdles. The Rana of Udaipur, who belonged to the oldest and most venerated of India's royal families, housed his guests in a marble palace that seemed to float on the waters of a large lake. He also sailed them around in a capacious, multicolored galley, rowed by a uniformed crew, while poets chanted and court musicians serenaded with ancient Indian music.

If the ladies felt bound to return home with new jewelry, the men had to bring back a few stuffed tigers, trophies to adorn their entrance halls or billiard rooms. Ever obliging, the princes were delighted to organize hunts on elephant back through the parched plains on which the gorgeous prey prowled before being reduced to near extinction. Shouting beaters—at the risk of their lives—flushed the big cats out of the bush and drove them into the range of the hunters, who were handed loaded guns by their turbaned bearers. On long treks, carpeted tents were set up at night; even so, everyone slept lightly among the disturbing sounds of the jungle. On less intrepid hunts, the party returned for a good night's rest in a fairy-tale palace with all the comforts of a Victorian house.

At the end of the season, the maharajas and their guests would head for Bombay on private trains to pick up a P&O liner back to Europe, usually stopping off for a few days in Alexandria or Cairo. The princes traveled with great, colorful retinues of servants and ministers, as well as numerous wives, and some even brought along huge vats of Ganges water for ritual purposes. As a consequence, crossings on the Indian Ocean could be nearly as glamorous as—if less comfortable than—the run across the Atlantic. Clearly, there could be no end to travel adventure and luxury for the happy handful who had those all-important assets—means and time.

SOCIETY

For most newly rich Americans, the ultimate goal was to gain a place in society. In 1861, the young nation could count only three multimillionaires—John Jacob Astor, Cornelius Vanderbilt, and Alexander T. Stewart, the founder of Wanamakers who made a fortune in real estate. By 1900, there were 4,000 of them, many with over $75 million, and they needed social classification. A vast fortune might buy education, the broadening effects of travel, beautiful houses, priceless furniture and paintings, Paris fashions, glittering jewels, race-horses, and yachts. Yet, such advantages served naught if one's family did not belong to or failed to make it into the group then setting the tone and ruling over the social life of the cities and resorts in which they lived. By and large, first-generation tycoons were so intent upon amassing money that the finer things of life took second place to getting even richer and gaining the respect of their peers in the business world. Social climbing was as rough and difficult a task as accumulating wealth, and the first generation often lacked the skill, the interest, and the concentration, or did not have the time to play the game.

After many years of Darwinian selection, the first American *Social Register* appeared in 1887. As a rule, the chosen few conformed to a life-style more or less modeled on that of Great Britain. Money was helpful, but not essential, and it had to be spent quietly with an emphasis on helping the less fortunate. Little sympathy or dialogue after business hours flowed between the narrow circle included in the *Social Register* and the many excluded for a host of reasons, among them religion, birth, business ethics, or simple boorishness.

BLUE BLOOD

For continental Europeans, the concept of American society—not to mention a nobility or aristocracy—seemed absolutely ridiculous. Across the pond there was a relatively easy answer to all this, as society was essentially feudal and clearly listed for all to see in the fat, red-leather book called *Almanac de Gotha*, which outlined in tiny print all the titled families of an ancient patchwork of duchies, principalities, kingdoms, and nations. For

Britain, the source was the equally large and detailed *Debrett's Peerage*. The font of honor everywhere, of course, sprang from reigning kings, queens, princes, czars, emperors, and empresses who had ennobled into their orbits first landowners and then those who had rendered long service to the crown, in battle, trade, or government. "Land is the basis of an aristocracy, which clings to the soil that supports it," wrote the nineteenth-century statesman Alexis de Tocqueville, "for it is not by privileges alone, nor by birth, but by landed property handed down from generation to generation that an aristocracy is constituted."

Throughout the Gilded Age, European monarchies and the nouveaux riches embraced with varying degrees of enthusiasm on both sides, although, as a rule, everyone was delighted to be ennobled, whatever the particle or prefix—de, von, Geheimrat, or Lord—added to the family name. In this way, the modern, dynamic, and often revolutionary forces that could have challenged the old order were instead brought into it, perpetuating an anachronistic system until 1914. Most of these largely idle grandees scorned the new entrepreneurs, fearing change and challenge, but chose to accommodate them as a matter of convenience. This was particularly true in Great Britain after the agricultural crisis decimated old landed fortunes, and on the Continent after World War I destroyed much of the traditional power structure, bringing down the German Kaiser, the Hapsburg Emperor, and the Russian Czar. The Gilded Age really ended in 1917, although it careened along in the United States until 1929. Meanwhile, before the curtain came down, many an aristocratic nest had been feathered by American heiresses whose ancestors would not have got by the gatekeeper a century earlier.

NEW WORLD ARISTOCRACY

If the basis of European nobility was land, that of New England's early Puritans was shipping and trade, the only means available owing to the British ban on manufacturing in the colonies. Indeed, there is hardly a great Boston family that cannot claim a sea captain in its ancestry. In 1846 a pamphlet entitled *Our First Men: A Calendar of Wealth,*

OPPOSITE: James Jacques Joseph Tissot (1836-1902), *La Mondaine*, c.1885. Having succeeded in both London and Paris as a painter of modern life at the top, the French artist James Tissot was well qualified to represent the expansive cosmopolitanism and complexity of his chosen subject. Here, a beautiful young woman of fashion, as dictated by the House of Worth, and her self-confident though delicate relationship with both her companion, an older man, and the world at large—note the Manet-like gaze straight into the viewer's eye—suggest not only the sumptuous elegance of the Gilded Age but also its eagerness to be simultaneously both exclusive and well publicized. The subject could be an American heiress wed by her socially ambitious parents to a penniless European artistocrat for the sake of his ancient title, or a courtesan, actress, or opera singer kept by a wealthy banker or industrialist for the macho cachet that such a liaison bestowed upon him. Whatever the situation, the scene radiates a sense of not only the opulence and ambiguity of the Gilded Age but also the growing interpenetration of the public and the private, even for the wealthy, who could neither escape this defining phenomenon of modern life nor resist contributing towards its accelerated development.

185

RIGHT: In the Puritan world of Boston society, the archetypal aristocrats were and remain the Cabots, a civic-minded family who allegedly speak only to the Lodges, who in turn speak only to God. Here, reading from the right, Senator Henry Cabot Lodge deigns to pose with U.S. Secretary of War Newton Diehl Baker and Harvard University President A.L. Lowell. New England's established families have made endless contributions to the public, philanthropic, and business life of their nation.

ABOVE: The archetypal aristocrat of the Old South was Robert E. Lee (1807-70), a plantation gentleman who led the Confederate Army during what Southerners still call the "War Between the States." Unlike the North, the antebellum South embraced a manner of living not so far removed from that of feudal Europe. Supported by wealth based on land, cotton, and slave labor, Southerners found the leisure to cultivate their minds, their manners, and their families. This meant careful intermarriage, accumulated riches, and an overweening sense of Southern superiority, especially in regard to the gruff, self-made tycoons of the urbanized, industrial North.
RIGHT: The Henry Grady house near Athens, Georgia, typifies the kind of gracious, Greek-Revival country house in which the South's plantation patriciate carried on their languorous, elegant lives.

Fashion and Gentility made its first appearance, unashamedly admitting that Boston's proper society was based on money. And rightly so, since the liberties granted by a proper fortune allowed the leading families to contribute heavily to the politics, religious affairs, and education of the fledgling United States. Puritans were expected to excel, both financially and educationally, and in its early days, entrance to Harvard University depended mainly on family rather than academic aptitude, indicating that, long before the American Revolution, an elite had emerged. Moreover, it was an elite distinguished by impeccable manners, consid-

eration for their fellow man, interest in civic affairs, and family life, religious devotion, and a yearning for higher knowledge, the last reflected in the many institutions of learning that quickly studded the cities and countryside of New England.

It is the antebellum South that most evokes an image of aristocratic American life, of large country estates or plantations, stately homes with white-columned porticoes, cigar-smoking gentlemen planters, and Southern belles in crinolines imported from Paris. The emphasis on elitism and the reliance on black slaves and poor whites to support the social and political aspirations of a few families might seem an oddity in a nation that produced the Declaration of Independence. In fact, the Civil War, referred to in the South as the War Between the States, was really a fight of the North against the great families of the South, a pitting of Dixie self-indulgence against Yankee self-denial. Convinced that elitist Britain and France would join them in a kind of triple entente against the democratic, vulgar, and commerce-driven North, the Confederates also believed that secession from the Union was the only way to save their opulent life-style, the life-style of families whose leaders had made significant contributions to the political wealth of the new nation.

All the cities of the Eastern Seaboard recognized certain families as their aristocracy, many of whom played a role in the history of the Republic. In Wilmington, Delaware, there were the Du Ponts de Nemours, whose gunpowder lit up battlefields for over two centuries. Quaker Philadelphia alone could boast the Cadwaladers, who founded the Philadelphia library with Benjamin Franklin, the Drexels, who took in J.P. Morgan as a partner, and the

Allens, who had financed Independence Hall, not to mention the Penns, Chews, Willings, Biddles, and Pembertons, among others. New York, meanwhile, had its "patroon" society, composed of old Dutch landowners such as the Van Rensselaers, who alone held 700,000 acres along the Hudson River, and such English landlords on the Hudson as the Pells, Livingstons, Morrises, and Philipses. The British crown gave these manorial holdings to important colonists who had proved useful to it, and along with the land went the title "Lord of the Manor."

Early arrival in the colonies served also as a perfectly valid claim to social acceptability, particularly if one's ancestors had been part of the scruffy lot that arrived on the *Mayflower*. And trade posed no barrier to inclusion, provided success had come before the 1800s. Only later did some of these founding dynasties go on to finance and real estate (or, in the case of Franklin Delano Roosevelt, to the destruction of his own class!). But once this had occurred, it is quite astonishing how the parvenu patriciate considered anybody in trade as socially unacceptable. New York society was therefore not as clean-cut as that to the North and South, which left it in a real quandary as to how aristocracy, meritocracy, and plutocracy could be welded into a homogeneous social unit lacking the authority of a royal family, a hierarchical institution that would have gradually separated the wheat from the chaff over the centuries.

MAKING LISTS

The first to try defining New York society was Mrs. John Jay, born Sarah Van Brugh Livingstone, a name that combined the Dutch patroon with the English lord of the manor. As the wife of the young republic's Secretary of Foreign Affairs (who later became its first Chief Justice [1789-95]), Mrs. Jay traveled to France, where she was found so beautiful and grand that some mistook her for Marie Antoinette. At home she proved both popular and lovable, qualities that helped make her the first recognized social arbiter in the United States. Everyone simply agreed that her "Dinner and Supper List" from 1787 to 1788 *was* New York society. The next person to whom the leadership role fell, quite literally, was the 300-pound carpenter and sexton of Grace Church, Isaac Hull Brown. His ascent to power came from the fifteen minutes he spent fixing the floor that collapsed at the old Academy of Music under the weight of the thousands attending a ball in honor of the Prince of Wales in 1860. Brown saved the day, and such was the gratitude of all the ladies present that they let him make up their dinner lists from then on. But even this power broker admitted that he could not control society beyond 50th Street!

Samuel Ward McAllister, the next person to inherit Mrs. Jay's crown, would enter history as the most celebrated of American social sorters, largely because of his association with Caroline Schermer-

horn Astor, whose patroon parents and immensely rich husband allowed her to straddle better than anybody else New York's odd mix of plutocracy and aristocracy. Born in Savannah in 1827, McAllister was a minor Southern gentleman who married a self-effacing Washington heiress, Sarah Gibbons. More important perhaps, his credentials for the

post of society's winnower included a short stint in London, where McAllister claimed that the Duke of Westminster had taken him under his wing and introduced him to the cream of British aristocracy. Moreover, he supposedly had enjoyed similar patronage and access in both France and England.

McAllister decided who had "the right to create and lead society," which he neatly divided into "nobs" and "swells," the nobs being the old distinguished families and the swells the parvenu newcomers. While a nob might get away with behaving like a swell, as long as his fortune permitted, a swell could become a nob only if McAllister touched him with his magic wand. In 1872 the great magician organized a ball committee of 25 men known as "Patriarchs," each of whom held the right of inviting to an annual ball four ladies and five gentlemen, including himself and his family.

Topping the alphabetical list of Patriarchs was John Jacob Astor III and his brother William, and the membership went on to

LEFT: Mrs. John Jay, the wife of the first Chief Justice of the U.S. Supreme Court. A well-born and socially prominent New Yorker, Sarah Van Brugh Livingston Jay cut such an attractive figure that she turned heads even in the Paris of Louis XVI, while abroad during Jay's tour of diplomatic duty. Back home her invitation list came to constitute New York society in the early years of the Republic.
BELOW: Ward McAllister, a minor Southern gentleman who managed, with the aid of Mrs. William B. Astor, to become the self-appointed arbiter of New York society at the height of the Gilded Age. A figure born to be caricatured, McAllister is seen here as "Our Society Chef" selecting the ingredients for a social soufflé even more exclusive than Caroline Astor's fabled 400.

The heirs of John Jacob Astor soon married into and made themselves the patriciate of New York City, using their vast inherited wealth to create a happy blend of breeding and money.

RIGHT: Not content merely to lead American high society, the Astor ladies vied with one another to be *the* Mrs. Astor. Here, Mrs. John Jacob Astor (*far left*) and Mrs. William B. Astor (*left center*) face off at the Assembly Ball of 1902, proclaimed by the press as "the greatest social event of the season in New York."

BELOW: Charles Carolus-Duran, *Mrs. William B. Astor*, 1890 (Metropolitan Museum of Art, New York). It was for Caroline Schermerhorn Astor that Ward McAllister selected the 400 socially desirable guests to fill her ballroom to comfortable capacity, thereby establishing what many considered to be New York's true *gratin*.

include the obvious manorial lords and patroons, plus a very generous sprinkling of Ward's Southern friends, who were attempting to make a new start in the nation's financial capital. John Jacob's wife, Charlotte Augusta, was far more interested in philanthropy, politics, and literature than balls, although—noblesse oblige—she did give an annual dance at Newport, where she appeared in $300,000 worth of diamonds. Her sister-in-law Caroline, however, had burning social ambitions, fueled by her marriage to the younger brother, William, who was only interested in his racehorses, his yacht, shooting at Ferncliffe, his Hudson estate, or loafing in Florida. Not only did Caroline Astor—*the* Mrs. Astor—yearn to be Queen of Society, she also had several daughters to marry. To advance her several causes, she even risked the wrath of other family members by sending cards reading simply "Mrs. Astor," as if there were none other. And in McAllister she found the companionship, frivolity, and snobbishness her husband was not able to provide.

In Caroline Astor, Ward McAllister met the locomotive he always cited as his "one and only," his "Mystic Rose." Together, they made a list of New York society, the famous Four Hundred that could fit into Caroline's Fifth Avenue ballroom. Beyond that number, he said, "you strike people who are either not at ease in a ballroom or else make other people not at ease." Essentially, the list expanded the Patriarchs' Ball with those members of the new plutocracy whom he and Caroline Astor believed ready to step into the social whirl, and when *The New York Times* published the list on the occasion of Caroline's ball in February 1892, the entire country paid attention. The Four Hundred were made up principally of bankers, lawyers, brokers, real-estate men, railroaders, and their spouses. It excluded politicians, people in trade, Jews, and the entire world of art and culture. On the whole, it was an extremely dull group totally disinterested in serious conversation at long, formal dinners that amounted to little more than eating contests. As for their other much-envied activities, the fabled Four Hundred liked showing off around the Metropolitan Opera's "Diamond Horseshoe," the ring of private boxes so named for the massively bejeweled socialites who sat in them every Monday night during the season. They also enjoyed competing with one another in ostentatiousness at an endless series of balls in New York, Newport, and later Palm Beach. For the benefit of this life, McAllister

ness the Commodore had crossed the Astors in 1867, with the result that for twenty years Caroline Astor and Alva Vanderbilt skated past each other on the New York scene without ever speaking. Goaded by frustration at not being part of the Four Hundred, Alva commissioned Richard Morris Hunt to build her the grandest possible mansion on Fifth Avenue. For the 1883 opening of the $3 million "Petit Château," she organized one of the most splendid balls ever held in the United States, with another Southern belle as guest of honor. This was Lady Mandeville, formerly Consuelo Yznaga and later the eighth Duchess of Manchester, whose social standing virtually guaranteed that the Four Hundred would dance attendance—right along

The funeral cortege for the social winnower Ward McAllister, making its way up Fifth Avenue in 1895. Social history describes the event as poorly attended, which may have been the case given the half-dozen carriages seen here. At the apogee of his power, McAllister had suddenly been ostracized for an act of hubris. This occurred when he published a book asserting his native belief in the superiority of Southern aristocracy over that of the North, where, quite astonishingly, he had persuaded society that he should decide who counted.

pursued his snobbist career quite happily until 1890, when, in a classic act of hubris, he wrote a book. Essentially a paean to Southern superiority and a satire on Northern parvenus, *Society as I Have Found It* succeeded mainly in offending the very culture Ward had so effectively helped to establish. Very much as café society did when Truman Capote abused the trust of his beloved "swans" in a short, silly story entitled "Côte Basque," the Four Hundred cut McAllister dead, and the great "Make-a-Lister" died of a heart attack in 1895 after dining alone at the Union Club.

For those who liked partying, publicity, and dressing up, the Four Hundred were the *nec plus ultra*, and not being included drove certain social ladies into a frenzy. Among the most frenzied of those excluded from the Astor set was Alva Vanderbilt, the indomitable wife of the Commodore's grandson, William Kissam, who was the richest man in America after John Jacob Astor III. In busi-

with the rest of the 1,200 invited members of *le tout New-York*, all of whom were dying to see the most famous house of its time. When it became evident that *the* Mrs. Astor had not been summoned, *the* Mrs. Vanderbilt replied that she could not invite a total stranger to her home.

Society was torn between curiosity and betrayal until Caroline came home to find her excited daughter and friends rehearsing the quadrille they expected to dance with electric lighted stars on their foreheads. Blithely assuming they would of course be invited, the girls had already settled on their dates, who were dressing in Henry VIII costumes. Caroline, unable to admit that an Astor daughter would not be welcome at the Vanderbilt party, dispatched a blue-liveried footman to deliver her card, corner turned down, to the Vanderbilts' maroon-liveried butler. Having thus broken the ice, she received back an invitation just in time to order for herself a Venetian dress of dark-colored velvet

RIGHT: George Stein (fl. 1900-20), *La Place de l'Opéra, Paris.* For the Gilded Age, the opera represented the ideal marriage of high art, high elegance, and high social cachet. Consequently, most of the world's great opera houses were built in the 19th century. In terms of Gilded Age aesthetics, the most splendid of the lyric theaters was the Paris Opéra commissioned by Napoleon III and designed by Charles Garnier. It called for grand opera on a heroic scale, generously supplied by the composers Giacomo Meyerbeer and Ludovic Halévy. Musically, it was still Milan's 18th-century Teatro alla Scala that reigned supreme.

BELOW: When New York's plutocracy found themselves excluded from the boxes at the Academy of Music—all held by "old" families—they retaliated by building the first Metropolitan Opera on Broadway at 39th Street. Thanks to the rich fees subsidized by wealthy patrons such as Otto Kahn, the Gilded Age Met could attract and hold the greatest operatic talents in what was a Golden Age of singing. They included Nellie Melba, Enrico Caruso, Rosa Ponselle, and Feodor Chaliapin.

and satin sewn with solid gold roses and hundreds of seed pearls. Now fashionable Fifth Avenue could emit a great sigh of relief, after which the two rivals reigned jointly. But if Caroline Astor had finally accepted the Vanderbilts, she kept her door closed to J.P. Morgan, John D. Rockefeller, the Goulds, Belmonts, and Harrimans, as well as to most of the other tycoons of the day. They, and others worthy of admission to the "charmed" circle, must have felt like James Gordon Bennett, Jr., who declared that "New York society consists mostly of people who don't invite me to their parties."

The social battleground was not limited to the ballroom. Throughout the world during the Gilded Age, the rich considered attendance at the opera the ultimate expression of interest in the arts. Here, however, the money princes generally paid attention only when the corps de ballet, with its pretty girls, appeared on stage; otherwise, they tended to snore, chat, or sup in their private boxes. Divas were the equivalent of today's pop stars, and few things carried greater cachet than keeping one as a mistress and covering her in diamonds. It is thanks to lavish private patronage that the great nineteenth-century opera houses were built: the Paris Opéra, a sublime summing-up of Second Empire luxury; the Teatro Colón in Buenos Aires; and, of course, New York's Metropolitan Opera. In New York, operas had been presented, until 1883, at the Academy of Music on Irving Place, where the eighteen boxes were reserved, from generation to generation, by the city's old guard of patrons and landlords, an elite dominated by Pierre Lorillard, August Belmont, and Robert L. Cutting. The nouveaux riches tried in vain to crash, and even William H. Vanderbilt suffered the humiliation of being turned down when he offered $30,000 for one of the temporarily available boxes.

In revenge, Vanderbilt enlisted the support of such fellow outcasts as Jay Gould, William Rockefeller, George F. Baker, and Collis P. Huntington to build a new opera house on Broadway and 39th Street—the Metropolitan—largely financed by 35 boxes priced at $60,000 each, a one-time fee that also granted the right to decorate the exclusive bit of property according to personal taste. One box-holder swathed her space in blue silk with silver stars,

another transformed hers into a bower of orchids. Together, the great tier of loges came to be known as the "Diamond Horseshoe," both for its shape and for the necklaces and tiaras that sparkled from the long necks and carefully coiffed heads of New York's richest and most elegant ladies. The glitter could be almost blinding on opening night, but also on Monday, the night of the Patriarch and Assembly balls. Needless to say, when these occurred, everybody left for the parties before the last curtain. On its inaugural night, the Met was boycotted by the old guard, but the joint fortunes of the new guard arrayed about the Diamond Horseshoe were totted

During the Gilded Age, much of New York's social life took place in two rather grand restaurants, Louis Sherry and Delmonico's. Both offered several different banqueting halls, all of which New Yorkers loved transforming into highly imaginative, sometimes even magical wonderlands.
ABOVE: The standard livery for Sherry's waiters was 18th-century tailcoats, brass-buckled pumps, and powdered wigs.
LEFT: Delmonico's could also serve relatively intimate dinner parties, as here on an occasion honoring Mark Twain. The great writer had turned seventy in 1905.

up at $540 million. Unable to beat such massed power, Lorillard, Belmont, et al., joined it, leaving the old Academy to be closed down.

SHOWING OFF

In New York, every large house gave at least one ball per season, at which the lords of the manor received their friends. Meanwhile, there were other parties for debutante daughters, dances in honor of visiting royals, or any other occasion that merited celebration. Since New York's social season went on for about six months, with time out for weekends at great country estates and a midwinter respite in Florida, this meant dressing up in white tie and tails nearly every night of the week for an extended period. Balls usually went into full swing only after midnight, inasmuch as they were preceded by interminable dinners at other people's houses. Everybody arrived more or less at the same time, the horse-drawn carriages standing in long lines to discharge their beautifully dressed and bejeweled passengers. To control the crowds of onlookers, the police set up barriers, while liveried coachmen queued in their top hats, waiting to take

RIGHT: Delmonico's around 1901. The mere size of this establishment, on the corner of Fifth Avenue and 44th Street, indicates the degree of success it enjoyed. More banqueting hall than bistro, Delmonico's encountered severe competition not only from Sherry's but also from the new grand hotels, such as the Waldorf-Astoria, the St. Regis, and the Plaza. BELOW: Sherry's, the great rival of Delmonico's, was the scene of a notorious stag party given by Chicago's C.K.G. Billings, a gas tycoon and renowned equestrian. For this dinner on horseback, a large banqueting hall was turned into an overdecorated stable, making the event one of the most bizarre in the history of American private entertaining.

their employers home, or to Louis Sherry's for breakfast, in the early hours of the morning. For real extravaganzas—events with guests numbering more than the few hundred possible in a private ballroom—hosts commandeered the fashionable restaurants and hotels: Delmonico's or Louis Sherry's, the Waldorf-Astoria, St. Regis, or Astor Hotel. Among the most famous *fêtes* in such public places were C.K.G. Billings's men's dinner, James Hazen Hyde's costume party at Louis Sherry's, and the Bradley Martin ball at the Waldorf-Astoria.

Billings, a natural-gas millionaire from Chicago, disguised Sherry's fourth floor ballroom as a wood-land garden complete with trees, shrubs, and sod on the floor. In the center stood a manger to which horses were to be tethered once brought up in the freight elevator. Overhead shimmered a blue-velvet ceiling studded with tiny electric stars, while live birds chirped in the bushes. Each horse had a small table slung over its back, and on its shoulders hung two saddlebags filled with ice and a bottle of champagne. Attired in riding habit or white tie and tails, the all-male guests mounted their horses where they were served a dozen courses by waiters dressed as grooms in scarlet coats and white breeches. They quenched their thirst by sipping champagne through long rubber tubes and remained in the saddle throughout the banquet. Presumably, conversation was limited, and it took a long time to clean up!

James Hazen Hyde was the immensely rich heir to the giant Equitable Life Assurance Society of New York, which brought with it directorships of 46 major American corporations. Instead of taking care of his affairs, Hyde spent most of his time in France, where society accepted him as an entertaining New World eccentric. A great lover of French art, literature, fashion, food, and actresses, he decided in 1905 to inspire his rougher American friends to emulate his Francophilia by inviting them to a $200,000 party at Sherry's (paid for by the Equitable) in honor of the French actress Gabrielle Réjane. For the theme of Louis XVI's court, the host had the ballroom converted into a wing of Versailles, with thousands of roses hung from lattices, screens, arbors, trellises, canopies, and arches. The assembled company rose grandly to the occasion.

Mrs. George Gould, daughter-in-law of the railroad robber baron, came dressed as Marie Antoinette, her green-velvet train lined in white satin and trimmed in real gold and emeralds, while Mrs. Clarence Mackay, whose mother-in-law had sewn and mended clothes for miners at the Comstock Lode, presented herself as Adrienne Lecouvreur. Hyde simply wore the dark-green evening tailcoat of New York's fashionable Coaching Club, covered with his French medals.

The entire Metropolitan Opera orchestra and

corps de ballet provided entertainment until midnight, when Mme. Réjane, dressed as a courtier, made her entrance on a sedan chair borne by four Nubian slaves. She and a few French thespians then performed a bedroom farce that nobody understood, after which the guests were piped, or trumpeted, to yet another wing of Versailles for supper. Next, they went back upstairs to dance until three in the morning. By that time, another supper had been prepared downstairs, and at six o'clock the waiters brought a breakfast of crab cakes and champagne. Photographs of costumed tycoons and stories of the ball filled the newspapers, prompting the Equitable's shareholders to holler and the government to launch an investigation into corporate irregularities. Soon Hyde left for France, where he died 40 years later, without ever again seeing his homeland.

The Bradley Martins suffered the same fate-in-exile following their 1897 affair that launched the new Waldorf-Astoria Hotel. Wanting to make a splash, this rich Troy, New York, couple kept the press apprised of all the plans for their great fancy-dress ball. These entailed 6,000 orchids spread around the ballroom, several orchestras, including fifty musicians from the 22nd Regiment Band, and supper served by waiters in royal livery with knee breeches and powdered wigs. Most of the Four

FAR LEFT: James Hazen Hyde with the renowned French actress Réjane, his guest of honor at a Sherry's party for which the assembled company dressed as if for an evening at the court of Louis XVI. So extravagant was the event that it caused a public scandal, prompting Hyde, an insurance heir, to expatriate and spend the rest of his life in France. ABOVE: As this program suggests, clown costumes were much in vogue during the Gilded Age, when the fortunate few loved to celebrate who they were by pretending to be someone else, often royalty. BELOW: The human comedy as *la commedia dell'arte*, with parvenu Pierrots and Pierrettes rehearsing their cotillion before the "Monkey Ball" given by James Hazen Hyde, again at Sherry's. To the delight of the tabloid press, the Gilded Age super-rich loved to have their social extravaganzas photographed and published. Otherwise, why bother to be ostentatious? The detailed reporting has also been the delight of subsequent generations, eager to find the Gilded Age even more absurd than their own.

OPPOSITE: John Jacob Astor III looking like a van Dyck portrait come to life. He was costumed—as Sir Walter Raleigh?—for an 1895 ball given by Mr. and Mrs. Bradley Martin, a couple who emigrated to Europe after their extravagant parties, during an economic depression, prompted an outraged city government to double their tax assessment.

RIGHT: The only existing color photographs of a costume party before World War I show Mr. and Mrs. Donn Barber at the 1913 Tiffany Ball dressed as "slave" and "slave driver."

BELOW: Fashionable Venice provided the Gilded Age with a favorite theme for fancy-dress balls. The lagoon city so captured the imagination of wealthy Harry Kessler that he had the ballroom at London's Savoy Hotel flooded, for the gondolas in which he and his guests floated and serenaded their way through the night.

Hundred decided to attend out of curiosity to see the new hotel, thereby helping to transform the event into a watershed in American social history, since it was the first grand ball to be given in a public place. Mrs. John Jacob Astor, Mrs. Henry Sloane, and Mrs. Livingston Ludlow invited New York's finest to dinner before the great occasion. Mrs. Oliver Belmont dressed up as yet another Queen of France, while her husband borrowed a priceless suit of gold-inlaid steel armor from the Metropolitan Museum. There were three George Washingtons, a few early patroons and Indians, and a pair of inevitable Marie Antoinettes. (The hostess even wore a ruby necklace valued at $75,000 that had belonged to the ill-fated Queen.) The Martins sat enthroned on a dais while a liveried lackey announced the name, character portrayed, and historical period of every guest. The publicity backfired, however, because the country was in the middle of a grinding depression, which left the party to become a symbol of plutocratic waste, frivolity, and indifference. Preachers ranted from the nation's pulpits, and the New York City tax authorities, upon learning that the evening had cost $369,200, doubled Bradley Martin's tax assessment. For their part, the hosts, who felt they had offered an unparalleled employment opportunity to New York's suffering florists, dressmakers, waiters, jewelers, and cooks, took such offense that they moved to England, but not before giving a dinner for 86.

In the United States, such follies were not limited to New York. Mrs. George Westinghouse gave a dinner in Washington where guests found a crisp, new $100 bill in their napkins, and in Philadelphia James Paul gave a coming-out party for his daughter Mary, at which 10,000 butterflies, imported from Brazil, were hung from decorative bags on the ceiling and released at a fixed time. Unfortunately, the heat rising from the ballroom asphyxiated the insects, all of which dropped dead onto the dancing guests. More successful as a party stunt was a giant swan that floated through another coming-out ball and all at once shot 10,000 pink roses into the air. For the grandest and most elegant of all such

RIGHT: The dining room at "The Elms," the Newport "cottage" of Edward Julius Berwind, provided a regal setting—albeit a sober one by Newport standards—for elaborate entertaining after a hectic day of drinking at Bailey's Beach, lunching on the terrace of some seaside mansion, riding about in a calèche, taking tea at Mrs. William K. Vanderbilt's, or watching a tennis match at the Newport Casino.

BELOW: Mrs. Robert Goelet, Jr., a lioness of New York and Newport society, accepts her corgi from a liveried coachman on Newport's Bellevue Avenue. Even on an August mid-afternoon, she wore a pearl-embroidered dress and a Paris chapeau.

soirées, Otto Kahn paid Enrico Caruso $10,000 to sing a pair of arias at his daughter Momo's debut, which took place on the family estate in Woodbury, Long Island. Kahn had also recruited 125 servants to look after the needs of guests housed in 100 bedrooms.

MADNESS BY THE SEA

For sheer fantasy and opulence, there was nothing like the parties given in Newport, where the wealthy from all parts of America gathered in the summer. After visiting this haven of the estivating rich, Russia's, Grand Duke Boris said: "I have never dreamed of such luxury as I have seen at Newport. We have nothing to equal it in Russia." Residents maintained enough permanent staff to serve dinner for a hundred with a butler behind nearly every chair. At one dinner, fish swam in a stream running down the center of a table, and a cage in the middle of another table contained parrots of all colors and sizes. Elsewhere, the centerpiece was a sandpile laced with thousands of dollars worth of rubies, emeralds, diamonds, and sapphires, which guests dug out between courses, using small silver spades provided for the occasion. Not only spent, money was constantly discussed. One Newport hostess refused to invite people with less than $5 million; another barred anyone whose house cost less than $1 million—not a consequential sum considering that hostesses regularly budgeted around $300,000 for summer entertaining.

Newport's social life started at 11 A.M., when everybody made an appearance at Bailey's Beach,

the exclusive club where one swam—more or less fully dressed—until lunch time. There were generally luncheon parties on the lawns of the enormous "cottages" or on the great oceangoing yachts often moored at the houses' private docks. Jackets and ties were de rigueur, and when James Hazen Hyde once turned up in a sport shirt, his hostess, the Newport locomotive Mrs. Stuyvesant Fish, loudly asked: "Who is that young man in a negligee?" In the afternoon, it was tennis and sailing for the young, or perhaps golf at Tommy Taylor's private course, while for the older ladies, dressed to the nines and topped with great feathered hats, it was a ride up and down seaside Bellevue Avenue in elaborate calèches. The men talked, drank, and occasionally took up a book at the Reading Room, Newport's most exclusive club. The evenings, of course, were reserved for elaborate entertainments. Mrs. Cornelius Vanderbilt would bring up the entire cast of a Broadway hit, *The Wild Rose*, or the violinist Fritz Kreisler to entertain her guests. Kreisler's fee was $13,000 until Mrs. Vanderbilt told him that her musicians never mixed with the guests, to which he replied that, such being the case, he would ask for

aristocratic European guests often provided the entire raison d'être of lavish entertainments.

In a famous contretemps, Mrs. Stuyvesant Fish invited 200 to dinner for Russia's Grand Duke Boris, who was staying at Ochre Court with Mrs. Goelet. The eccentric Mrs. Fish refused to invite one of the Goelets' guests, which left the Imperial party no choice but to stay at home, whereupon

LEFT: The eccentric Mrs. Stuyvesant Fish (*right*) with Lola Robinson at a Newport garden party in 1910. Tightly corseted and attired in heavily embroidered white muslin, veils, and ostrich feathers, these dreadnaughts of high society forfeited much of summer's pleasure in order to present an image of ironclad propriety.

only $500. Dinners were of the greatest formality, every bit as grand as those given on Fifth Avenue. For the opening of Marble House, Alva Vanderbilt invited 120 to dine, in preparation for a ball honoring the Duke of Marlborough, the future (and mismatched) husband of her daughter Consuelo. Fought over by their American hostesses, royal or

Mrs. Goelet invited to her house the same well-mannered group expected at Mrs. Fish's. They all declined, given that they had accepted a previous invitation. According to Ward McAllister, if you died after having accepted a dinner invitation, your executor should attend in your place. That night, Mrs. Fish—who called everybody "little lamb" and greeted people at the door with "Howdy-do, howdy-do. Make yourselves at home and, believe me, there is no one who wishes you were there more than I do"—told her group that royalty "is better never than late." As the suspense grew, she finally stood at the top of the stairs in all her diamonds. "I could not get the Grand Duke Boris," she said, "but I have someone far better. Lambs and pets, His Most Gracious Imperial Majesty, the Czar of all the Russias." The ladies went into a deep curtsy, the gentlemen bowed and then rose to see a popular local jester, the foppish Harry Lehr, dressed in scarlet regalia and holding a scepter. Guffaws of laughter broke out as Lehr, spluttering broken English, toured the room with his hostess on his arm. The joke was such a success that a year later Mrs. Fish invited everybody to meet the

BELOW: Almost catatonic with upper-crust dignity, Mr. and Mrs. Van Allen go for a ride in a new-fangled contraption known as the automobile. One assumes the driver wears the black overalls while his employer takes the wheel, but one can never be sure in a would-be democratic society.

Such was the obsession with formality at Newport that even sporting life seems to have unfolded in slow motion. RIGHT: Delivered by their liveried coachmen, Newport grandees observe a regatta in 1900. A fair, flawless skin being essential to Gilded Age beauty, the ladies have protected themselves with parasols.

BELOW: Mrs. William K. Vanderbilt, the owner of Marble House, one of the very grandest of the Newport "cottages" (see page 116), takes a dip in the sea at Bailey's Beach fully clothed, corseted, and even hatted against the sun. Being the mother of the Duchess of Marlborough, Alva Vanderbilt had a certain position to maintain.

RIGHT: At the Newport Casino, a group of ladies and gentlemen have gathered for a tennis match in 1888.

LEFT: Daringly stripped of shirts and ties, William Vanderbilt and friends prepare for a mattress race at Bailey's Beach.
BELOW: With his crisp and deftly stylized engravings, Charles Dana Gibson established the ideal beauty of the period. A distinctly American beauty, it was largely inspired by the Langhorn sisters of Virginia, one of whom became Mrs. Gibson and another, Lady Astor, the first female member of the British Parliament. The Gibson girl epitomized the healthy, sleek, casual, rich, and beautiful young women of the New World whose affluent parents brought them up to be confident and winning. An admiring European writer, Paul Bourget, asserted that an American beauty "must be very tall, very well formed, the lines of her face and figure must lend themselves to that sort of reproduction of which the newspapers are so fond. She must also know how to dress with magnificence, which here is inseparable from elegance."

Roman Prince del Drago at a splendid, formal dinner. The "Prince" turned out to be a monkey in evening dress, who drank lots of champagne, leaped to the chandelier, and bombarded guests with light bulbs. The foreign royalty bug went so far that one dowager put a sign outside her cabana at Bailey's Beach: "English spoken here."

AMERICANS INVADE EUROPE

All this was as much a lark as social commentary on title hunger, but once the newly rich had crashed into American "society," they felt a need to be accepted in Europe as well. There were two possibilities: spending lots of money or selling a daughter to a nobleman for his coronet. Europeans made no distinction between Americans, totally disregarded the social hierarchy the latter had so carefully established, and cheerfully agreed to be bought or entertained. As a consequence, Europe's highly stratified society often proved more open and hospitable to rich Americans than to their own. The unconventional James Gordon Bennett and James Hazen Hyde were adopted by the French *gratin* and had a far better time abroad than at home. Jay Gould's family, suspect in America by reason of the patriarch's unscrupulous business practices, entered French society in a permanent way thanks to the marriage of their daughter Anna, first to the spendthrift Marquis Boni de Castellane and then to his grander cousin Hélie de Talleyrand-Périgord, Prince de Sagan. The most famous marriage was forced by Alva Vanderbilt on her daughter Consuelo, who thus became Duchess of Marlborough.

Levi Leiter, a Mennonite merchant from Chicago, totally skipped over *all* the barriers put in his way by disapproving dowagers in both Chicago and New York. Mrs. Leiter, one of the most bumbling of America's social climbers, told friends that her husband was going to a fancy-dress ball "in the garbage of a monk" and encouraged Mrs. Roosevelt to dig into her tea sandwiches as "you don't get anything like this at home." Nonetheless, thanks to an enormous fortune, the Leiters launched their daughter Mary Victoria in Europe. There she found herself courted not only by the Marchese Rudini but also by the Count of Turin, who was in direct line of succession to the Italian throne. Finally, Mary Victoria wed the ambitious and brilliant George Curzon, with the result that she eventually became Vicereine of India and Marchioness of Kedleston. By then, all those who once snubbed her had long since lived to regret it. The eighth Duke of Manchester married Consuelo Yznaga, whom he met in Saratoga Springs, while the ninth Duke found a wife in Helena Zimmerman, also an American. Mary Goelet became Duchess of Roxburghe, a match accompanied by New York newspaper headlines clamoring: "England's Poorest Duke after our Richest Heiress." It is no wonder that an eager British nobleman placed an ad in *The Daily Telegraph* reading as follows:

OPPOSITE: Consuelo and Sunny Marlborough, with their children, King Charles spaniels, and ducal trappings, as portrayed magnificently by John Singer Sargent in 1905 Although considered a brilliant match, the Vanderbilt/ Marlborough union proved to be the saddest and most cynical of the transatlantic alliances formed during the Gilded Age. BELOW: As the illustrator seems to have perceived in the image reproduced here, Consuelo Vanderbilt wept so bitterly before being led to the altar that the ceremony had to be postponed for an hour until she could compose herself. The unhappy couple did produce an heir and a spare, but eventually Consuelo got a papal annulment on the grounds of coercion. ABOVE: When Mary Goelet married the Duke of Roxburghe, the tabloid press announced in tall headlines: "England's poorest Duke after our Richest Heiress." It guaranteed a throng of curiosity-seekers as the wedding party entered St. James's on Fifth Avenue.

An English Peer of very old title is desirous of marrying at once a very wealthy lady; her age and looks are immaterial, but her character must be irreproachable; she must be a widow or spinster—not a divorcee. If among your clients you know such a lady, who is willing to purchase the rank of a peeress for £25,000 sterling, paid in cash to her future husband, and who has sufficient wealth besides to keep up the rank of a peeress, I shall be pleased if you will communicate with me in the first instance by letter when a meeting can be arranged in your office. I beg you to keep this confidential. The peer will pay handsomely for the introduction when it is arranged.

By 1915 nearly 500 American women had married into the European aristocracy, which included 42 American princesses, 17 duchesses, 19 viscountesses, 33 marchionesses, and hundreds of baronesses and countesses, almost all of them in Britain and France. Meanwhile, an American grandee like William K. Vanderbilt could be accepted in Paris and London by virtue of his splendid stable. One branch of the Astors became British and even entered the peerage under their own name, thanks to massive philanthropy. All in all, the American invasion of European society was extremely fortuitous. The women not only replenished coffers and thickened blue blood; they also proved to be distinct social assets. Young American ladies were far better educated than their British counterparts, purposely kept ignorant as these were of anything but sewing and housekeeping in a world totally dominated by

men. Frances, Countess of Warwick, put it quite succinctly: "As a class, we did not like brains."

In France, aristocratic daughters either grew up in châteaux among the peasantry or with nuns, prior to being pushed into arranged marriages the night after learning the facts of life. As a consequence, the more liberated Yankees could talk or flirt circles around European girls, and once married they played important roles in the cultural and political life of their adopted countries. All the marriages were not unhappy, despite their having been mostly dictated by overweening parents eager for the daughters to return home on occasional visits, thereupon outranking the other girls with whose parents the family constantly competed in boardrooms and ballrooms. The elders also wanted to participate in the brilliant "seasons" abroad, where, as part of the family, they could not be refused. But for some young women, the price paid to satisfy their parents' social objectives was terrible.

RIGHT: An artist's conception of a glittering soirée at the Palais de Marbre Rose, the great mansion built on Paris's Avenue du Bois by the Marquis Boni de Castellane with money from his marriage to the rather unattractive Anna Gould, granddaughter of Jay Gould, "the Mephistopheles of Wall Street." Unlike Consuelo Vanderbilt, Anna did not have to be forced into an alliance with old European nobility. Still, after Boni squandered and then philandered, Anna sought a divorce in order to make a still more prestigious marriage, this time to Boni's uncle, the Duc de Talleyrand-Périgord. In the end, therefore, the Goulds obtained value for their money, which Anna's titles seemed to launder clean of the robber-baron taint that had long clung to it.
BELOW: Charles Édouard Boutibonne (1816-79), *Getting Dressed*, 1869. This *belle parisienne* could be preparing to attend one of Boni de Castellane's geat balls at the Palais de Marbre Rose on Paris's Avenue du Bois.

THE RULES OF THE GAME IN EUROPE

Once established and the mothers of children, the American heiresses became part of European aristocracy, unless they returned home for good or behaved scandalously. They might also attempt to bring their relatives into society, a goal achieved with varying degrees of success. Boni de Castellane, for example, proposed his father-in-law, George Gould, for the aristocratic Jockey Club in Paris, only for the son of the notorious robber baron to be blackballed. Outside the proper marriage, elevation into European nobility could be achieved only by royal decree. In France, there was no legitimate font of honor after the Revolution, and nobody took the honors distributed at Napoleon III's court terribly seriously. However, daughters of France's newly rich industrialists and bankers married into old families and brought their titled husbands into the realm of business and on to the boards of the country's important companies and financial institutions. Eugène Schneider, France's steel lord, found titled husbands for his four daughters, and one of his grandsons married into the House of Orléans. New champagne, sugar, and banking fortunes refilled the coffers of such princely families as the Broglies, Poniatowskys, Brissacs, or Breteuils, as well as those of the Uzès, the premier Dukes of France. By the end of the nineteenth century, more than thirty American heiresses had become the consorts of grand and titled Frenchmen.

South American and Mexican money played the same role in Paris society as South Africa's mining fortunes had in London, bringing large infusions of cash to the social scene. Eventually Latin Americans married into such important families as the de Ganays, and the arrival in Paris of Simon Patiño—the colossally rich Bolivian mestizo tin king—proved to be a bonanza even for the Spanish royal family, into which his son married. French aristocracy, despite their lack of a court around which to revolve, was extremely proud—even haughty—and French remained the lingua franca of higher society throughout Europe until World War II. The literary, musical, and artistic salons of the French capital were really courts of a sort, informal institutions that forged a unique interrelationship between the arts and society. Crucially, they helped make Paris the cultural center of Europe during the Belle Époque. The perfect diarist of all this was Marcel Proust, who, in *Le Côté de Guermantes*, described the aristocratically dominated salons and clubs that melded intelligence, art, and birth into a new ruling class.

Vienna, the capital of the Hapsburg Empire, had a far more hidebound and tedious social scene, its aristocracy pretty much closed to newcomers either by marriage or by ennoblement. A perceptive *fin-de-siècle* visitor, Virginia Gayda, described Viennese society as "fused into a disdainful little circle, closely bound to the court in time of need, impassive and indifferent to changing times, unfriendly and opposed to things and people foreign to its kingdom." Definitely not *hoffähig*, or eligible to enter Franz Joseph's stuffy, family-like inner circle, were intellectuals, newly rich industrialists and bankers, or Jews, and the last Hapsburg Emperor was extremely stingy with major patents of nobility. Given the all-important role played by Jews in the arts, sciences, banking, and commerce, a society as isolated and aloof as the Viennese court

been wise enough to dine earlier in the *chambres privées* at Sacher's. However, social life could be quite brilliant in the splendid city palaces of such old Viennese princely families as the Liechtensteins, Schönburgs, Schwarzenbergs, Metternichs, Lobkowiczes, or Dietrichsteins. But they too received only those Austro-Hungarians considered *hoffähig* or else foreigners of an equivalent class. Shockingly rich from vast landholdings in the Empire as well as in Central Europe, these

could not but be dull and even irrelevant. As a result, the dynamic, ambitious money-makers directed their energy, fortune, and wit toward art and culture, thus giving rise to the intellectual renaissance of Vienna in the years before World War I. The brightest moments of life at the Hofburg, the Imperial palace, were dinners served at a long table where the Emperor generally cleared his plate before some of his guests had been able to raise a fork. Yet, according to protocol, nobody could eat once His Imperial Majesty had finished, leaving many to go home hungry, had they not

grandees could in no way be tempted to pollute their blue bloodlines with anyone less than 24 quarters noble, the standard applied by the *Almanac de Gotha*. Below these great princes was a less elevated nobility who were *hoffähig* but also open to a larger group viewed as *salonfähig*. Here too the intelligentsia and Jews were deemed too ill at ease to interact in a proper Viennese salon. Country weekends at the great estates were totally devoted to forestry and blood sports, and thickets of noble stag horns sprouted from every inch of wall space in many a vast and breezy *schloss*.

The great families of the Hapsburg Empire also had castles in Prague and around the Central European countryside, where they received their peers and excluded everybody else. World War I, of course, shattered this cozy, protected world, which changed dramatically after the fall of the Empire. Since then, even non-*salonfähig* heiresses—including many Americans—were welcomed as mates and could soon be found wearing dirndls and studying their *Gotha*. During the Gilded Age, however, social climbing in the Austrian part of the Empire was *streng verboten*—out of the question. Curiously, a quite different situation prevailed in the

LEFT: Wilhelm Gause (19th century), *The Court Ball* (Historisches Museum der Stadt, Vienna). At the epicenter of Austro-Hungarian society reigned Emperor Franz Joseph (1830-1916) for almost a full half-century. The antiquated "Spanish" etiquette rigidly observed at the Hapsburg court must have seemed quite odd when set against the vigorously innovative artistic and intellectual life of Vienna at the turn of the century. Here, the Emperor receives the homage of his lady guests at a court ball in the Hofburg. As usual, he stands alone, since his Empress, the beautiful Elisabeth of Bavaria, preferred being almost anywhere— especially the Greek island of Corfu—other than Vienna.
FAR LEFT: Emperor Franz Joseph entertains Czar Nicholas II at Schönbrunn Palace on 30 September 1903. The autocratic regimes of Russia and Austria could not unbend sufficiently to acknowledge the newly rich, who thus directed their considerable energies towards the arts, with happy results, as well as towards politics, with decidedly mixed consequences.

Imperial Germany—the Reich—was a concoction of numerous small, ancient fiefdoms or principalities cobbled together in nationhood by Prussia's "Iron Chancellor" Bismarck and Kaiser Wilhelm I. Dominated as it was by the large aristocratic military, German society adhered to a strict code of Teutonic values, which left little room for the kind of glamour that sparkled elsewhere during the Gilded Age, especially in Paris, London, New York, and Newport. With his shrunken arm, vanity, and paranoia, the stiff-necked Wilhelm II (r. 1888-1918) was more feared and ridiculed than welcomed on Europe's royal circuit. Instead of leading society as his uncle, Edward VII of Britain, did, "Kaiser Willy" drove Europe into the suicidal morass of World War I, thereby destroying his own class.

ABOVE: Snappily uniformed Prussian cavalrymen salute their officers, who seem to be enjoying themselves in the company of a beautiful but aloof young lady.

RIGHT: A rather self-satisfied, foppish German officer revels in the attention paid him by the old and the young alike at a Berlin tea party in 1897.

Hungarian part of Franz Joseph's realm, where the Magyar ruling classes, having no interest whatever in business, opened up the country to foreign entrepreneurs, whom they supported, encouraged, and brought into the establishment. By 1914 Jews made up 25 percent of Budapest's population; moreover, they totally controlled finance, commerce, and light industry. The new bourgeoisie received titles in the thousands, and 28 Jews even became hereditary barons. Yet, despite its cosmopolitan upper crust, Budapest remained a province of the Hapsburg Empire, and, as elsewhere in that realm, its social life generated few if any sparks.

Nor did the social doings of Germany's stiff-necked Hohenzollern court and vast feudal aristocracy radiate much interest at the end of the century. A few generations earlier, there had been enchanting courts led by cultivated electors and princes who followed eighteenth-century France in sponsoring musicians, composers, artist-decorators, and porcelain manufacturers. These enlightened autocrats commissioned elegant palaces and made them the setting for delightful musicales, *fêtes champêtres*, and other entertainments. All this changed, however, when Germany's gaggle of independent principalities came together as a single, federated state under the leadership of Prussia. The new nation rediscovered its Teutonic, warrior past and began yearning for a return to a Holy Roman Empire, stretching from the Baltic to the Adriatic and ruled over by a patrician caste led by the Kaiser in Berlin. Young aristocratic males, as a consequence, spent their student years bashing one other's heads with sabres, slashing cheeks with dueling swords—eager to win the prized *mansur* scar—drinking beer and schnapps, and studying von Clausewitz's military strategies. This left little time or energy for dances and flirtations in ballrooms. Beginning with Otto von Bismarck, the Prussian "Iron Duke," all of Germany's chancellors belonged to the nobility, from

1871 to the end of World War I. So too did most of the Imperial cabinet, leaders of the Foreign Ministry, and 90 percent of the country's ambassadors. Monocle-popping, heel-clicking nobles were in charge of the armed forces, and crisp uniforms, feather-crested eagle helmets, and polished boots lent a snappy air to Berlin's elegant Unter den Linden. The Kaiser did make an effort to bring into his circle industrialists and bankers who would be useful to his ultimate purpose, but receptions in town and shooting weekends on country estates had little of the bonhomie so characteristic of Paris, Newport, and London. Germany's aristocracy, however, was beautifully mannered, adhered as a rule to a strict moral code, and had the means to live in grand style. Foreign heiresses, however, were not tempted to become soldiers' wives, and Berlin held slight allure for the fun-loving.

The same could not be said of Imperial Russia, particularly of its capital, St. Petersburg. Here, the great titled families lived in enormous palaces on the banks and canals of the Neva and entertained one other nonstop, starting with the Christmas Bazaar of the Circle of the Nobility and ending at Lent, when most of the well-off departed for Nice and Monte Carlo. Every night there were splendid balls and receptions, as well as wonderful ballets and operas at the blue and gold Marjinsky Theater. Nowhere were jewels bigger, tables more sumptuously set, liveried servants more numerous, and distinguished foreigners more welcome (if properly introduced). Society, however, was absolutely fixed, and the reactionary autocracy refused to expand it to include the new industrial and financial bourgeoisie. Not a single merchant prince was ever ennobled, yet an astonishing 7 percent of St. Petersburg's population bore some form of official czarist recognition, and by 1897 Russia had a grand total of 1,373,000 nobles of both sexes. This, like much else in the reigns of Alexander III and Nicholas II, was a colossal blunder, since much of the industrial elite sympathized with and financed the revolutionary left rather than joining the aristo-cratic far right. There were practically no marriages between old families and new money, and the mere idea of a rich foreigner appropriating a grand title by marriage would have seemed an absurdity. This, of course, changed radically in 1917, when Russian grand dukes, princes, and counts found that the only alternative to driving a taxi or selling jewels and paintings was to capture an heiress.

Dressing Up

International social life involved a mind-boggling outlay for dresses and jewels, particularly since a desire for sartorial ostentation was shared by royalty, aristocracy, and the newly rich. There was only one place for women to shop—Paris—which clothed almost every female member of the *beau monde*. Dressmakers in New York, Buenos Aires, and St. Petersburg did their best to copy the splendid creations they saw in *L'Illustration*, *Gazette du Bon Ton*, and other fashion magazines published in the French capital. But no self-respecting lady of means would put up with anything less than a Paris original that bore the label of Charles Frederick Worth, the first great couturier and the virtual dictator of fashion from 1860 until his death in 1895. In his salon at 7 Rue de la Paix, Worth laid down the law for queens, empresses, divas, actresses, grand courtesans, and international millionairesses, telling

In 1907, a well-heeled and thoroughly bedecked client selects fabric for her new gown at the Worth salon on Paris's Rue de la Paix. Owing to the number of orders he had to fill, Worth—the Englishman who founded the French couture industry—did not radically alter the cut of his clothes in any one season; rather, he assured one-of-a-kind dresses by the variety of materials—textiles, embroidery, embellishments such as pearls, jet, brilliants, feathers, etc.—with which he made them. The stuffs most favored by Worth were silk, tulle, velvet, brocade, lace, gauze, and cloth of silver, often trimmed in bows and fringes. The House of Worth filled orders from all over the world, but the great pioneer couturier had a particularly high regard for American women, who, he said, "had faith, figures, and francs. Faith to believe in me, figures that I can put in shape, and francs to pay my bills."

ABOVE: Franz Winterhalter (1806-73), *Pauline Sandor, Princess Metternich*, 1860. The bearer of one of Europe's most illustrious names, acquired through marriage to the Austrian ambassador to France, Princess Metternich had the beauty, style, and prestige to lead society and fashion in Paris. Stunning in ball gowns made by Worth, well before any other lady patronized his small salon, Pauline Metternich persuaded Empress Eugénie to take the revolutionary step of allowing herself to be dressed by a man. RIGHT: Franz Winterhalter, *Empress Eugénie Surrounded by Her Ladies in Waiting* (Château de Compiègne). The consort of Napoleon III became Worth's most important and influential client. Under the Second Empire (1852-70), France enjoyed twenty years of peace, stability, and prosperity, a period that saw the rise of railroads, heavy industry, great joint-stock companies, and banks. Such well-being provided an ideal climate for the flowering of the couture industry, which Worth invented and virtually dominated for the remainder of the 19th century. In the group portrait reproduced here, the ladies of Eugénie's court are all dressed by Worth, making the scene a kind of seated *defilé de mode*.

them what to wear, choosing the colors and materials *he* felt were most appropriate to their personalities and physical attributes. The master even insisted that, prior to attending a grand ball, they pass by made up, fully dressed, and coiffed for a final inspection under candlelight. Before Worth, a lady bought material and took it to a seamstress to be made into a dress. Worth invented fashion, made it respectable for a man to dress women, became,

dered whether it would not be smarter to return to the more stable environment of his homeland.

In 1849 Prince Charles-Louis Napoleon—son of the Corsican arriviste's brother Louis, the former King of Holland, and his wife, Queen Hortense de Beauharnais (the daughter of the former Empress Josephine, the first wife of Napoleon I)—was elected Prince-President of France. Two years later he engineered a coup d'état that metamorphosed

with his wife Marie, as much part of society as his clients, and grew richer than many of them.

In numerous ways, Worth enjoyed a success story that stands up to that of the titans of industry and finance whose wives he dressed. He was born in the small market town of Bourne, south Lincolnshire, on October 13, 1825, the son of a solicitor who paid him little attention. While still a boy, Charles started working as a clerk at Swan and Edgar in London's Regent Street, sorting materials by day and sleeping under the counter at night. Here he stayed for seven years before moving to Lewis and Allenby, silk mercers by Royal Appointment to Her Majesty Queen Victoria. As a young man about London, Worth made many visits to the National Gallery, paying particular attention to the attire of grandees in portraits by major artists, a lesson that was to serve him well throughout his life. Realizing that Paris was the center for beautiful and luxurious materials, he crossed the Channel in 1845 and, after a year of living from hand to mouth, got a job selling material at Gagelin, the city's leading silk mercers who also marketed shawls and a few ready-made garments. These were turbulent years in Paris, fraught with all manner of rebellion that culminated in the revolution of 1848, and the young Englishman often won-

France's Second Republic into the Second Empire, whose seat of power was at the Château de St. Cloud and the Tuileries Palace. Suddenly, Paris became an Imperial capital after having guillotined aristocrats a mere sixty years earlier. The Emperor Napoleon III admitted to Princess Metternich, wife of the Austrian ambassador who went on to lead the Concert of Europe: *"N'oubliez pas, princesse, que je suis un parvenu dans le véritable acceptation du mot."* That was hardly a secret, and in some ways the new court was a bit of a joke; nonetheless, under Louis Napoleon France enjoyed twenty years of peace, stability, and incredible prosperity. The parvenu Emperor benevolently watched the rise of railroads and heavy industry, as well as the creation of the great joint-stock companies and banks, and he brought the makers and shakers of his time into the royal orbit. Everything boomed, the universal expositions drew visitors from all over the world, and Paris was rebuilt, becoming for nearly a quarter-century the center of the civilized world. In January 1853, the Emperor surprisingly married a mere Countess, Eugénie Maria de Montijo de Guzman, a Spanish-Scottish beauty with great chic and charm. For her wedding, Gagelin supplied the trousseau, affording Charles Worth his first glimpse of the lady who would become his most significant client and inspiration.

Another important marriage had taken place two years earlier. In 1851, the year of London's Great Exhibition, Charles Worth married a beautiful model, Marie Augustine Vernet, for whom he produced gorgeous dresses that Gagelin exhibited under his own name in Paxton's Crystal Palace. His creations—including a revolutionary court train that dropped from the shoulders rather than the waist—appeared at other expositions, and by 1858 Worth decided to set out on his own with a fellow *commis*, the Swede Otto Bobergh, as a partner. Shortly thereafter, Mme. Octave Feuillet, wife of the writer, was so displeased with a dress delivered to her the day before a grand ball at the Tuileries that she decided to try Worth and Bobergh. Overnight the avid new firm ran up a splendid gown of lilac silk covered with tulle of the same color gathered by knots of lilies-of-the-valley. Much taken by the ravishing creation, the Empress asked who had designed it. When told, she was stunned to learn of Worth's nationality and sex. A British tailor, Henry Creed, made her riding habits, but the idea of a man draping crepe and silk around the naked shoulders of an aristocratic lady seemed outrageous. Worth clearly needed a major push from a social engine, and in 1860 he sent Marie, sketches in hand, to see Princess Metternich, wife of the Austrian ambassador. The Princess said she would buy two gowns, neither to cost more than 300 francs, and Worth's staff immediately came to take her measurements. In a week, the dresses were ready, and they dazzled the Hungarian beauty, who particularly liked the extraordinary fit achieved in one visit, rather than the six or seven she was accustomed to. Princess Metternich decided to wear the evening dress to a state ball in the Salle des Maréchaux at the Tuileries.

The Empress once again inquired about the dress, and this time caved in. Mme. Feuillet might not be taken seriously in matters of fashion, but the Princess Metternich was a great arbiter of style. Eugénie summoned Worth to the Tuileries and ordered her first dress from him, whereupon the couturier turned out a particularly sumptuous creation in heavy Lyons brocade. Eugénie would have preferred light tulle, but the Emperor believed the dress would create new markets for the silk manufacturers in Lyons—a city he was soon to visit. Thus came into being what the Empress called her "political toilettes." It was also the birth of the haute couture industry.

In 1861 Queen Victoria's consort, Prince Albert, died, and life at the British court abated. Instantly, Paris became the only place to be for social action. Worth was lucky once again, since the Paris season, lasting from Epiphany to Shrove Tuesday, generated some 125 balls, on average, and no *grande dame* could be seen twice in the same dress. Meanwhile, Worth and Bobergh had emerged as the sole *fournisseurs* of the Empress's evening gowns, with the result that every lady on the social circuit had virtually no choice but to head for the Rue de la Paix.

A ball given in 1857 at Catherine de' Medici's Tuileries Palace, which Napoleon III and Empress Eugénie made their official residence in Paris. Only the Russian Imperial court in St. Petersburg could match the four state galas staged at the Tuileries during the Second Empire. On these spectacular occasions, the great Renaissance halls were thronged with 4,000-5,000 people.

After the collapse of the Second Empire, social excitement returned to London, for a host of reasons. First, it was the capital of the world's greatest empire and thus a major center of power and money. Further, the monarchy was quite open to the idea of expanding the titled classes by ennobling the newly rich industrialists and bankers. Businessmen and captains of industry of every religious persuasion received their fair share of peerages, even if the bulk went to the landed gentry. Although rigid codes of behavior, dress, education, and manner of speech excluded several freshly elevated tycoons from the bosom of society, their sons attended public schools and universities where, chameleon-like, they absorbed upper-class tics and formed the lifelong friendships that gave them the solid entry their parents lacked. With agricultural income declining, high-born Englishmen also started to covet the remunerative corporate directorships that involved little work. They were also open to the business advice that the powerful newcomers could give them before regulatory authorities invented inside trading. The transaction was rather similar to the dollar-heiress industry, in that feudal aristocrats gave parvenus the gift of their name and presence in return for money, perks, and stock-market tips. Not only did they grace the dining rooms of wealthy commoners; they even, occasionally, invited them back to their often less opulent residences in town or country. Thus, business boards and rich men's tables sparkled with lofty titles, and society became increasingly more varied. But what really made London an enjoyable place to be at this time was the Prince and eventually monarch who gave the jolly period in Britain its name.

Albert Edward, as Prince of Wales and later King Edward VII, was merry, gregarious, open to change, enamored of beautiful women and social

RIGHT: For their wedding in 1864, the Prince and Princess of Wales posed with his mother, Queen Victoria, still in deep mourning for her consort, Prince Albert, who had died in 1861. The bride, Princess Alexandra of Denmark, brought beauty and sweetness into the British royal family, greatly improving the life of Prince Edward, who had barely survived the unhappiness of his earlier life.

RIGHT: The Indian Room at Marlborough House during the residence there of Edward and Alexandra of Wales. Following their marriage, the great mansion—built on the Mall by Sir Christopher Wren in 1709-11 for the first Duke of Marlborough—became the center of London society, from which Queen Victoria had withdrawn into solemn widowhood. The royal couple also bought Sandringham, a great house in game-rich Norfolk, where they entertained at weekends and during the Christmas holidays. ABOVE: A caricature of Wales as a cock among hens. Thanks to his complaisant wife, Edward could more or less freely indulge his appetite for good food and spirited women, especially in Paris.

LEFT: The 1902 coronation procession of Edward VII, who had the good fortune to reign during a brief decade when the British Empire reached the zenith of its power and prestige. A monarch of gargantuan scale, Edward was entirely equal to the occasion, if not to his own coronation as originally scheduled for 1901. Despite abdominal pains on the eve of the event, the King gave way to gluttony as usual, thereby bringing on an attack of appendicitis, from which he nearly died. By the time His Majesty recovered the host of crowned heads and other dignitaries had returned home, some of them as far away as India and Japan. When it finally took place, the ceremony could scarcely have been more splendid, even if short on royal attendance from abroad.

FAR LEFT: Archibald Stuart Wortley (1849-1905), *Edward VII* (Forbes Magazine Collection, New York).

subjects. The courtier Lord Granville got it right when he surmised that Edward was loved because he had all the faults of which the Englishman is accused.

London society gravitated quickly into what would soon be known as "the Marlborough House set," joining the Prince and Princess of Wales in a seemingly endless merry-go-round of banquets, balls, operas, music halls, and private suppers. The heir to the throne and his truly beautiful, sweet-tempered consort were the center of fashion, and everything they did was copied. When Bertie had an attack of rheumatism and was obliged to shake hands with his elbow pressed to his side, or when Alexandra became temporarily lame, everybody shook hands oddly or limped. And when the Prince once forgot to secure the bottom button of his waistcoat, a fashion was established which survives today. Being somewhat out of official life, the Prince had a fairly free choice of friends and hangers-on. The two things he hated most were discomfort and boredom, which drove him to take up with people eager to spoil or entertain him. Thomas Lipton did both, and the Kaiser simply could not understand why his very grand uncle was always "boating with his grocer."

Keeping up with Wales was an extremely expensive proposition and ruined such courtiers as Sir Christopher Sykes, whose reward was to have brandy poured over his head and cigars put out on

life, and constantly in need of money, at least until the death of his long-lived mother, Queen Victoria. Although seemingly a monument to self-indulgence, Edward the King proved to be quite intuitive about foreign policy. Moreover, he managed to establish himself as a royal sun around which all other European sovereigns revolved. And at home—despite scandals as well as almost perpetual absence abroad—he was absolutely adored by his

RIGHT: Young ladies being presented at court during the reign of Edward VII and Queen Alexandra. This ritual annually launched the London season, with its taxing round of lunches, breakfasts, teas, dinners, balls, horse races, regattas, and long country weekends. The King's avid interest in money and chronic need for entertainment guaranteed access to the court—including its titles and privileges—for the rich and successful as well as the high-born.

BELOW: King Edward and Queen Alexandra arriving to lay the foundation stone for King's College Hospital.

OPPOSITE: A.E. Harris (d. 1917), *Edward VII Receiving Maharajas and Dignitaries Prior to His Coronation*. Indian royals were probably the most colorful element in London's June season. They came to play polo at Sandringham, race their horses at Ascot, and pay tribute to their King Emperor, who gained their loyalty by a liberal sprinkling of Imperial decorations and titles.

the back of his hand while he groaned to the guffawing Prince: "As Your Royal Highness desires." The atmosphere was hilariously funny until somebody forgot his or her place. During a raucous billiards game at Sandringham, the fun-loving Prince put his hand on a friend's shoulder and remarked in a kindly manner, "Freddy, Freddy, you're verrry drunk," rolling his Hanoverian R's. Sir Frederick, pointing at Bertie's great girth, roared: "And Tum Tum, you're verrry fat." The Prince froze, the room suddenly turned silent, an equerry was called, and Sir Frederick's bags were packed.

THE SEASON

Edward Grey perceptively wrote that the Prince of Wales's "capacity for enjoying life was combined with a positive and strong desire that everyone else should enjoy life too." Yet, despite what would appear to be a fairly useless existence devoted entirely to pleasure, Edward harbored a strong sense of duty and a sincere—if generally frustrated—desire to serve his country. He also had a high energy level that, failing a serious outlet, made London an extremely entertaining place to visit during "the season," that early summer whirl of social and sporting events which culminated in the regatta at Cowes in early August. The very clear division between Queen Victoria ruling her Empire and the Prince of Wales reigning over society was unique, and it encouraged a degree of informality and openness that could not be found elsewhere in Europe or, for that matter, in the supposedly more democratic United States. The name of the game in Edwardian England was *inclusion*, at a time when fashionable New Yorkers were principally busy with *exclusion*, which explains why there were no free suites on the great ocean liners beginning in mid-May.

Americans who could not have got past the first gate of Vienna's Hofburg might even present their daughters at the English court, a ritual that was traditionally the first great event of the season. In May, fiacres would roll up to the porte cochère of

Buckingham Palace before 11 A.M., leaving daughters and parents to be ushered up the grand staircase by the palace staff in full court livery of knee breeches, crimson tailcoats, gold braid, and decorations. The debutantes, coiffed in three white plumes and dressed in long, white gowns, each with a train of specified court length, were ushered into a waiting room and brought out one by one to make a deep curtsy before the entire royal family. After rising slowly, they had to exit backward, no mean feat with a train threatening to trip them up at any instant. Light refreshments were served, after which all went off to "breakfasts" in the great houses and embassies of London.

COUNTRY WEEKENDS

The presentation of debutantes was followed by a seemingly endless series of entertainments. Lady Dorothy Neville remembered a season in which she attended fifty balls, sixty parties, about thirty dinners, and twenty-five afternoon "breakfasts," not to mention elaborate country-house parties during which exhausted socialites pretended to recover from the week. The most desirable parties, of

RIGHT: Edward VII at one of the many house parties he enjoyed on the country estates of the wealthy and the well-born who could afford it. However, playing host to this gregarious monarch could fray both nerves and pocketbook. Even putting together a list of guests interesting enough to gain the King's approval demanded great savoir-faire and diplomacy. No snob, Edward welcomed the company of his "Jewish court" of successful bankers and entrepreneurs— the Rothschilds, Baron de Hirsch, Sir Ernest Cassel, Sir Albert Abdullah Sassoon—upon whom he did not hesitate to bestow knighthoods and peerages. The kitchen had to be up to preparing the King's favorite dishes, including oysters, caviar, quail eggs, Scotch lobster, and game birds stuffed with foie gras and served in a rich, gluttonous Madeira sauce. But the monarch of dishes for Edward consisted of a turkey stuffed with a chicken, stuffed with a pheasant, stuffed with a woodcock and finally with a quail, all baked into a pie. There was a good chance the King might have shot the quail and the woodcock.
RIGHT: William Powell Frith (1819-1909), *The Fair Toxophilites* (Royal Albert Memorial Museum, Exeter). While weekending at some wealthy subject's country house, the easily bored King Edward would occasionally tolerate a visiting head of state; on every occasion, however, he would insist upon the presence of amusing, pretty, and sporting young women, particularly if safely married.

course, were those graced by the presence of the Prince and Princess of Wales, for which entire houses were often redecorated, an expense some hosts could barely afford. Weekends started on Saturday afternoon, when guests and servants arrived by train for the final journey by horse and carriage to the main house.

When shown to their rooms, guests would find their names in silver frames attached to the proper doors. This courtesy was essential for a successful weekend whose purpose was mostly late-night trysts, and it would not have done for a gentleman to wander into the wrong lady's room during the wee hours of the morn. There was an elaborate ritual concerning signals to be left outside the door to indicate free sailing or stormy weather. Upon arrival in the country house, meanwhile, the private servants, joined by the permanent staff, would immediately unpack, press the clothes, and lay out evening wear while the guests descended to an afternoon tea, weather permitting served in far pavilions in the formal garden. In many cases, tented follies were set up, to which servants brought cake, sandwiches, and a silver tea service in a procession along the neatly cut lawn. Otherwise, it was a cozy ceremony in the elaborately furnished drawing room, where great logs burned in late afternoon. In due time, everyone returned upstairs, where zinc tubs had been laid in the rooms, to be filled from large jugs of hot water brought up the service stairs. After the advent of modern bathrooms, servants engaged in a life-and-death struggle to get their employers in first.

Dinner was as elaborate as any occasion in the great houses of London, with seating arranged strictly according to protocol. This meant that the Prince and Princess of Wales or another royal guest

had to sit next to the same person for the entire weekend. (In the case of a Wales visit, the weekend generally became the larger part of a week). Boredom could often be relieved only by practical jokes, such as replacing the cheese with soft soap, a trick that Consuelo, Duchess of Marlborough, much enjoyed at Blenheim. A guest list always had to be reviewed in advance by the Prince or King, who often deleted names. A favorite victim was William Waldorf Astor, royally scratched as "too boring." After dinner came billiards, cards, conversation, and a bit of music. Despite the gargantuan dinner, served jointly by house and personal servants wearing livery prepared in all sizes, there would be another round of sandwiches, fruit, cakes, and drinks before retiring.

Without the presence of the Waleses, weekends could be somewhat less grand as well as a bit more relaxed, since hostesses no longer had to fear the icy wind of royal ennui or displeasure. And, of course, Edward and Alexandra reciprocated even more grandly at Sandringham and Windsor, the latter particularly during Royal Ascot, and also at many balls in Marlborough House. These were the most remarkable of the London season, evenings that began with a Scottish gillie in plaids greeting guests in the entrance hall before passing them on to scarlet-coated footmen with powdered wigs. After their capes had been taken by a porter in a short red coat with a band of leather across the shoulders, they were escorted upstairs by a page in a dark-blue coat and black trousers. For a costume party on July 21, 1872, over 1,400 guests were invited to appear in disguise and Sir Frederick Leighton to do the decorations. The Prince dressed as Charles I in a great curled wig and white-plumed black felt hat highlighted by diamonds. Benjamin Disraeli described the event as "gorgeous, brilliant, fantastic."

The great private London balls may very well have climaxed in the fancy-dress pageant given by the Duchess of Devonshire on the occasion of Queen Victoria's Diamond Jubilee in 1897. Three thousand invitations were sent out, at a time when the British capital was filled with visiting royals and grandees from all over the world. The Duchess's guests went to extraordinary trouble and expense, each of them spending several hundred pounds on their finery and bringing out the very largest of their important jewels. The theme was "allegorical or historical costume before 1815," and the hostess suggested that there be processions of royal courts. The Prince of Wales came as the Grand Prior of the Order of St. John of Jerusalem and Princess Alexandra as Marguerite de Valois, the Duke and Duchess of Westminster as Emperor Charles V and Queen Zenobia of Palmyra. The two resplendent couples stood at the top of the Devonshires' grand staircase to receive the homage of, among others, three Queens of Sheba and two Cleopatras, as well as the real Lady de Grey and Mrs. Arthur Paget, the latter from the United States and "a marvelous study in white and gold and literally covered in jewels."

LEFT AND BELOW: Early-18th-century Blenheim Palace, designed by Sir John Vanbrugh for the Duke of Marlborough, was a favorite weekend haunt for Edward VII. While grander than almost any other country mansion of its kind, Blenheim epitomized the environment in which the elect of the Gilded Age reveled away their weekends of sport, politics, high finance, gourmandise, and amorous adventure.

FAR RIGHT: The extraordinarily
elegant salesroom of Fouquet,
at 6 Rue Royale in Paris, was
created by the Spanish artist
Alfonso Mucha in 1901. Paris
was the Mecca for rich
grandees who were constantly
searching for splendidly
designed jewellery.

BELOW: The Maharaja of Patiala
was among Cartier's most
important customers, and is
seen here wearing a necklace of
pearls as well as a diamond and
ruby turban ornament designed
and made at the firm's
headquarters on the Place
Vendome.

ABOVE AND CENTER: For those
unable to splurge on such
baubles, Bapst and Falize
supplied retour à l'antique
bracelets, while Castellani
produced in Rome hardstone
cameo brooches imitating
Greek and Roman originals.

JEWELRY

The second half of the nineteenth century was one of the most brilliant eras for beautiful jewelry since the establishment of the Medici workshops in Renaissance Florence. Stones of particular magnificence were coming out of South Africa's mines, at the same time that maharajas were arriving at the Rue de la Paix jewelers to have vast quantities of family treasures redesigned in more contemporary taste. Not only had the Arts and Crafts movement spawned a new generation of designers, but all around the world rich clients were eager to give flattering presents to their wives and mistresses. In response to this demand, great new jewelers came forward to offer their talents and services—Cartier, Mellerio, Boucheron, Lalique, and Georges Fouquet, the latter with his storefront on the Rue Royale designed by the Art Nouveau painter Alphonse Mucha. Fortunately, these masters could count on the craft and ingenuity of seasoned workshops all over the French capital. They helped make Paris the undisputed center of the jewelry industry at the end of the century, although St. Petersburg shone brightly with the fabulous creations of Fabergé, Tiander, Ovchinnikov, and many minor but interesting designers, all of whom worked for both the court and the new bourgeoisie.

In design, historicizing eclecticism competed with nature-inspired modernism, which was essentially Art Nouveau. Among the most accomplished of the eclectic jewelers were Castellani and Giuliano. The Castellanis started as goldsmiths on the ground floor of the Palazzo Raggi in Rome and then went on to engender the revival of Italian archaeological jewelry that could subsequently be found displayed, along with antique Greek and Roman vases, in a shop on the Piazza Fontana de Trevi. Affluent visitors were thrilled to bring back these gold souvenirs, often embellished with tiny mosaics and semiprecious stones, that evoked the Classical and Byzantine worlds. In the 1860s, prior to opening his own establishment at 115 Piccadilly, Carlo Giuliano arrived in London with Castellani and sold his less literal copies after antique prototypes to various jewelers. In Paris, the leading exponent of the *retour à l'antique* was certainly Eugène Fontenay, whose young and brilliant disciple, Henri Vever, started in the same vein before going on to create gold and enamel masterpieces in the Art Nouveau manner.

Greek pieces enjoyed a great vogue in the last decade of the Second Empire, and the Empress Eugénie gave Fontenay her custom as did a few Oriental potentates, such as the Shah of Iran, whose commissions the French jeweler studded with large stones supplied by Fontenay's associate, Joseph Halphen. Other French "antiquarians" of the moment were Mellerio and Baugrand, but

ABOVE: The main salesroom of Tiffany's, on New York's Fifth Avenue, was where rich Americans bought the jewelled trifles they liked to hide in guests' dinner napkins. It also had the world's largest stock of important diamonds and a brilliant designer in Louis Comfort Tiffany, son of the firm's founder.
BELOW: The greatest art nouveau designer, however, was René Lalique, whose enamel and gold brooch, with two girls and swallows, seems to be in flight thanks to typical sinuous and sensuous curves.
BELOW: A gold bracelet by Giuliani, inspired by ancient Greek jewellery, seems tame in comparison.

undoubtedly the most spectacular homage to antiquity came from the London jeweler Hancock, who remounted the world-famous collection of ancient cameos belonging to the Duke of Devonshire. Hancock set them in enameled gold to make a multipart parure that would be worn by Countess Granville, wife of the sixth Duke of Devonshire's nephew, at the coronation of Alexander II of Russia (to whose court the Earl of Granville had been appointed ambassador). Even the Russians, who owned the grandest jewelry of all, were impressed by the parure, a superb ensemble that included diadem, coronet, stomacher, necklace, comb, and bracelet.

The revival of enamel became one of the great achievements in jewelry design during the second half of the nineteenth century, an instance of eclecticism that involved looking beyond the ancient world to the Middle Ages and Renaissance. French master enamelers specializing in revival pieces were Lucien Falize, Cartier, and Christofle, but the undoubted genius was Peter Carl Fabergé, who made frames, cigarette boxes, Imperial Easter eggs, pocket watches, cane handles, cufflinks, and even service bells gleam with all the colors of the rainbow. Their special iridescence derived from underlying patterns engraved in silver and gold, all highlighted by diamonds and other precious stones. While parents ordered these exquisite concoctions at the Fabergé shop off the Nevsky Prospekt, their children played with small animals carved by Fabergé in the semiprecious stones so plentiful in Russia's mountains. Although Fabergé endowed his jewelry with Art Nouveau qualities, he essentially looked backward to the courts of the eighteenth century in order to satisfy the taste of his aristocratic and rather decadent clientele.

LALIQUE, TIFFANY, CARTIER

In Art Nouveau jewelry, no one came close to René Lalique, who, for brilliance of design, can certainly be put in the class of Benvenuto Cellini, the great Renaissance goldsmith. The main difference is that while Cellini used only precious materials, Lalique employed horn, crystal, glass, and such inexpensive stones as amethyst, opals, and aquamarines. Diamonds, when they did appear, were tiny and utilized to generate a bit of glitter. Like all Art Nouveau masters, Lalique sought his models in nature, where he found the crisp autumn leaves,

RIGHT BELOW: Alfred Cartier, seen here with his sons Louis,Pierre and Jacques, created a veritable empire of fine jewellery, with branches in Paris, London and New York prior to World War I. Like the Rothschilds, the Cartiers found strength in numbers and were extremely active in Czarist Russia.

BELOW: The Grand Duchess Vladimir is seen dressed as a Boyar's wife for the last and grandest of the Imperial Costume Balls in 1908. Cartier made her extraordinary kokoshnik headdress and also sold her the 107 carat emerald brooch. After the Russian Revolution of 1917, Cartier repurchased many of the gems they had sold, permitting such grand ladies a few more comfortable years in exile.

tree roots, petals and flowers, iridescent butterflies, swans, and even serpents that abound in his work. Lalique, whose technical inventions in both jewelry and glass were manifold, cast a magic spell over the most ordinary materials and subject matter, creating pieces of sublime lightness. He was one of the stars of the universal expositions, and critics thought him the most remarkable designer of his day, after Vever and Fouquet, both of whom made extensive use of gold, pearls, and high-priced gems. Lalique's great contribution to the history of jewelry lay in debunking the notion that a truly desirable piece had to be materially valuable.

However beautiful Lalique's work, most wives of newly rich husbands preferred priceless rather than worthless jewelry and headed for Tiffany's or Cartier's. The former opened in New York City in 1837 and were renowned for their use of big, costly stones. The firm bought a girdle of diamonds reputedly once owned by Marie Antoinette and brilliants from noble estates, like that of Prince Esterhazy. Using such assets, Tiffany's offered creations on the order of "Peacock Feather," a hair ornament with a 30-carat yellow diamond surrounded by a plumed encrustation of 600 smaller white diamonds. When great stones came out of Kimberley, Tiffany's were first in line, their major purchase being the 287.4-carat Tiffany diamond, still the pride of the store. In 1887 they bought up most of the French crown jewels left behind by the fleeing Empress Eugénie, and by that year their vaults held over $40 million in precious stones. Tiffany and Co. had salesrooms in London and Geneva and served the royal houses of Europe and Asia with the same zeal they displayed toward rich American heiresses. In addition to being stone ped-

dlers *extraordinaires* to the very wealthy, the firm hired excellent designers, particularly after the 1902 arrival of Art Nouveau master Louis Comfort Tiffany, son of the founder.

If one wanted the finest stones and best designs, the place to go was Cartier, the king of jewelry for gala occasions. Founded in Paris in 1847 by Louis-François Cartier, who was joined by his son Alfred in the 1870s, the house originally catered to the taste of France's nouveaux riches. It advanced by leaps and bounds with the arrival of Alfred's sons—Louis, Pierre, and Jacques—who were sent around the world both to buy materials and to sell the beautiful finished products to their international clientele. In 1899 they opened a large shop on the Rue de la Paix, following it with another in London, on New Bond Street (1902). Six years later Pierre took charge of a "salon" on New York's Fifth Avenue, while also setting up a St. Petersburg branch, this one with the support of the Grand Duchess Xenia, the Grand Duke Vladimir, and Prince Felix Yussupov.

Louis Cartier, who assumed responsibility for design worldwide, had exquisite taste. He invented the graceful, curvilinear garland style, which evoked eighteenth-century glamour, and the mystery clock, which tells time seemingly without a mechanism. In 1910 Louis brought into the company an extremely talented designer, Jeanne Toussaint. Mme. Toussaint and Louis Cartier sought their inspiration in ancient Egypt, China, India, and Russia, and their close relationship, as both buyers and sellers, with the legendarily rich Indian maharajas and Russian grand dukes gave the house an unparalleled touch of opulence.

ADIEU

It was hats rather than parures, however, which were the most noticeable accessories at that centrally important annual event for the British upper crust: the mid-June, week-long equestrian-cum-fashion feast known as Royal Ascot. Ascot lies near Windsor, and the royal castle all but exploded with guests during racing week in the spring. The closing event of the three-month social season was Cowes, toward which every millionaire and royal steam yacht set course in mid-August, followed by an armada of the world's finest sailing ships. Then the waters of the Solent, shimmering mirror-like in the high-summer sun, bristled with a forest of bobbing, brilliantly flagged rigging. Farther out at sea lining the course were the enormous steam yachts—viewing platforms in the day and the center of brilliant entertainments after dark.

At the end of the season, sheets were thrown over the furniture, silver and gold plate stored in vaults, summer dresses packed in mothballs, and windows sealed shut, after which most London houses remained in suspended animation until the following May. The new grand hotels became the venue for short visits to town in the fall and winter. After Cowes, Bertie went off to his cures in Marienbad, Carlsbad, Bad Homburg, and Baden-Baden before setting out for the bracing air of Biarritz. But all this therapy could not keep the jolly royal alive forever, and, as King Edward VII, he died, at age 69, in 1910.

Britain would never again have a sovereign who managed so perfectly to combine pleasure and duty, or indeed one who so completely embodied the spirit of his time. George V was rather dour, his son and heir Edward VIII a good-looking, sweet, but irresponsible disaster, and his forced replacement, George VI, a stammering though steadfast leader in difficult times. Free of snobbishness, Edward VII evinced a lust for life, a passion for comfort and luxury, an appreciation of the upwardly mobile, and an international flair that truly made him monarch of monarchs, the uncle of Europe, and the leader of all society. The year of his death everyone wore black at Ascot, establishing the color as fashionable.

The Gilded Age continued for a while longer, thanks to the hallucinating momentum of more than half a century of fortune-building, industrial development, and prosperity. Before King Edward's death, however, there was the first inkling of catastrophe to come in the Russian Revolution of 1905, after czarist troops opened fire on the well-meaning procession of Father Gapon, who requested little more than an acknowledgment of the problems suffered by Old Russia's legions of have-nots. Jealous Wilhelm II—who as a bratty child had revealed his character at the wedding of Edward and Alexandra, where he bit the leg of an English uncle, the bridegroom's brother—could not be controlled once the Merry Monarch had gone. It was then that Kaiser Willy launched an unprecedented shipbuilding program designed to challenge Britain on the high seas. Shortly before his death, King Edward correctly predicted to Countess Greffulhe: "I have not long to live. Then my nephew Willy will make war."

Europe rolled inexorably on to a useless conflict that was to bring its old order as well as its Gilded Age to a bloody end. In 1917, the United States became a world leader, but its Gilded Age ended on black Black Tuesday, October 29, 1929. Since American society had so largely been built on money, it was quite appropriate that its Waterloo should be fought on the New York Stock Exchange. As bodies plummeted from skyscraper windows, the Jazz Age began.

ABOVE AND OPPOSITE: A 1910 Cartier diadem and a 1908 choker necklace, both in platinum and diamonds, were designed in the highly appreciated "style guirlande" that was particularly popular before the First World War. Rich and titled ladies in both the United States and Europe would have felt naked at a ball without such embellishments. Cartier took its inspiration from all parts of the world and all civilizations, blended perfectly the beautiful with the priceless, and remain among the greatest jewellers of all time.

EPILOGUE

It seems just yesterday that Jean Paul Getty, when asked what it felt like to be the world's only billionaire, replied quite prophetically that a billion dollars was not what it used to be. As of late 1991, there were 311 of the species in the world, but the only descendants of the Gilded Age moguls presently eligible for the *Fortune* magazine list are Baron Edmond de Rothschild and William Randolph Hearst, Jr., the former in 189th place with a meager $1.1 billion, the latter in 42nd place with $3.4 billion. It is also interesting to note that a scant 57 of the world's billionaires are American, although they do occupy seven of the top seventeen slots.

What caused the demise of our financial giants' descendants was mostly incompetence combined with estate and income taxes. As a rule, the great driving force of the patriarchs diminished through several generations, which progressively devoted far more effort to spending money than to making it. In most cases, heirs who tried to prove themselves blessed with their ancestors' business acumen ended up laying terribly expensive eggs and, at the same time, very much exploited by ruthless associates. In other words, they wasted more money on bad deals than on fine yachts. Then, of course, absent a strict system of primogeniture, fortunes were endlessly subdivided until they petered out. Most descendants of the very rich remain comfortably well-off, but they have lost their power. The two world wars were also grim decimators of fortunes, particularly in Europe, where property was destroyed, frontiers redrawn, and governments overthrown. The immense cost of destruction and reconstruction could only be covered by ever-larger tax assessments. Accordingly, the post-Depression Democrat governments in the United States, as well as the postwar Socialist governments in Europe and Britain, firmly believed that inherited wealth constituted an aberration, and so shaped laws to favor earned over unearned income and created important legislation to curb what they saw as the excessive abuses inherent in the capitalist system.

Philanthropy also played a major role in the liquidation of private wealth since many hard-earned fortunes were given away. Thus, nearly all of Andrew Carnegie's money went for, among other things, an international system of libraries, splendid auditoriums, and Carnegie Tech. The Astor fortune was largely used to put back into New York City what the family had taken out. The Rockefellers have been extraordinarily magnanimous in many areas of public welfare, while the Ford Foundation has played a major role in shaping modern times.

In most cases, the only way wealthy American families could maintain control of their empires and escape the long arm of the Internal Revenue Service was to leave their holdings tax-free to foundations they would control. Thus, the limited number of Americans on the *Fortune* list is irrelevant, since many heirs still direct foundations whose value far exceeds the holdings of all but the richest of the new crop of parvenus. All said and told, things worked not so badly. The public has benefitted from the wealth amassed by the few, and, in the aftermath of World War II, the developed world enjoyed the longest period of peace and economic expansion it had ever known. There was a new multinational world order under generally benevolent

American domination, and all the blocks were kept nicely in their places until the vast transfer of wealth from Europe, the United States, and Japan to a few tiny desert kingdoms ruled over by sheiks whose grandfathers were mostly horse thieves. Soon, hundreds of billions of dollars were being telexed around the world on round-the-clock call instead of being invested long term—and stagflation raised its ugly head.

The solution proposed by Ronald Reagan, the 40th President of the United States, as well as by his close ally, Prime Minister Margaret Thatcher of Great Britain, was a return to Adam Smith and laissez-faire. These powerful leaders wanted to make the 1980s into the 1890s, believing quite seriously that the rich would work harder and invest more if they paid fewer taxes and had less interference. Controls built up over decades were removed, causing stock markets to soar, at the same time that new fortunes were made by takeovers and by trading borrowed money on 24-hour exchanges. The price of paintings, resort homes, yachts, and all luxury goods skyrocketed; meanwhile, young people forgot there was any future outside Wall Street or the law firms that charged exorbitant fees to assist in the deconstruction of international industry.

The country allowed itself to be ruled by what economist John Kenneth Galbraith has so brilliantly identified as "the culture of contentment," in which the ease and security of a large middle and upper class are perpetuated by politicians of both parties to the detriment of a disenfranchised, increasingly poorer lower class who do not vote, largely out of inertia fueled by despair and a lack of truly committed representation. Harlem is the new Lower East Side, and illegal immigrants from the Third World peddling drugs have replaced the upwardly mobile Jewish pushcart merchants who became the backbone of American banking and retailing.

What the 1890s and 1980s really shared was the "conspicuous consumption" so entertainingly described by Thorstein Veblen in his classic treatise of 1899, *The Theory of the Leisure Class*. According to Veblen, prosperity is a trophy of success to be emulated, abstention from productive work, evidence of wealth, and a mark of social standing. Moreover, footmen in large numbers doing very little demonstrate their master's wealth and power, and it is par for the course for people in cold climates to "go ill clad in order to be well dressed." But Veblen's humor has a sharp edge when it comes to the inevitable crooks, lethal albeit smooth operators who turned up in the second Gilded Age just as in the first. "The thief or swindler who has gained great wealth by his delinquency has a better chance than the small thief of escaping the rigorous penalty of the law: and some good repute accrues to him from his increased wealth and from his spending the irregularly acquired possessions in a seemly manner".

Both the 1890s and 1980s suffered no shortage of ruthless, unprincipled, and occasionally dishonest moguls. The great difference, however, is that the gift of the 1890s was optimism, hope, and the industrial base of the twentieth century, while that of the 1980s seems to be bloated debt, tottering markets, intense anxiety, and no sense of the future whatsoever.

BIBLIOGRAPHY

Adams, Henry. *The Education of Henry Adams*. Boston and N.Y.: Houghton Mifflin, 1918.

Alexander, Grand Duke of Russia. *Once a Grand Duke*. N.Y.: Farrar & Rinehart, 1932.

Allfrey, Anthony. *Edward VII and His Jewish Court*. London: Weidenfeld & Nicolson, 1991.

Amory, Cleveland. *The Last Resorts*. N.Y.: Harper, 1952.

—-. *Who Killed Society?* N.Y.: Harper, 1960.

Anderson, R.D. *France, 1970-1914: Politics and Society*. London: Routledge & Kegan Paul, 1977.

Andrews, Wayne. *Architecture, Ambition, and Americans: A Social History of American Architecture*, rev. ed. N.Y.: Free Press, c. 1978.

—-. *The Vanderbilt Legend*. N.Y.: Harcourt, Brace, 1941.

Ashburn, Frank D. *Peabody of Groton: A Portrait*. N.Y.: Coward-McCann, 1944.

Auchincloss, Louis. *J.P. Morgan: The Financier as Collector*. N.Y.: Abrams, 1990.

Baedecker, Dietrich. *Alfred Krupp und die Entwicklung der Gussstahlfabrik zu Essen*. Essen, 1889.

Baldwin, Charles C. *Stanford White*. N.Y.: Dodd, Mead, 1931.

Balsan, Consuelo Vanderbilt. *The Glitter and the Gold*. N.Y.: Harper, 1952.

Baltzell, E. Digby. *Philadelphia Gentlemen*. Chicago: Free Press, 1958.

Bater, James H. *St. Petersburg: Industrialization and Change*. Montreal: McGill-Queens U. Press, 1976.

Beebe, Lucius. *The Big Spenders*. Garden City, N.Y.: Doubleday, 1966.

Behrens, C.B.A. *The Ancien Régime*. N.Y.: Harcourt Brace Jovanich, 1967.

Behrman, S.N. *Duveen*. N.Y.: Random House, 1951.

Bernstein, Victor Heine. *Final Judgment*. N.Y., 1947.

Birmingham, Stephen. *America's Secret Aristocracy*. Boston and Toronto: Little, Brown, c. 1987.

—-. *California Rich*. N.Y.: Simon and Schuster, c. 1980.

—-. *Our Crowd*. Boston: Little, Brown, 1968.

—-. *Real Lace: America's Irish Rich*. N.Y.: Harper & Row, 1973.

—-. *The Right People: A Portrait of the American Social Establishment*. Boston: Little, Brown, 1968.

Brandon, Ruth. *The Dollar Princesses: Sagas of Upward Nobility, 1870-1914*. N.Y.: Knopf, 1980.

Bridge, James H. *The Inside Story of the Carnegie Steel Company*. N.Y., 1903.

Brodrick, George C. *English Land and English Landlords*. London: Cassel, Pettre, Galpin, 1881.

Burnham, Alan. "The New York Architecture of Richard Morris Hunt," *Journal of the Society of Architectural Historians*. May, 1952.

Burnley, James. *Millionaires and Kings of Enterprise*. London and Philadelphia, 1901.

Cabanne, Pierre. *The Great Collectors*. N.Y.: Farrar, Straus, 1963.

Cable, Mary. *Top Drawer: American High Society from the Gilded Age to the Roaring Twenties*. N.Y.: Atheneum, 1984.

Calvert, George. *The Gentleman*. Boston: Ticknor and Fields, 1863.

Campbell, Edward G. *The Reorganization of the American Railroad System, 1893-1900*. N.Y., 1938.

Camplin, Jamie. *The Rise of the Plutocrats: Wealth and Power in Edwardian England*. London: Constable, 1978.

Canfield, Cass. *The Incredible Pierpont Morgan: Financier and Art Collector*. N.Y., 1974.

Carnegie, Andrew. *The Autobiography of Andrew Carnegie*. Boston, 1920.

Castellane, Boni de. *How I Discovered America*. N.Y.: Knopf, 1924.

Choules, John Overton. *The Cruise of the Steam Yacht North Star*. Gould and Lincoln, 1854.

Clapham, J.H. *The Economic Development of France and Germany: 1815-1914*, 4th ed. Cambridge, England: Cambridge U. Press, 1945.

Clark, George T. *Leland Stanford*. Stanford, Calif.: Stanford U. Press, 1931.

Clews, Henry. *Fifty Years in Wall Street*. N.Y.: Irving, 1908.

Cotter, Arundel. *The Authentic History of the United States Steel Corporation*. N.Y., 1916.

Cowles, Virginia. *Edward VII and His Circle*. London: Hamilton, 1956.

—-. *The Rothschilds: A Family of Fortune*. N.Y.: Knopf, 1973.

Crabtree, Reginald. *The Luxury Yacht from Steam to Diesel*. Newton Abbot: David & Charles, 1973.

Crawford, Mary Caroline. *Famous Families of Massachusetts*, 2 vols. Boston: Little, Brown, 1930.

Curl, Donald W. *Mizner's Florida: American Resort Architecture*. Cambridge, Mass.: MIT, c. 1984.

Cust, Sir Lionel. *King Edward VII and His Court: Some Reminiscences*. London: Murray, 1930.

Davidson, Bernice, Edgar Munhall, and Nadia Tscherny. *Paintings from the Frick Collection*. Intro. by Charles Ryskamp. N.Y.: Abrams, 1990.

Davis, John Hagg. *The Guggenheims: An American Epic*. N.Y.: Morrow, 1978.

Demeter, Karl. *The German Officer Corps in Society and State, 1650-1945*. N.Y.: Praeger, 1965.

Dodd, William E. *The Cotton Kingdom*. New Haven: Yale U. Press, 1921.

Donaldson, Marshall B. *The American Heritage History of Notable American Houses*. New York, 1971.

Donzel, Catherine, Alexis Gregory, and Marc Walter. *Grand American Hotels*. Intro. by Paul Goldberger. N.Y.: Vendome, 1989.

Drummond, Maldwin. *Salt-Water Palaces*. N.Y.: Viking, 1980.

Duff, David. *Eugénie and Napoleon III*. N.Y.: Morrow, 1978.

Duveen, James H. *The Rise of the House of Duveen*. N.Y., 1957.

Eliot, Elizabeth. *Heiresses and Coronets: The Story of Lovely Ladies and Noble Men*. N.Y.: McDonnell, Obolensky, 1959.

Ellet, Mrs. *The Queens of American Society*. N.Y.: Scribner, 1867.

Engelmann, Bernt. *Krupp*. Munich: Goldmann, 1978.

Erickson, Charlotte. *British Industrialists: Steel and Hosiery: 1850-1950*. Cambridge, England: Cambridge U. Press, 1959.

Farrer, David. *The Warburgs: The Story of a Family*. N.Y.: Stein and Day, 1975.

Folsom, Merrill. *Great American Mansions*. N.Y.: Hastings House, 1963.

Girouard, Mark. *Life in the English Country House: A Social and Architectural History*. New Haven: Yale U. Press, 1978.

Gregory, Alexis. *The Golden Age of Travel*. N.Y.: Rizzoli, 1991.

Grodinsky, Julius. *Jay Gould: His Business Career*. Philadelphia, 1957.

Gulbenkian, Nubar. *Portrait in Oil: The Autobiography of Nubar Gulbenkian*. N.Y.: Simon and Schuster.

Halévy, Élie. *The World Crisis of 1914-1918*. Oxford: Clarendon, 1930.

Hamm, Margherita Arlina. *Famous Families of New York*. N.Y.: Putnam, 1901.

Harvey, George. *Henry Clay Frick, the Man*. N.Y., 1928.

Hastings, Thomas, et al. "The Work of Messrs. Carrère & Hastings," *Architectural Record*. Jan., 1910.

Heckstall-Smith, Anthony. *Sacred Cowes*. London: Allan Wingate, 1955.

Hewins, Ralph. *Mr. Five Per Cent: The Story of Calouste Gulbenkian*. London: Hutchinson, 1957.

Hibbert, Christopher. *Edward VII, a Portrait*. London: Allen & Lane, 1976.

Hime, H.W.L. *Gunpowder and Ammunition*. London, 1904.

Hitchcock, Henry Russell. *The Architecture of H.H. Richardson and His Times*. N.Y., 1936.

Hobsbawm, E.J. *Industry and Empire: The Making of Modern English Society: 1750 to the Present Day*. N.Y.: Pantheon, 1968.

Holbrook, Stewart H. *The Age of the Moguls*. N.Y., 1953.

Hoyt, Edwin P. *The Guggenheims and the American Dream*. N.Y., 1977.

—-. *The Vanderbilts and Their Fortunes*. New York: Doubleday, 1962.

Johnson, William Weber. *The Forty-Niners*. New York: Time/Life, 1974.

Josephson, Matthew. *The Robber Barons*. N.Y.: Harcourt, Brace, 1934.

Kean, Beverly Whitney. *All the Empty Palaces: The Merchant Patrons of Modern Art in Pre-Revolutionary Russia*. London: Barrie & Jenkins, 1983.

Kennan, George. *Edward H. Harriman: A Biography*, 2 vols. Cambridge, Mass., 1922.

King, Robert B. *Vanderbilt Houses*. N.Y.: Rizzoli, 1989.

Kolodin, Irving. *The Metropolitan Opera*. N.Y.: Oxford, 1936.

Kruedener, Jürgen von. *Die Rolle des Hofes im Absolutismus*. Stuttgart: Gustav Fischer, 1973.

Krupp, Alfred. *Generalregulativ (Vorbemerkungen und Kommentar von Ernst Schroeder)*, in *Tradition: Zeitschrift für Firmengeschichte und Unternehmerbiographie*. 1956.

Laver, James. *Edwardian Promenade*. Boston: Riverside, 1958.

Lehr, Elizabeth Drexel. *"King" Lehr and the Gilded Age*. Philadelphia, 1935.

Lewis, Oscar. *The Big Four: The Story of Huntington, Stanford, Hopkins, and Crocker, and of the Building of the Central Pacific*. N.Y. and London, 1938.

—-. *The Silver Kings*. N.Y.: Knopf, 1947.

Longford, Elizabeth. *Queen Victoria: Born to Succeed*. Harper & Row, 1964.

Loth, David. *Public Plunder: A History of Graft in America*. N.Y.: Carrick & Evans, 1938.

Low, Will H. *A Monograph on the Work of McKim, Mead & White*, 4 vols. N.Y., 1925.

Lucie-Smith, Edward, and Celestine Dars. *How the Rich Lived*. N.Y.: Two Continents, 1976.

Machtan, Lother, and Dietrich Milles. *Die Klassensymbiose von Junkertum und Bourgeoisie in Preussen-Deutschland: 1850-1878/79*. Frankfurt: Ullstein, 1980.

Manchester, William. *The Arms of Krupp, 1587-1968*. N.Y.: Bantam, 1968.

Marly, Diane de. *Worth: Father of Haute Couture*. N.Y.: Holmes and Meir, 1980.

Mayer, Arno J. *The Persistence of the Old Regime: Europe to the Great War*. N.Y.: Pantheon, 1981.

McAllister, Ward. *Society as I Have Found It*. N.Y.: Cassell, 1890.

McCagg, William O., Jr. "Ennoblement in Dualistic Hungary," *East European Quarterly 5* (13-26). 1971.

Menne, Bernhard. *Krupp, Deutschlands Kanonenkönige*. Zurich, 1937.

Morris, Lloyd. *Incredible New York*. N.Y.: Random House, 1951.

Muhlen, Norbert. *The Incredible Krupps: The Rise, Fall, and Comeback of Germany's Industrial Family*. N.Y.: Henry Holt, 1959.

Muhlstein, Anka. *Baron James: The Rise of the French Rothschilds*. London and N.Y., 1983.

Myers, Gustavus. *History of the Great American Fortunes*. N.Y.: Modern Library, 1964.

Nicolson, Nigel. *Mary Curzon*. London: Wiedenfeld & Nicolson, 1977.

Noffsinger, James Philip. *The Influence of the École des Beaux-Arts on the Architects of the United States*. Wash., D.C.: Catholic U., 1955.

O'Connor, Harvey. *The Astors*. N.Y.: Knopf, 1941.

O'Connor, Richard. *The Golden Summers: An Antic History of Newport*. N.Y.: Putnam, 1974.

Olivier, Fernande. *Picasso et ses Amis*. Paris: Librairie Stock, 1933.

Painter, George. *Marcel Proust*. London and N.Y., 1959 (vol 1), 1965 (vol 2).

Patterson, Jerry E. *The Vanderbilts*. N.Y.: Abrams, 1989.

Perkins, J.R. *Trails, Rails and War*. Indianapolis: Bobbs-Merrill, 1929.

Pitkin, Albert H. *The Morgan Collection*. Hartford, 1918.

Platt, Frederick. *America's Gilded Age: Its Architecture and Decoration*. N.Y.: A.S. Barnes, 1976.

Pomeroy, Elizabeth. *The Huntington: Library, Art Collections, Botanical Gardens*. London: Philip Wilson, 1983.

Proust, Marcel. *À la recherche du temps perdu*, 15 vols. Paris: Gallimard, 1919-1927.

Quiett, Glenn Chesney. *They Built the West*. N.Y.: Appleton-Century, 1934.

Robinson, Bill. *Legendary Yachts*. McKay, 1978.

Rothschild, Dorothy de. *The Rothschilds of Waddesdon Manor*. N.Y.: Vendome, 1979.

Rousmaniere, John. *The Luxury Yachts*. Alexandria, Va.: Time-Life Books, c. 1981.

Saarinen, Aline B. *The Proud Possessors: The Lives, Times and Tastes of Some Adventurous American Art Collectors*. N.Y.: Random House, 1958.

Sackville-West, Vita. *The Edwardians*. London: Hogarth, 1930.

Schezen, Roberto, Jane Mulvagh, and Mark A. Weber. *Newport Houses*. Intro. by Robert A.M. Stern. N.Y.: Rizzoli, 1989.

Schumpeter, Joseph A. *Capitalism, Socialism, and Democracy*, 3rd ed. N.Y.: Harper, 1962.

Schuyler, Montgomery. *American Architecture*. N.Y., 1892.

Seligman, Germain. *Merchants of Art*. N.Y., 1961.

Seton-Watson, Hugh. *The Decline of Imperial Russia, 1855-1914*. N.Y.: Praeger, 1956.

Sinclair, Andrew. *Corsair: The Life of J. Pierpont Morgan*. Boston and Toronto: Little, Brown, 1981.

—. *The Last of the Best: The Aristocracy of Europe in the Twentieth Century*. N.Y.: Macmillan, 1969.

Sirkis, Nancy. *Newport Pleasures and Palaces*. N.Y.: Viking, 1963.

Smith, Arthur D. Howden. *John Jacob Astor, Landlord of New York*. Philadelphia: Lippincott, 1929.

Snowman, A. Kenneth. *Master Jewelers*. London: Thames & Hudson, 1990.

Stadiem, William. *A Class by Themselves: The Untold Story of the Great Southern Families*. N.Y.: Crown, c. 1980.

Sykes, Christopher. *Nancy: Life of Lady Astor*. London: Collins, 1972.

—. *Private Palaces: Life in the Great London Houses*. N.Y.: Viking, 1985.

Taylor, Francis Henry. *Pierpont Morgan as Collector and Patron, 1837-1913*. N.Y., 1970.

Tebbel, William John. *The Life and Good Times of William Randolph Hearst*. N.Y.: Dutton, 1952.

Thorndike, Joseph J., Jr. *The Very Rich: A History of Wealth*. N.Y.: American Heritage, 1976.

Tomkins, Calvin. *Merchants and Masterpieces: The Story of the Metropolitan Museum*. N.Y., 1970.

Tuchman, Barbara W. *The Proud Tower: A Portrait of the World Before the War: 1890-1914*. N.Y.: Macmillan, 1966.

Van Rensselaer, Mrs. J.K. *The Social Ladder*. N.Y.: Henry Holt, 1924.

Veblen, Thorstein. *Imperial Germany and the Industrial Revolution*. N.Y.: Macmillan, 1915.

—. *The Theory of the Leisure Class*. N.Y.: Macmillan, 1934 (reprint).

Walker, John. *National Gallery of Art*. N.Y.: Abrams, 1984.

Walker, Martha E. *John Jacob Astor, the Richest Man in the United States*. c. 1849.

Wechsberg, Joseph. *The Merchant Bankers*. Boston and Toronto: Little, Brown, 1966.

Wecter, Dixon. *The Saga of American Society*. N.Y.: Scribner, 1937.

Wharton, Edith. *The Age of Innocence*. New York: Scribner, 1920.

—. *French Ways and Their Meaning*. London: Macmillan, 1919.

—, and Ogden Codman. *The Decoration of Houses*. N.Y.: Scribner, 1897.

Wheatcroft, Geoffrey. *The Randlords*. London: Weidenfeld & Nicolson, c. 1985.

Williamson, Jefferson. *The American Hotel*. N.Y.: Knopf, 1930.

I N D E X

A

Academy of Music, 190, 191
Accessory Transport Company, 42
Acquavella Galleries, 140
Adam, Robert, 123
Aga Khan, 177
Agnew (gallery), 135, 137, 140-141
Agnew, Thomas, 140
Albert, Prince, 207, 208
Alcazar (hotel), 120
Alexander I, Czar, 170
Alexander II, Czar, 215
Alexander III, Czar, 205
Alexandra, Princess of Wales, 208-213, 217
Alexandria, 179, 182
Almanac de Gotha, 185, 203
Altman, Benjamin, 135, 138, 150, 156
Aluminum Company of America (Alcoa), 100
Alvarado, Juan Batista, 71
Amalgamated Copper Company, 70
Amélie, Queen, 53, 154
American Express, 63
American Revolution, 186
American Smelting and Refining Company. *See* ASARCO
Anaconda. *See* Amalgamated Copper Company
Anatolian Railways, 61
ancien régime, 104, 151
Andrews, Samuel, 57
Anglo-Austrian Bank, 54
Anvers, Cahen d', 88-89
Apsley House, 128
Aquitania, 168
Art Institute of Chicago, 156, 157, 158
Art Nouveau, 214, 215
Arts and Crafts movement, 214
ASARCO, 70
Ascot, 177, 181, 210, 213, 217
Asiatic Petroleum Company, 61, 62
Aston Clinton House, 124, 126
Astor
Caroline Webster Schermerhorn, 25, 28, 116, 118, 157, 187, 188, 189, 190
Charlotte Augusta Gibbes, 25, 28, 188
John Jacob, 9, 12, 17, 21, 22, 21-28, 32, 39, 42
John Jacob, Jr., 25, 44, 185
John Jacob, III, 28, 29, 187, 189, 194
John Jacob, IV, 25, 29, 30, 32
Rebecca Armstrong, 28
Vincent, 28
William Backhouse, 25, 28, 29, 133
William B., Jr., 25, 187, 188
Viscount William Waldorf, 28 32, 33, 122, 212

Astor Foundation, 33
Astor Hotel, 30, 31, 192
Astor House, 24, 29
Astor Library, 28
Astor Place, 24
Astoria (hotel), 179
Astoria (Queens, N.Y.), 24
Aswan, 180
Atchison Topeka Banana Line, 52
Atlantic and Pacific Steamship Company, 42
Augustus the Strong, 133

B

Baccarat, 181
Bache, Jules, 134
Baden-Baden, 163, 177, 181, 217
Bad Homburg, 217
Bailey's Beach, Newport, R.I., 196, 198, 199
Baker, George F., 13, 66, 97, 190
Baker, Newton Diehl, 186
Balfour Declaration, 83
Ballin, Albert, 123, 124
ballrooms, 109
Baltimore & Ohio, 97
Balzac, Honoré de, 83, 85
Bank of England, 87
banking, 81-101
Barber, Donn, 194
Barbizon School, 156, 157
Baring Brothers, 78, 81, 85, 87, 93, 95, 96
Barnato, Barney, 76, 77, 78, 79, 122
Barnato Brothers, 78
Barnes Collection, 159
Barry, Sir Charles, 124
Bates, Joshua, 96
Bath, Marquess of, 79, 122
bathrooms, 110
Battery, 10
Baudelaire, Charles, 160
Baugrand (jeweler), 215
Beard, William H., 14, 99
Beauharnais
Hortense de, 206
Josephine de, 206
Beaux-Arts, architecture, 103, 111, 114, 115, 116, 120, 131, 146, 148, 172
Bedford, Duke of, 171
bedrooms, 110
Behrman, S.N., 135, 138
Beit, Alfred, 78, 79, 134
Beitz, Berthold, 130
Belcourt Castle, 115
Bell, Isaac, Jr., 111
Belle Époque, 10, 122, 202
Belmont
August, 92, 96, 97, 115, 190, 191
Mrs. Oliver, 194
Bennett, James Gordon, Jr., 23, 111, 170, 171, 190, 199
Beraud, Jean, 177
Berenson, Bernard, 134, 137, 138, 139, 147
Bergdorf-Goodman, 115
Berkman, Alexander, 66
Bernard, George, 133
Bernhardt, Sarah, 177
Bertie, Ivor, 122
Berwind, Edward Julius, 196
Bessemer, Henry, 64, 67
Biarritz, 217
"Big Bertha," 67
"Big Four," 46
billiard rooms, 109
Billings, C.K.G., 192
Biltmore, 118
Birmingham, Stephen, 89
Bischoffsheim, Clara, 54
Bischoffsheim and Goldschmidt (bank), 54
Bismarck, Otto von, 88, 204
Black Tuesday, 14, 48, 217
Blake, Theodore, 121
Bleichröder, Gerson von, 88
Blenheim Palace, 213
"Blue Train," 166
Bobergh, Otto, 207
Bode, Dr. Wilhelm von, 137
Boesky, Ivan, 12
Boggis, Bertram, 138, 140
Bokelman, Christian Ludwig, 163
Boldt, George, 30
Boleyn, Anne, 123
Boris, Grand Duke, 196, 197
Borne, Robert, 22
Boucheron, 214
Bourget, Paul, 199
Boutibonne, Charles Édouard, 202
Bowery, 24
Bowman, John, 142
Breakers, The, 112, 116, 118
Breakers Hotel. *See* Palm Beach Inn
Britannia, royal yacht, 168, 170, 171
British Museum, 139
Brown, Capability, 79, 122, 123
Brown, Isaac Hull, 187
Bruce, Ailsa Mellon. *See* Mellon, Ailsa
"The Buccaneer." *See* Robinson, J.B.
Buchan, John, 19
Buckhout, Isaac C., 44
Buderus, Carl, 83, 84, 86
Burden, James H., 104
Burr, Aaron, 23
Bush, G.C., 43
Bute, Lord, 123
Butt, Major Archie, 32
Byron, Thomas F., 29

C

Cabanel, Alexandre, 156
Cadbury, George, 18, 19
Cafferty, James, 81
Cairo, 179-180, 182
"California Quartet," 47, 52

Callow, William, 82
Camondo, Count Moïse Nissim de, 153-154
"Cannon King." *See* Krupp, Alfred
Capote, Truman, 189
Carême, Antoine, 85, 88, 126
Carlotta, Empress, 70
Carlsbad, 164, 217
Carlton (hotel), 175
Carnarvon, Lord, 179
Carnegie, Andrew, 57, 63-64, 66, 109, 141, 177
Carnegie Brothers & Company, 64
Carnegie Hall, 66
Carnegie Tech, 66
Carrère and Hastings, 33, 120, 121, 138, 142
Carrère, John Merven, 120
Cartier
Alfred, 216
Jacques, 216
Louis, 216
Louis François, 78, 168, 180, 214, 215, 216
Pierre, 216
Caruso, Enrico, 290, 196
Cassatt
Alexander 157
Mary, 156, 157, 158
Cassel, Sir Ernest, 89, 122, 212
Castellane, Marquis Boni de, 103, 104, 199, 202
Castellani (jeweler), 214
Cataract Hotel, 180
Catherine the Great, 133, 134, 151
Cellini, Benvenuto, 215
Central of Georgia, 97
Central Pacific Railroad, 47, 48, 51, 52
Central University. *See* Vanderbilt University
Cernuschi, Henri, 154
Chaliapin, Feodor, 109, 160, 178, 190
Chanel, Coco, 171
Charing Cross (hotel), 172
Charles-Louis, Prince. *See* Napoleon III
Château de Ferrières, 87, 124, 126, 128
Château Lafite, 88
Château de Maisons-Laffitte, 116
Château Mouton-Rothschild Pauillac, 88
Château de Prégny, 124, 126
Chemin de Fer du Nord, 53
Chicago, Rock Island & Pacific Railway, 38
Chief Sitting Bull, 51
Choate, Joseph H., 29
Chopin, Frédéric, 85 109, 154
Christie's, 10
Christmas Bazaar of the Circle of the Nobility, 205
Christofle, 215

City, the (London), 17, 78, 81, 96
City Hotel (N.Y.), 24, 172
Civil War, 14, 35, 45, 186
Claridge's, 177
Clark, Alfred Corning, 157
Clark, William, 110
Clark & Rockefeller, 57
The Clermont, 40
Cleveland, President Grover, 97
Cliveden, 122
Clore, Sir Charles, 12
Club Le Polo, 181
Coaching Club, 193
Cognacq, Ernest, 154
coke, 64
Colesberg Kopje, 75, 77
collectors, 133-161
Collins, George K., 42
Colnaghi (gallery), 135, 140, 145
Columbian Exposition, Chicago, 14, 111, 157
Combe Court, 123
Compagnie Générale Trans-atlantique (CGT), 168
Compagnie Internationale des Wagons-Lits (CIWL), 166
Comstock, George, 74-75
Comstock Lode, 74-75, 97, 121, 193
Connelly, Senator Tom, 146
Cook, Thomas, 19, 179, 189
Cooke, Jay, 51, 52
Cooper-Hewitt Museum. *See* Carnegie, Andrew
Corbin, A.R., 45
"Corner House," 78
Corsair, yacht, 170, 171
Cosine Farm, 23
country weekends, 210-213
Court of St. James, 100
court, presentation at, 210
covered wagons, 57
Cowes, 168, 171, 217
crash of 1873, 48, 51, 64, 65
Crash of 1929, 9, 13, 16
Credit and Finance Corporation, 48
Crédit Mobilier, 48, 87
Creed, Henry, 207
Crocker
Charles, 46, 47
William H. 157
Cross, Henri-Edmond, 159
Crystal Palace, 9, 14, 124, 207
Cullinan diamond, 79
Cullinan, Thomas, 79
Cunard, Samuel, 42
Cunard Line, 168
Curzon, George, 199
Cutting, Robert L, 190
Cutty Sark, yacht, 171
Cuypers, P.J.H., 128

D

Dabney, Morgan & Company, 96
The Damned, film, 131
Damrosch, Walter, 29

Davies, Joseph, 145
Davis, Arthur, 122, 123, 124, 175
De Beers, 75, 76, 79
Debrett's Peerage, 185
Delmonico's, 191, 192
Demidoff, Prince, 112
Denis, Maurice, 159
Denton, Frank R., 99
Destailleur, G.-H., 126
Deterding, Henkrijk W.A., 61, 62
Deutsche Bank, 55
Deutschland über Alles, 67
Devonshire, Duchess of, 213, 215
de Wolfe, Elsie, 109
Diaghilev, Sergei, 156, 179
"Diamond Horseshoe," 189, 190
Diamond Jubilee, 79, 213
Diaz, Porfirio, 70, 165
Dickens, Charles, 19
Dietrich, George, 22
dining rooms, 109
"Dinner and Supper List," 187
Disraeli, Benjamin, 86, 87, 88, 128, 213
Dodd, Samuel C.T., 59
Drew, Daniel, 12, 41, 42, 43, 44, 45, 46, 52
Drexel, Anthony, 51, 95, 96, 170, 186
Drexel, Morgan and Company, 51, 99
Du Camp, Maxime, 180
Dudley, Earl of, 75, 122
Durand-Ruel
  Jean, 156
  Paul, 156, 157, 158, 159, 160
Durant, Thomas, 47
Dutoitspan, 75
Duveen Brothers, 135-140, 141
  Dorothy, 139, 140
  Henry, 135-136, 138
  Joseph (Joe), 134, 135-136, 137, 138, 139, 140, 141, 145, 146, 147, 156, 177
  Joseph Joel, 134, 135, 136, 137, 138

E

Eagle's Nest, 114
Eastern Seaboard Trust, 98
Eckstein, Herman, 78
École des Beaux-Arts. *See* Beaux-Arts
Eden Farm, 23
Edward VII, 18, 54, 55, 79, 83, 88, 89, 126, 148, 168, 170, 171, 174, 177, 180, 187, 204, 208-213, 217
Edward VIII, 217
Edwardian society, 10, 208-213
Egypt, 179-180
Eiffel Tower, 14
Electrical Building, 15
Elisabeth of Bavaria, Empress of Austria, 203
Ellis Island, 10, 16, 89
Elms, The, 196
Empire State Building, 25, 30
Empire Transportation, 63
Employees' Benefit Fund, 18
Employees' Holiday Club, 18
Ennery, Adolphe d', 154
Equitable Life Assurance Society, 192-193
Erie Canal, 23
Erie Railroad, 44, 46, 58, 92
Erie & Reading, 97
Erin, 168, 171
Escoffier, Auguste, 174, 177
Eugénie, Empress, 179, 206, 207, 214, 216
European palaces, 121-131

F

Fabergé, Peter Carl, 145, 178, 214, 215
Fair, James G., 74, 75
Falize, Lucien, 215
Federal Steel Company, 66
Ferncliffe, 188
Feuillet, Mme. Octave, 207
"FFF," 109
Field, Marshall, 32
Finley, Davis E., 146, 147
First National Bank, 97
Fish, Mrs. Stuyvesant, 196, 197
Fisk, James (Jim), 44, 45, 46, 52
"Five Arrows," 84
Flagler, Henry Morrison, 58, 59, 120, 121, 165
Flandrin, Hippolyte, 87
Flaubert, Gustave, 180
Flèche d'Or. *See* Golden Arrow
Flood, James C., 75
Florham, 114
Fontenay, Eugène, 214
"Foreign Masterpieces Owned by Americans," 157
Fortune (magazine), 10
Fortune 400, 9
fossi oil, 58
Fould, Achille, 53, 87
Fouquet, Georges, 214, 215
"Four Hundred," 28, 133, 187, 189, 193-194
Frances, countess of Warwick, 201
Franco-Prussian War, 67, 156
Franklin, Benjamin, 186
Franz Joseph, Emperor, 203, 204
Frederick the Great, 151
French Line, 168
French Revolution, 19, 134, 142, 151, 154, 202
Frère, Charles Theodore, 179
Frick Collection, 10, 120, 142, 146
Frick, Henry Clay, 10, 65, 66, 99, 120, 133, 134, 141, 142, 147, 148, 150, 156
Frith, William Powell, 212
Fuler, Loïe, 177
Fulton, Robert, 40, 41

G

Gagelin, 206
Galerie Georges-Petit, 133
Gapon, Father, 217
Garden, Mary, 109
Gardner, Isabella Stewart, 134, 137, 138
Garnier, Charles, 172, 174
Gary, Elbert H., 66
gasoline, 59
Gates, John W., 66
Gause, Wilhelm, 203
Gayda, Virginia, 202
Gazette du Bon Ton, 205
General Electric, 97
Generalregulativ, 68
George V, 79, 217
George VI, 217
German Customs Union, 67
German Empire, 68
German society, 204-205
Gerry, Elbridge T., 118
Gezireh Palace, 179
Gibbons, Sarah, 187
Gibbons, Thomas, 40
Guiliano, Carlo, 214
Gneisenau, 69
Goelet, 32
  Mary, 199, 201
  Ogden, 115
  Robert, 111, 164, 197
  Mrs. Robert, 196, 197
Gold Rush, 38, 42, 71-74

Golden Arrow, 166
Golden Horn, 55
Goldman
  Bertha, 93
  Louise, 93
  Marcus, 89, 91, 92, 93
  Rosa, 93
Goldman, Sachs & Co., 93
Goldschmidt, Maximilian, 88
Goodall, John S., 180, 181
Gould
  Anna, 104, 199, 202
  George, 171, 193, 202
  Jay, 9, 12, 28, 44, 45, 46, 52, 92, 97, 99, 104, 157, 164, 165, 190 199, 202
Grady, Henry, 186
Grand Central Hotel, 45
Grand Central Station (Terminal), 35, 44, 45, 165
Grand Hotel (Paris), 172, 174
Grand Hotel (Rome), 174-175
Grand Palais, 14
Grand Tour, 134, 175-177
Grant, President Ulysses S., 45, 51, 74
Granville, Lord, 209, 215
Great Depression, 9, 87
Great Exhibition, 9, 67, 164, 207
Great Indian Peninsula Terminus, 182
Great Northern Railroad, 52
Great Temple of Amun, 180
Great Western Hotel, 172
Greene, Belle da Costa, 148
Greenwich Village, 24, 25
Greffulhe, Countess, 217
Gretton, John, 171
Grey, Lady de, 213
Grosch
  Allen, 74, 75
  Hosea, 74, 75
Grosvenor Hotel, 172
Guggenheim, 13, 69-71, 89
  Benjamin, 70
  Daniel, 70
  Isaac, 70
  Meyer (father), 69
  Meyer (son), 69
  Murray, 70
  Peggy, 70
  Simon, 70
  Solomon, 70
  William, 70
Guggenheim Exploration Company (Guggenex), 70
Guinness, Sir Edward Cecil, 135, 136, 137, 140, 141, 171
Gulbenkian, Calouste, 61, 62, 145
Gulf Oil, 100

H

Hainauer, Oskar, 137, 138
Halphen, Joseph, 215
Hamilton, Alexander, 23
Hamilton, Duke of, 122
Hammond, John Harp, 71
Hampton Court, 114
Hancock (jeweler), 215
Hapsburg Empire, 202, 203, 204
Harding, President Warren, 101
Hardouin-Mansart, Jules, 116
Hardwick, P.C., 172
Harkness, Stephen V., 58
Harlem Railroad, 42, 43
Harriman, Edward Henry, 52, 55, 94, 97, 190
Harris, A.E., 210
Harris, David, 78
Harvard University, 186
Hastings, Thomas R., 104, 120
Haussmann, Baron Georges-

Eugène, 33, 87, 103, 109, 121, 128
Havemeyer, Henry O., 157, 158
H.C. Frick and Company, 65
Hearst
  George, 121
  William Randolph, 112, 121
Heine, Heinrich, 83, 85, 154
Hennessey, Richard, 171
Henry, Edward Lawson, 35
Hermitage, The, 133, 134, 145, 146, 159, 160, 161
Hever Castle, 32, 123
Hill, James Jerome, 52, 55, 97
Hirsch, Baron Maurice de, 54, 55, 89, 212
Hofburg Palace, 203
Hohenzollern court, 204
Holy Roman Empire, 91, 204
Homestead Mill, strike at, 65-66
Hopkins, Mark, 46, 47
Hoppner, John, 137
Hôtel Continental, 172
Hôtel de l'Europe, 179
Hôtel de Villars, 125
Hôtel du Louvre, 172
hotels, 172-175
Hudson River Railroad, 43
Hunt, Richard Morris, 29, 109, 114-119, 121, 175, 189
Huntington
  Collis P., 46, 47, 134, 139, 190
  Henry E., 47
Huntington Library, 47, 139
Hurlingham, 181
Hyde, James Hazen, 1942-193, 196, 199

I

Illustration, L', 205
Imperial State Crown, 79
India, 180-183
Industrial Revolution, 10, 14, 19, 35, 91
Interstate Commerce Commission (ICC), 38
"Iron Duke," *See* Bismarck, Otto von
Isaacs
  Barnett, 77. *See also* Barnato, Barney
  Harry, 77, 78

J

Jackson, William H., 48
Jacquemart
  Édouard André, 104, 154
  Nélie, 104, 154
James, Henry, 118, 120
Jameson Raid, 79
"Jay Cooke's Banana Belt," 51
Jay
  Mrs. John, 187
  Louise, 154
Jazz Age, 217
Jefferson Memorial, 146
jewelry, 214-217
"Jewish Court," 54, 55, 89, 212
Jiménez, Luis, 141
Jockey Club, 104, 202
Johnson, John G., 150, 157
Johnson, John Taylor, 35
Jones, Captain Bill, 64
Jones and Laughlin Steel, 63
Josephine, 71
J.S. Morgan & Company, 96
"Jubilee Jim," *See* Fisk, James
Judah, Theodor Dehone, 47
Jullian, Phillippe, 126

K

"Kaffirs," 75
Kahn, Otto, 94, 134, 177, 196

Kahnweiler, Daniel-Henry, 160, 161
Kaiser Ferdinand Nordbahn, 53
Kann
  Maurice, 138
  Rodolphe, 138
Karnak, 180
Kasteel de Haar, 128
Kedleston, Marchioness of. *See* Leiter, Mary Victoria
Kenan, Mary Lily, 121
Kent, William, 122
Kenwood House, 141
Kessler, Harry, 194
Keynes, John Maynard, 14
Khedive of Egypt, 128
Kimberley Diamond Mine, 75, 76, 77, 78, 79
Kirstein, Lincoln, 139
Kloman Brothers, 63
Knickerbocker Hotel, 30
Knight, John Prescott, 140
Knoedler (gallery), 134, 140, 141, 142, 145, 177
Koppers Company, 100
Kreditanstalt, 87
Kreisler, Fritz, 197
Kress, Samuel H., 135, 138, 145, 147, 156
Kruger, President, 79
Krupp
  Alfred, 67, 130
  Bertha, 69, 130
  Friedrich, 68
  Friedrich Alfred (Fritz), 68, 130, 131
  Marga, 68, 69
Krupp von Bohlen und Halbach
  Alfred, 130
  Gustave, 68, 69, 130
Kruppianers, 68, 69
Kuhn, Abe, 89, 91, 92, 93, 94
Kuhn, Loeb & Company, 38, 93, 94, 97, 134

L

La Farge, John, 115
Lafayette Place, 24
la haute juiverie, 81, 88-89
Lake Shore Railroad, 58
Lalique, René, 14, 214, 215, 216
Lami, Eugène, 126
Lane, Frederick, 61, 62
Langham (hotel), 172
Latrobe, Benjamin Henry, 104
Laugrand-Dumonceau, André, 54
Law, George, 42, 43
Lazard Frères, 88
Lecouvreur, Adrienne, 193
Lee, Robert E., 186
Leeds Castle, 123
Lehigh University, 91
Lehman Brothers, 89, 91, 92, 93
  Emmanuel, 92, 93
  Henry, 92, 93
  Mayer, 92, 93
  Robert, 150
Lehr, Harry, 197
Leigh, John Shaw, 123
Leighton, Sir Frederick, 213
Leiter
  Levi, 199
  Mary Victoria, 199
Leopold, King of the Belgians, 71
Lever, William Hesketh, 18
Lewis and Allenby, 206
Lewisohn Brothers, 70, 89, 91
libraries, 66
libraries in houses, 109
Lido, 177
Lippert, David, 78
Lipton, Sir Thomas, 17, 18, 168, 171, 209

Livingston, Robert R., 40
Livingston, Sarah van Brugh. *See* Jay, Mrs. John
Lodge, Senator Henry Cabot, 186
Loeb, Solomon, 89, 91, 92, 93, 94
Longacre Square. *See* Times Square
Longchamp, 181
Lorillard, Pierre, 32, 190, 191
Louis Philippe, King, 53
Louis Sherry, 191, 192
Louvre, 133
Lowell, A.L., 186
Lower East Side, 16, 24, 91
Ludlow, Mrs. Livingston, 194
Luton Hoo, 79, 122, 123
Lutyens, Sir Edwin, 181
Luxor, 180
Lysistrata, 170

M
Mackay, John W., 74, 75, 193
Maharajahs
 Bikaner, 182
 Dhuleep Singh, 182
Majestic (hotel), 175
Manchester, Duchess of. *See* Yznaga, Consuelo
Mandeville, Lady. *See* Yznaga, Consuelo
Maple's, 181
Marble House, 112, 116, 188, 197, 198
Margarita, 170
Marienbad, 217
Marjinsky Theater, 205
Marlborough, Duke of, 126, 197, 201, 208, 213
Marlborough House, 208, 209, 213
Marmottan, Jules, 154
Marquet, 159
marriage, 199-201
Marshall, Justice John, 40
Martin, Bradley, 192, 193-194
Marx, Karl, 14
Mary, Queen, 79
Maximilian, Emperor, 70, 87
Maxwell, Robert, 79
Mayflower, 187
Mead, William Rutherford, 111
Medici
 Catherine de', 207
 Cosimo de', 10, 118, 133
Melba, Dame Nellie, 109, 174, 190
Mellerio, 214, 215
Mellon
 Ailsa, 101, 144, 145
 Andrew, 9, 99-101, 134, 138, 141, 142-144, 145, 146, 147, 148, 150, 156, 159
 Paul, 101, 134, 144, 145
 Judge Thomas, 99
Mellon Bank, 65, 99
Mendelssohn, Felix, 88
Mentmore Towers, 124, 125
"Mephistopheles of Wall Street." *See* Gould, Jay
merchant princes, 158-161
Metropol, 179
Metropolitan Museum, 139, 148, 150, 156, 157, 158, 179, 194
Metropolitan Opera, 94, 134, 189, 190, 193
Metternich, Prince, 86, 88
Metternich, Princess, 203, 206, 207
Meurthe, Henri Deutsch de la, 88
Mewès, Charles, 122, 123, 124, 175
Milken, Michael, 12
Miller, Tom, 63
"Mr. 5 Percent." *See* Gulbenkian, Calouste
Mizner, Addison, 121

Monte Carlo, 163, 205
Montefiore, Moses, 86
Montijo de Guzman, Countess Eugénie Maria de. *See* Eugénie, Empress
Morgan
 John Pierpont (J.P.), 13, 38, 51, 52, 57, 64, 65, 66, 92, 94, 95-99, 134, 135, 139, 141, 142, 148-150, 151, 156, 164, 170, 179, 186, 190
 John Pierpont II (Jack), 150
 Julia, 121
 Junius (father), 95, 96, 148
 Junius (son), 13
 "Morganization," 95
Morgan Library, 100, 148, 150, 151
Morozov, Ivan, 158, 159, 161
Morse, Charles W., 98
Mount Stephen, Lord, 52
Mucha, Alphonse, 214
music rooms, 109
McAllister, Ward, 28, 157, 187, 188, 189, 197
McKim, Charles Follen, 111, 112, 114
McKim, Mead & White, 100, 111, 112, 114, 148
McMullen, Nora, 101

N
Nabisco, 100
Nagelmackers, Georges, 163, 166-167
Namouna, yacht, 170
Napoleon I, 206
Napoleon III, 33, 53, 67, 87, 103, 118, 122, 124, 133, 154, 172, 179, 202, 206, 207
National Archives, 146
National City Bank, 13, 97
National Gallery (London), 139, 140, 144, 206
National Gallery of Art (Washington), 100, 101, 144, 145, 147, 150
National Portrait Gallery (London), 139
Nationale (hotel), 179
Netherlands Trading Society, 61
Neuman, Sigismund, 78
Neville, Lady Dorothy, 210
New Jersey Central, 35
Newmarket, 181
Newport
 Casino, 111-112, 196, 198
 Reading Room, 111, 112, 196
 season, 196-199
New Rush, 75, 77, 78
New York Central Railroad, 44, 45, 46, 58
New York Harbor, 10, 39, 40, 41
New York Herald, 22, 111, 170
New York Herald-Tribune, 171
New York Life Insurance Company, 97
New York Palace Hotel, 52
New York Philharmonic, 29
New York Public Library, 28, 33, 120
New York Stock Exchange, 93, 96, 217
New York Times, 188
New York Yacht Club, 170, 171
New Yorker, 135
Nice, France, 163, 205
Nicholas I, Czar, 87, 112
Nicholas II, Czar, 38, 78, 203, 205
Niekerk, Schalk Jacobus van, 75
Nobel, Robert, 61
"nobs," 187
North Star, yacht, 42, 168-170
Northern Pacific Railroad, 51, 52, 97

O
O'Brien, William S., 75
ocean liners, 167-168
Ochre Court, 115, 297
Ogden, Henr A., 40
Ohio Life and Trust, 96
oil, 57-62
Old Delhi, 181
Olivier, maître d'hôtel, 175
Olmsted, Frederick Law, 118
Olympic, 167
1 London Wall, 79
Oppenheim, Moritz Daniel, 82
Oppenheimer
 bank, 83
 Ernst, 79
 Harry, 79
Orient Express, 61, 111, 166
Ottoman Empire, 54-55
"our crowd," 81, 89-94, 96
Our First Men, 185-186
Ovchinnikov, 214

P
Pacific Associates, 47
Pacific Railway Act, 47
Packer, Asa, 91
Paddington Station, 172
Paderewski, Ignace, 109
Paget, Mrs. Arthur, 213
Palais de la Légion d'Honneur, 124
Palais de Marbre Rose, 103, 104, 202
Palazzo Pisani, 118
Palm Beach, 163, 164, 165, 172, 177, 189
Palm Beach Inn, 120
Palmer
 Berte (Mrs. Potter), 14, 157, 158
 Potter, 32
Paris Opera, 172, 174, 190
parties, 187-199
Patiño, Simon, 202
"Patriarchs," 187-188, 190
Paul, James, 194
Pavlova, Anna, 179
Paxton, Joseph, 9, 14, 124, 126, 207
Peabody, George, 95, 96
Pellegrini, Giovanni Antonio, 118
Pennsylvania Railroad, 63, 64
Péreire, Émile, 87, 88
"Petit Château de Blois," 112, 114, 115, 189
Petit Palais, 14
Petit Trianon, 103, 116
Philadelphia Museum of Art, 150
Phipps, Henry, 63, 66
Picasso, Pablo, 156, 158, 159, 160, 161
picture galleries in houses, 109
Pierce, Henry Clay, 59
Pinkerton Detective Agency, 66
Pissarro, Camille, 156, 157, 158
Pittsburgh Glass, 100
Pittsburgh Reduction Company, 100
Plaza Hotel, 115, 192
P&O, 181, 182
Pocantico Hills, 60
Poiret, Paul, 109
Polesden Lacey, 123
polo, 181, 210
Ponce de León Hotel, 120
Ponselle, Rosa, 190
Pope, John Russell, 142, 146
Populist Party, 97
Porgès, Jules, 78, 79, 124
"posh," 181
Post, George Browne, 115
Post, Marjorie Merriweather, 145
"PPP," 104
Pratt, Charles, 59

Prester John, 19
Preziosi, Count Amadeo, 55
Promontory, Utah, 51
Proust, Marcel, 174, 175, 202
Public Ledger, 51
Pullman, George, 9, 163, 164-165, 166
Punch, 104
Pushkin Museum, 158, 161

R
Rachmaninoff, Serge, 160
racing, 177
railroads, 35, 38, 39, 42-55, 59, 64, 93, 94, 96, 97, 164-167
Rambagh Palace, 181
Rana of Udaipur, 182
Randlords, 79
Ranney, William Tyler, 91
real estate, 21-34
Red Fort, 181
Reform Club, 124
Réjane, Gabrielle, 192, 193
Reichmann Brothers, 12
Reinhardt, Max, 134
Remington, Frederic, 22, 51
Renoir, 157, 158, 159, 161
resorts, 163, 165, 172
Rhodes
 Cecil, 77, 79
 Herbert, 77
Richardson, Henry Hobson, 111
Richelieu, Cardinal, 121
Ring of the Nibelungen, The, 14
Ripley, William Z., 47
Ritz, César, 122, 123, 174-175
Ritz Hotel (London), 174, 175, 177
robber barons, 16, 24, 35, 39, 43, 57, 65, 95, 98, 100
Robinson, J.B., 122
Robinson, Lola, 197
Rockefeller
 John Davison, 14, 17, 28, 57-60, 61, 62, 64, 70, 76, 82, 104, 190
 William, 70, 190
Rockefeller, Andrews & Flagler, 58
Rockefeller Center, 60, 147
Rockefeller Trust, 59
Rogers, Henry, 59, 70
Romano, Giulio, 121
Roosevelt
 Franklin Delano, 187
 President Theodore, 98
Rosanova, Olga, 159
Rosenberg, Charles, 81
Rothschild, 12, 13, 19, 52, 61, 78, 81, 82-88, 93, 134, 136
 Adolphe de, 126
 Albert de, 128
 Alice de, 126, 153
 Alphonse de, 87, 124
 Amschel Mayer von, 84
 Anselm de, 87
 Anthony de, 86, 124
 Beatrix Ephrussi, 126, 128
 Betty de, 109, 126, 154
 Carl (Kalmon) de, 53, 84, 86, 126
 Edmond de, 83, 153, 171
 Édouard de, 89, 154
 Ferdinand de, 126, 153
 Gutele, 82, 83
 Guy de, 154
 Hélène Betty de, 128
 James de, 53, 84, 85, 86, 87, 88, 109, 126, 128, 153, 154
 Jimmy, 153
 Julie de, 126
 Lionel, Lord, 86, 87, 128
 Louis, 87-88
 Mayer, 86
Mayer Amschel, 53, 83-84, 124, 125, 128

Mayer Carl, 87
Nathan, 52, 84, 85, 86, 153
Nathaniel, 83, 86, 128
Salomon von, 53, 84, 86, 128
Rothschild houses, 124-129
Roxburghe, Duke of, 201
Royal Academy, 133
Royal Dutch Company, 61
Royal Dutch Shell, 60-62
Royal Pionciana, 120
Royal Sceptre, 79
Rubinstein, Anton, 109
Rudd, Charles Dunell, 77, 79
Rudini, Marchese, 199
Rüppell & Harnier, 84
Russian Revolution
 1905, 217
 1917, 161
Russian season, 205
Russian society, 205
Ryan, Thomas Fortune, 70, 71
Ryerson, Martin A., 158

S
Saarinen, Aline, 148
Sacher's, 203
Sachs Collegiate Institute, 93
Sachs, 89, 91, 92, 93
 Joseph, 93
 Julius, 93
 Sam, 93
 Sophie, 93
Sagan, Prince de, 199
St. Donat's, 121
Saint-Gaudens, Augustus, 115
St. Gilles, 115
St. James, 201
St. Regis, 21, 30, 192
Salon d'Automne, 160
"Salon des Tapisseries de Leprince," 104
salons, 109
Salt Lake City, 48
Samaritaine, La, 154
Samuel, Marcus, 61, 62
Sandor, Pauline. *See* Metternich, Princess
Sandringham, 208, 210, 213
San Simeon, 121
Sans Souci, 151
Santayana, George, 137
Sapphire, yacht, 171
Saratoga Springs, 172, 199
Sargent, John Singer, 137, 201
Sassoon, Sir Albert Abdullah, 89, 212
Savile Row, 10, 94
Savoy, 177, 194
Savoy Plaza, 21
Scharnhorst, 69
Schiff, Jacob, 38, 71, 89, 91, 94, 97
Schilersdorf, 128
Schloss Charlottenburg, 151
Schloss Enzesfeld, 128
Schneider, Eugène, 67, 202
Schönbrunn Palace, 203
Schönburg, 203
Scott, Thomas A., 63
Scottish Rite Temple, 146
seasons, 163-164, 175-178, 179, 180-181, 189, 191, 201, 210, 217
Sears, William T., 138
Second Empire, 33, 48, 177, 190, 206, 207, 208, 214
Seligman, 89-92
 Abraham, 92
 David, 89-91
 Fanny, 91
 Henry, 92
 Isaac, 92
 James, 91, 92
 Jesse, 92

Joseph, 89, 91, 92, 94
Leopold, 92
William, 91, 92
servant's quarters, 110
Shah of Iran, 214-215
Shamrock, 168, 171
Sharon Steel, 100
Shchukin, Sergei, 158, 159, 160, 161
Shell Transport and Trading Company, 61
Shepheard's, Cairo, 179, 180
Sherry-Netherland, 21
shooting, 177, 181, 182, 204
Siemens, William, 67
Simpson, Wallis Warfield, 128
Skibo Castle, 64
Skoda, 68
Sloane, Mrs. Henry, 194
Smith, Calvin Rae, 168
Social Register, 185
Solomon R. Guggenheim Museum, 70
South Improvement Company, 58
South Sea Bubble, 51
Southern Pacific Railroad, 47, 52
Southey, Richard, 75
Spencer, Earl of, 122
stagecoaches, 38
Standard Oil Company, 58, 59, 60, 61, 62
Stanford, Leland, 47, 47, 164
Star of Africa, 75
"Star of Egypt," 166
Staten Island, 39, 41, 46, 112, 115
State Island Ferry, 41
steamboats, 40-41
steel, 62-64, 65, 66, 67
Stein
  Gertrude, 158, 159, 160-161
  Leo, 58, 159, 160-161
Stewart, Alexander T., 12, 32, 185
Stillman, James, 97, 98
Stotesbury, Mrs. Edward T., 165
Strathmore, Lord, 52
Stravinsky, Igor, 156
Suez Canal, 86, 87, 128, 179
Sultan Abdul Aziz, 55
Sultan Abdul Hamid, 55, 61

Sultan Murad, 55
Sutter, John Augustus, 71
Swan and Edgar, 206
"swells," 187
Sykes, Sir Christopher, 209-210

T
Talleyrand-Périgord, Duc Hélie de, 199, 202
Tate Gallery, 139
Taylor, Tommy, 196
Teatro alla Scala, 190
Teatro Colón, 190
Temple of Abu Simbel, 180
Temple of Amenhotep, 180
Tetrazzini, Luisa, 174
Texaco, 57
Texas & Pacific Railroad, 51
Texas Spindletop, 100
Thaw, Harry, 111
Thomire, Pierre, 112
Thomson, J. Edgar, 64
Thyssen, Baron, 67, 150
Tiander (jeweler), 214
Tiffany, Louis Comfort, 115, 216
Tiffany and Co., 215, 216
Times (London), 32
Times Square, 30, 31
Tissot, James Jacques Joseph, 185
Titanic, 25, 32, 70, 167
Tocqueville, Alexis de, 185
Toussaint, Mme. Jeanne, 216
transportation, 35-55
Trans-Siberian railroad, 71, 167
travel, 163-183
Tremont House, 24
Trinity Church (Boston), 111
Trinity Church (N.Y.), 23
Triple Mansion, 112, 115
Troubetskoy Palace, 160, 161
Tuileries, 207
Turin, Count of, 199
"Türkenhirsch." *See* Hirsch, Baron Maurice de
Twain, Mark, 191
Tweed, "Boss," 43
Tweedmouth, Lord, 122
Twombly, Hamilton McKown, 114

U
Uffizi, 133
Union Club, 189
Union Iron Mills, 63, 64
Union Pacific Railroad, 47, 48, 51, 52
Union Savings Bank, 100
Union Steel, 100
Union Trust of Pittsburgh, 100
United Metals Selling Company, 70
United States Steel, 57, 63, 66, 70, 95, 97, 141, 142

V
Valhalla, 14
Valley of the Kings, 179, 180
Van Allen, Mr. & Mrs., 197
Vanbrugh, Sir John, 213
Vanderbilt
  Alice, 115
  Alva, 112, 114, 115, 116, 126, 189, 197, 198, 199
  Consuelo, 197, 199, 201, 202, 212
  Cornelius ("Commodore"), 9, 10, 12, 17, 32, 39-46, 52, 55, 112, 114, 115, 164, 168-170, 185, 189, 190
  Cornelius II, 115, 116, 118
  Florence Adèle, 114
  Frederick William, 114
  George Washington, 118, 142
  Louise, 114
  Margaret, 114
  Sophia Johnson, 46
  William Henry, 9, 43, 112, 115, 190
  William Kissam, 28, 60, 114, 115, 124, 177, 189, 196, 201
  William K., Jr., 114
Vanderbilt six-part formula for making money, 42
Vanderbilt University, 46
Vanity Fair, 54, 58, 76, 86
"varnish," 164-165
Vernet, Marie Augustine, 206, 207
Versailles, 103, 104, 109, 116
Vever, Henri, 214, 215
Victoria, Queen, 68, 79, 87, 88, 124, 126, 168, 170, 172, 206, 207, 208, 209, 210, 213
Victoria and Albert I and II, royal yachts, 168

Victoria Station, 172, 177
Viennese society, 202-204
Villa Hügel, 130-131
Villard, Henry, 51, 52
Viollet-le-Duc, Eugène-Émmanuel, 104
Visconti, Luchino, 131
Viscount Bearstead. *See* Samuel, Marcus
Viscount Leverhulme. *See* Lever, William Hesketh
Vladimir, Grand Duke, 216
Voisin, 177
Volksbank. *See* Crédit Mobilier
Vollard, Ambroise, 158, 159, 160, 161
Vooruitzigt, 75
Vuitton, Louis, 10, 177

W
Waddesdon Manor, 126, 153
Wadsworth Atheneum, 150
Wagner, Richard, 14
Wagner Palace Car Company, 164
Waldorf Hotel, 29, 32
Waldorf-Astoria Hotel, 29, 30, 31, 32, 165, 192, 193
Wallace, Sir Richard, 134
Wallace Collection, 141
Wall Street, 13, 14, 51, 66, 70, 71, 92 96, 98
War of 1812, 39, 40
"watering cattle," 41
"watering stock," 41, 42, 44
Watson, George, 170
Webb, Beatrice, 122
Weir, John Ferguson, 62
Welles, Orson, 121
Wellington, Duke of, 128
Wernher, Beit & Company, 78
Wernher, Sir Julius, 78, 79, 122, 123
Westinghouse, Mrs. George, 194
Westinghouse Electric, 98
Westminster, Duke of, 33, 122, 139, 171, 187, 213
whale oil, 58
White, Stanford, 111, 114, 121, 175
White Star Line, 167
Whitehall (London), 17
Whitehall (Palm Beach), 120, 121

Whitney, William, 70
W.H. Smith, 18-19
Wildenstein (gallery), 134, 140, 154
Wildenstein
  Georges, 154, 177
  Nathan, 154
Wilhelm I, Kaiser, 67, 204
Wilhelm II, Kaiser, 68, 79, 124, 126, 131, 204, 209, 217
Wilkenson, Sam, 51
William, Landgrave of Hesse-Cassel, 83, 84, 86
Williams, Tennie, 46
Williams, Victoria, 46
Windsor, 181, 213 217
Winterhalter, Franz, 206
Winter Palace Hotel, 180
Witwatersrand, 75, 79
Woodlawn Cemetery, 114
Woodlea, 114
Woodruff Palace Car Company, 63
World War I, 9, 28, 32, 67, 131, 133, 167, 194, 203
World War II, 61, 175, 202
Worth, Charles Frederick. *See* House of Worth
Wortley, Archibald Stuart, 209
Wren, Sir Christopher, 114, 208
Wyk, Adriaan van, 75
Wyllie, William Lionel, 69
Wynton, 121

X
Xenia, Grand Duchess, 216

Y
yachts, 168-171
Ysaye, Eugène, 109
Yusupov, Prince Felix, 134
Yznaga, Consuelo, 189, 199

Z
Zaharoff, Sir Basil, 67
Zanetti, Vittorini, 140
Zatzenstein, F., 145
Zeckendorf, William, 12
Zimmerman, Helena, 199
Zum Römischer Kaiser, 128
Zuylen van Nyvelt, Baron van, 128

P I C T U R E   C R E D I T S

African Library ©, Kurckirles: 76 far right below, 78 top far right; Arcaid: 213; Agnew's, London: 140 below, right; Mrs Vincent Astor: cover, 26, 27; Avant-Garde Publishing House, Moscow: 158 below, 159 bottom, 160, 161; Beken of Cowes, Ltd: 169; Berenholz ©: 100 below, 105, 106-107; C. Bergholz, Geneva: 124 far right; Bettmann Archive, New York: 9, 10, 11, 21, 22, 23 bottom, 24 bottom, 25 below, 31 top, 41 bottom, 43 bottom, 44 top, 45 center and bottom, 46 far right, 47 top right, 48 top and far right, 51 bottom, 54 top, 63 above, 65 top and bottom, 67 above, 72 bottom and far right, 84 top (*Harper's New Monthly Magazine*, 1973), 90, 91 top, 93 top and right, 95, 96 top, 99 top, 111 top, 112 bottom, 114 far left, 115 top, 118, 121 bottom right, 133 bottom, 150, 157 bottom right, 167 bottom, 171 bottom left, 182 bottom left, 186, 187 above, 195, 197 bottom, 201 bottom; Bilderdienst, Munich: 131; The Biltmore Company: 41 top, 119; Boissed Collection: 172 top; Bridgeman Art Library, London: 8 (Victoria & Albert Museum), 38 bottom, 46 top, 53 top (National Railway Museums), 55 (Christie's), 69 botom, 79, 81 (Musée Carnavalet), 82 top and bottom, 92, 103: Cartier, Paris; 214 below, 216, 217, (Christie's), 132, 133 top, 141 top, 162 (Guildhall Library), 163 bottom, 164 top (Guildhall Library), 167 above right, 168 top, 176 (Musée Carnavalet), 178 top and bottom, 179 top center, 180 top, 181 top and below (Paul Breman Collection), 182 top (India Office Library) and bottom left (National Army Museum), 190 top, 202 left, 203 above, 206 center, 209 below, 211, 212 bottom; Brown Brothers: 15 top, 29 top, 31 bottom, 64 top and far right, 120 top, 136 bottom, 148 bottom, 170 top, 171 top, 191 top, 193 above left and bottom, 197 bottom, 210 bottom; Cape Archives ©: 76 far right above; Chicago Historical Society, 15 bottom; Sterling and Francine Clark Art Institute, Williamstown, Mass.: 134 bottom, 135, 138 bottom; The Clayton Corporation, Pittsburgh: 66 top, 141 center and bottom; Cliché Salaun: 175 top; Compagnie Internationale des Chemins de Fer: 54 center; Compagnie Intrnationale des Wagons-Lits: 166, 167 top left; Courtauld Collection ©: 122 top; Culver Pictures, New York: 23 above, 24 far left, 28, 29 below and bottom, 32 bottom, 33 bottom, 39 above, 41 center, 43 above, 44 bottom, 46 bottom, 47 top left and below (2), 48 bottom, 51 top, 52 top and far right, 56, 57, 58, 59 top and below, 60, 63 bottom, 64 bottom, 66 bottom, 68 top, 73, 74, 77 top, 83, 84 far left, 85 bottom, 97 far left, 98, 100 top, 112 top, 113, 114 bottom, 115 below, 126 top, 159 top, 165 top, 188 bottom, 189, 190 bottom, 193 above right, 198 bottom, 199 bottom, 201 bottom, 208 bottom, 210 top; dpa Bild, Munich: 130 top and far right above; Duke of Marlborough: 200; Durand-Ruel, Paris: 156; Mary Evans Picture Library, London: 17 below, 18 bottom, 53 bottom, 54 bottom, 61 center, 62 bottom left, 75, 76 bottom,

77 bottom, 78 far right below, 86 bottom left, 97 above and bottom, 103 top 140 bottom, 203 below, 204, 207, 2 far left; The Frick Collection: 142, 143; Isabella Stewart Gardner Museum, Boston: 137 top, 138 top and far right; Giga ©: 177 (cav. Scarabello Giovanni); David Heald: 69 far right; Henry E. Huntington Library and Art Gallery, San Marino, Calif.: 38 right, 47 left, 52 bottom, 139; Hearst San Simenon Historical Monument © (photo: John Blades): 121 top and center; Keystone, Hamburg: 130 far right bottom; Keystone Collection, London: 174 bottom; Samuel H. Kress Foundation, New York: 147 below; Mr. Mrs. Noel Levine: 49, 180 far right; Maharaja of Bikaner Trust, 183; Metropolitan Museum of Art: 35 below, 36-37, 62 below, 149, 150 below, 151; Mentmore Trust: 124 right, 125; Mansell Collection: 16 top and bottom, 17 top, 19 top, 86 bottom right, 124 bottom, 136 far left, 164 bottom, 208 top right, 212 top; National Gallery of Art, Washington: 144 above, 145; New York Historical Society; 14, 40, 99 below, 100 below; Pierpont Morgan Library: 148 top and far left; (accession number 1958. 24 and 1950.12); 151 (accession number M.1, FC); Museum of the City of New York: 12, 13, 14, 24 top, 33 top (Wurtz Collection), 59 far right, 71 bottom, 80, 108, 109, 136 top, 194 top (2); Museum of the City of New York (Byron Collection): 20, 25 top, 30, 31 center, 191 below, 192, 194 bottom; National Gallery of Art (Photographic Archives): 147 below; National Monument Record ©, London: 123; National Trust, Waddesdon Manor, Aylesbury, Bucks, England: 126, 152; Newport Historical Society: 111 center, 198 top and far left, 199 top; Preservation Society of Newport: 116, 117, 196 top; Rizzoli: 120 below; Roger-Viollet, Paris: 85 far right, 87, 89 far left, 102, 104, 153, 170 top, 172 bottom, 202 right, 205; Lord Rothschild: 84 right, 86 far right; Baron Guy de Rothschild; 35 left above, 154, 155; Baron Edwind de Rothschild: 124 far right; Baron David de Rothschild; 127 (photography Delorme); Mrs Thomas Fortune Ryan; 94 below, 134 far right; Royal Commission on Historical Monuments (Crown copyright), London: 124 top (photo: E. Elerahon), 125; Sayford City Art Gallery (photo: Entwistle, Thorpe & Co.), Manchester: 140 far left; Scott Brown Photography, New York: 49, 180; Shelburne Museum, Inc.: 42 top; Shell Photographic Services ©: 61 far right (2), 62 top; Sotheby's: 184, 214 above and center, 215 right; Sotheby's, London: 89 top; Studio Lourmel (photo: Routhier), Paris: 155; Raleigh Treveman ©: 78 far left; Ullstein Bilderdienst, Berlin: 130 far left bottom; UPI Bettmann: 32 top, 44 center, 45 top, 67 bottom, 68 top, 96 bottom, 110, 114 top, 121 bottom left, 122 bottom, 137 bottom, 146 top, 154 bottom, 165 far left, 171 bottom right, 196 bottom, 209 top, 213 above; Marc Walter: 17 above, top left, 88 far right, below, 163, 166, 172, 173, 174, 175, 176 left, 179 above, left below; Jeremy Whitaker MCSD, Hants, England: 200; Windsor Castle, courtessy Her Majesty the Queen: 16 top; Baron and Baroness van Zuylen, Kasteel de Haar: 128, 129.

ACKNOWLEDGMENTS

My first regret, as must be apparent to any reader of this book, is that I did not live in the Gilded Age. My next regret is that there are no survivors who could be interviewed to corroborate the endless books written about this extraordinary period. The finest contemporary literary chroniclers were, of course, Edith Wharton, Henry James, and Marcel Proust, but most of the bibliography listed at the end of the present narrative was written after the fact. Many legends concerning the Gilded Age have been perpetuated throughout this century, and there are endless discrepancies of fact and dates among the various commentators. Today, therefore, the most a scrupulous writer can do is read the main sources, exercise his judgment, and hope for the best. As the Italian dictum goes, *"se non è vero, è ben detto."* The books mentioned here are but the tip of an iceberg, and obviously some provided far more information than others. Among these, I should like to cite, first of all, a few authors whose work proved especially helpful: Stewart Holbrook, Matthew Josephson, and Gustavus Myers for general background on robber barons; Arthur Smith on the Astors; Wayne Andrews and Jerry Patterson on the Vanberbilts; Oscar Lewis on the Big Four; Anthony Allfrey on Maurice de Hirsch; James Bridge, Cotter Arundel, and George Harvey on Frick and Carnegie; Bernt Engelmann and William Manchester on the Krupps; John Davis on the Guggenheims; the Editors of Time-Life and Oscar Lewis on the Gold Rush; Geoffrey Wheatcroft on the Randlords; Virginia Cowles and Anka Muhlstein on the Rothschilds; Joseph Wechsberg on merchant bankers; Andrew Sinclair on J.P. Morgan; and Stephen Birmingham on "Our Crowd." For the spending section of this book, I should like to pay particular tribute to Wayne Andrews for his brilliant analysis of Gilded Age architecture; Robert King for Vanderbilt houses; Dorothy de Rothschild for her information on Waddesdon Manor; Aline Saarinen and Pierre Cabane for great American and European collectors; Sam Hunter for Andrew Mellon and his purchases of Old Master art from the Soviet government; S.N. Behrman for Duveen; John Walker for Andrew Mellon and the National Gallery of Art; and Beverly Keane for Moscow's merchant-prince collectors, Sergei Shchukin and Ivan Morozov. It would be impossible to write anything about American society of the period without three great social observers—Lucius Beebe, Stephen Birmingham, and Cleveland Amory—but the most revealing document of the entire period was certainly written by one of its leading players, Consuelo Vanderbilt. As for the composition and quirks of society in Europe, I relied heavily on Arno Mayer, as well on Ruth Brandon for the fascinating phenomenon of American social-climbing in Europe. Edward VII is splendidly treated by both Virginia Cowles and Christopher Hibbert; Charles Frederick Worth by Diane de Marly; and there is no better source for the jewelry of the period than Kenneth Snowman. Joe Thorndike's book proved to be an invaluable precursor of the present tome. Finally, I should like to thank my library researcher, Joanne Polster, and the delightful staff at the New York Society Library for granting me the run of their stacks, which *must* be haunted by some of the protagonists in this book.

The search for illustrations was a transatlantic venture, and I wish to thank Donna Thynne in London and Bernice Gelzer in New York for their sterling efforts, as well as Peter Simmons at the Museum of the City of New York, Ron Brenne at the Bettmann Archives, and Allen Rubin at the Culver Picture Service. Among those who generously contributed photographs from their archives and other sources were various members of the Rothschild family, including Lord Rothschild in London, Baron Guy and Baron Éric in Paris, and Baroness Edmond in Geneva. Baroness Élie was a mine of useful information and a perfect guide to the whereabouts of family treasures, while Baroness Gabrielle van Zuylen has been magnanimous in allowing me to use photographs of Kasteel de Haar before publication of the official book on that splendid castle of Rothschildian origin. My warmest thanks go as well to His Grace the Duke of Marlborough for providing portraits of his grandparents, Sunny and Consuelo, and to Mrs. Vincent Astor for permitting me to photograph the family group on pages 26-27. Immensely helpful were the curators of W.R. Hearst's San Simeon, George Vanderbilt's Biltmore, the Frick family's Clayton Foundation, and the Newport Historical Society as well as the Newport Preservation Society. The Museum of the City of New York was a rich source for period pictures, as was the New York Historical Society, which will hopefully soon find a better-feathered nest for their magnificent collection. Among those who provided dazzling photographs of period jewelry were John Block of Sotheby's, Edward Green of Asprey's, and the staff of Cartier in Paris, and I sincerely regret that we could not reproduce more of their treasures. Alex Apsis of Sotheby's in New York ferreted out many interesting paintings used throughout the book, and Pierre Christian Brochet in Moscow provided most of the transparencies of the great modernist pictures collected by Moscow's merchant princes, all now in Russian museums, where photography is invariably a nightmare. Among the institutions without whose help this book would have lacked its brightest imagery are the Metropolitan Museum of Art, the National Gallery of Art in Washington, D.C., the Frick Collection, the Morgan Library, and the Isabella Stewart Gardner Museum. Mr. and Mrs. Noël Levine provided several old photographs from their superb collection. However, my favorite find is the picture of the great banker Otto Kahn wearily puffing his cigar after a day's work on the railroad as he sits between masterpieces by Rembrandt and Patinir. This quintessential image of the tycoon-collector was generously provided by his daughter, the ever-helpful Nin Ryan, and we proudly publish it here for the first time. While thanking grandees, my appreciation must also be extended to His Highness the Maharaja of Bikaner for the wonderful image on page 183 of his grandfather and the Viceroy standing over a slain beast.

There is no way I can sufficiently thank my valiantly attentive editor, Daniel Wheeler, and that most genial of all book designers, Marc Walter. I am profoundly grateful to my old friend and skiing companion, John Kenneth Galbraith, for reading the manuscript, for gracing my book with his foreword, and for sharing my tongue-in-cheek attitude towards the super-rich. And last, but certainly not least, without my faithful publishers—Gian-Franco Monacelli at Rizzoli, Rolf Heyne, Ingeborg Meier, and Harry Olechnowitz at Munich's Wilhelm Heyne Verlag, and both Claire Howell and Chris Fagg at Cassell in London—this book would have never seen the light of day.

Alexis Gregory